Building a Legacy

Women in Social Education 1784-1984

EDITED BY

Margaret Smith Crocco
O.L. Davis, Jr.

NCSS BULLETIN 100

National Council for the Social Studies

8555 SIXTEENTH STREET ▸ SUITE 500 ▸ SILVER SPRING, MARYLAND 20910
301 588-1800 FAX 301 588-2049 WWW.SOCIALSTUDIES.ORG

EDITORIAL STAFF ON THIS PUBLICATION: Steven S. Lapham, Michael Simpson
ART DIRECTOR: Gene Cowan GRAPHIC DESIGNER: Kami Renee Price

Library of Congress Control Number: 2002107482
ISBN 0-87986-091-x

DEDICATED TO ALL WOMEN SOCIAL EDUCATORS,
PAST, PRESENT, AND FUTURE.

Table of Contents

Preface

Margaret Smith Crocco

This book has been a long time in the making. Why that is so needs explaining, because the reasons are historically significant. They suggest larger truths about the state of historical research, gender equity, race relations, and of course, social studies as an academic enterprise. This preface and the chapter narratives that follow are an effort to lay out these issues so that the story of women working in the social studies can be placed within a broad intellectual and social context.

Social studies education is most commonly conceived of as citizenship education. Since the birth of the republic, women have contributed towards this end in a variety of formal and informal ways. When women of the late 18th century took on the role of "republican motherhood" by developing civic virtue in their offspring, they practiced citizenship education. As compulsory education spread across the country during the 19th century, numerous female authors and educators undertook the task of laying out suitable form and content for the history and geography of formal schooling. By the time social studies took its contemporary shape in 1920, teaching had become a feminized profession. Women teachers and teacher educators embraced the new discipline of social studies, developing its theory, method, and practice in distinctive ways.[1] Today, women find themselves well represented across all domains within the social studies, serving as the majority of all social studies practitioners in kindergarten through twelfth-grade teaching. Women also represent a sizable proportion of all social studies teacher educators working in colleges and universities. Over the last twenty years, the increasing number of female presidents of the National Council for the Social Studies (NCSS) offers further evidence of women's enhanced visibility within the field.

Using the words "enhanced visibility" is a deliberate choice, but one requiring comment. We might have used an alternative phrase such as "enhanced presence," especially if we were writing about the history of math, science, law, or medicine. It is quite clear that women have always been a presence in social studies. By contrast, "visibility" implies "one who sees" as well as "something to be seen." This word choice underscores our

belief that a kind of intellectual fog, for which words such as "sexism" and "patriarchy" have been used, inhibited until quite recently the seeing of women as contributing agents to the social studies.

This "insight" has made itself painfully obvious to anyone bringing feminist sensibilities to reading the histories of the social studies. As a result of the 75th anniversary of the founding of NCSS, several important works were published.[2] This research has been valuable in establishing an "official history" of the social studies, as manifest through the development of the premiere organization of the field, NCSS. These narratives have focused on "great men" from elite universities responsible for shaping the field in institutionally sanctioned ways. These works have neglected the roles played by women, whose contributions in advancing the social studies were made more commonly at the grassroots level — in schools, as supervisors and textbook authors, and at the margins of institutions such as NCSS and elite universities. What is dismaying, however, is that none of the authors of these historiographic works problematized, at least in print, the portrait they painted of a field seemingly dominated by men or questioned what the women were doing as far as social education was concerned.

Although this oversight surprises less than it disturbs, the social studies field has features that make its narrative different from those of law, medicine, science, or even academic history. For example, Bessie Pierce, the first female president of NCSS, took over the reins of the organization in 1926. Between that date and 1984, fourteen women in all led NCSS. Numerous others served in leadership roles at the county and state levels and as curriculum developers, supervisors, theorists, teacher educators, and classroom practitioners. If we think more broadly about social studies by considering forms of social education antedating the establishment of the formal domain of social studies in 1921, the number of women who have shaped the field grows even larger.

Using the term "social education" suggests that education about democracy and citizenship has occurred in a variety of settings beyond the school. In this book as well as in previous work,[3] we have defined social education as teaching and learning about how individuals construct and live out their understandings of social, political, and economic relations—past and present—and the implications of these understandings for how citizens are educated in a democracy. Women such as Jane Addams and Eleanor Roosevelt have been intimately and prominently involved in social education.

Likewise, school-based social studies, unlike traditional academic fields such as history, has always had a hybrid status, with strong attachments across institutional boundaries of school and university. As a result, there have always been more avenues for involvement of women than was the case in disciplines identified more prominently with postsecondary education. Over the last several decades, as women's roles have moved towards greater equity of opportunity, women have assumed leadership positions in even larger numbers in academic disciplines, at least within the humanities, and to a lesser extent, the social sciences. At the same time, the feminist movement has resulted in spreading consciousness by many women and men of the gender dynamics shaping modern society.

Nevertheless, the major historiographic works within the social studies have largely ignored these developments. Even those written by women, such as Hazel Hertzberg's significant publication *Social Studies Reform, 1880-1980* feature very few women.[4] To the degree that such monographs rely on one another in outlining the important figures and crucial milestones in the evolution of the social studies, they perpetuate a monolithic vision. Clearly, more primary research needs to be done about the many questions that remain unanswered concerning our field's origins and development, especially the forms of citizenship education found among diverse groups in the United States.

If we widen our gaze and move beyond the record found in conventional histories, we see that women's contributions to the field have been significant. Archival data, anecdotal information, oral histories, and other forms of communal memory, especially as seen from within the landscape of the feminization of teaching, indicate that women played crucial roles in shaping the social studies. Why, then, this invisibility? In sum, we believe that women's absence from the historical record derives less from a lack of sustained contribution to the social studies than from historians' unwillingness or inability to perceive and acknowledge that contribution.

In this book, we write a history of the social studies that owes much to the expansive approach represented by the work of Bernard Bailyn and Lawrence Cremin. These scholars believed the history of education should be written as social history, encompassing the array of institutions and agents that contributed to the socialization of youth.[5] We recognize that since the mid-19th century in most parts of this country, the formal pedagogy of schooling has been the fulcrum of citizenship education. Nevertheless, we also consider settlement houses during the progressive era and citizenship schools associated with the civil rights movement as alternative means by which diverse groups transmitted their concern for citizenship education. These shadow institutions functioned to raise questions about who gets recognized as a citizen and what a citizen's rights are during critical periods in American history when such issues were hotly contested. At such moments, in settings such as segregated schools, the equitable reach of the traditional agencies of citizenship education was indicted, and the verdict rendered that schools had failed in their mission to promote "advanced ideas about democracy."[6] In our effort to write this more inclusive history of our field, we acknowledged the exclusions that have been part of our shared history, and we attempted to compensate for them by casting a wide net, which moved us into the realm of social education.

Making Choices

In selecting the women to be included in this book, we started by establishing the following criteria: The women included should be those (1) whose careers as educators concerned with citizenship education covered a sizable span of years in the 19th and 20th centuries, but who had retired by the mid-1990s, which allowed their full career paths to be described; (2) whose work influenced the offerings, instruction, or conceptualization of the social studies or those school subjects ordinarily included in the social studies; (3) whose influence had at least a strong regional, but preferably national impact within these areas; and (4) whose impact can be assessed through documentary or testimonial evidence of a sufficient scope to allow for well-grounded historical accuracy of biographical treatment.

We devised a proposed list of candidates generated by an initial exchange of candidates' names with a group of experts in the field. We then mailed ballots to a larger group of twenty-six experts, all of whom taught social studies education at the college and university level and were familiar with its history. The response we received from these consultants largely governed selection for the book and provided an enthusiastic endorsement for its concept. Several new names were also added as a result of this process. Throughout the nomination phase, we were struck that our experts (both men and women) often did not recognize several of what we took to be the more "prominent" names on our list. This observation supported the guiding assumption behind this book: The major female social studies educators of the past, even women deemed pre-eminent by their contemporaries, are not well remembered today.

This collective amnesia was compounded when we turned our attention to the matter of race and ethnicity during the nomination process. We were committed to including a diverse representation of women in this book, but were dismayed so few names of women of color emerged. We placed calls for nominees with appropriate online listservs and newsgroups affiliated with the American Educational Research Association, the College and University Faculty Assembly (CUFA) of NCSS, and Special Interest Groups related to these organizations in an effort to solicit names of nominees from more diverse backgrounds. Unfortunately, we achieved little success with these efforts. Our failure raised a set of interesting historiographic questions about the particular invisibility of women of color within the social studies and our own inability, as white authors, to deal effectively with a legacy of racism and discrimination.

We considered whether it was the case that cultural and institutional racism had prevented minority women from achieving prominence and/or whether we simply didn't know of these women's efforts. Over the past two centuries, *de jure* segregation in the South and *de facto* segregation in the North prohibited many women of color from achieving the kind of national prominence we called for in our selection criteria. For example, we know that many women of color worked diligently within their own communities to promote Black history and citizenship education. They have labored often times under the auspices of organizations like the Association for the Study of Negro History and Life, the National Council of Negro Women, the National Association of Colored Women, and the Black sororities. Moreover, their efforts generally escaped notice by white society. Perhaps this legacy of indifference toward the work black women have done was manifesting itself once again in our shared lack of awareness as "experts" in the field of social studies education.

To some extent, we mitigated this problem by adopting a broad perspective of work in social education. Our primary goal was to feature women in this book who would be recognized as working "within" the social studies field. However, bearing in mind the broader tradition of social education, we decided to include a few women, some white and some black, who were not conventionally associated with social studies education. The contributions of figures such as Jane Addams, Ella Baker, Septima Clark, and Eleanor Roosevelt to citizenship education were simply too great to be left out, despite their lack of formal ties to mainstream organizations within the field.

Still, we must acknowledge our own acute sense of failure to identify more women of color for this book, those who taught social studies and citizenship education in the barrio, on the reservation, and in the segregated schools of the South. We are not satisfied with the limited number of more recognizable names included here who must "stand in" in a sense for those less well known. Although our nomination process attempted to be systematic, we are aware of the role of serendipity (in this case related to geography) in bringing to our attention the names of black women such as Deborah Partridge Wolfe. But what of Chicana and Native American women who also served to promote citizenship education? Despite extensive efforts over the last several years, we were unable to identify a more diverse pool of candidates for this book. If education is indeed life, rather than merely preparation for life, as John Dewey believed, then education has an obligation to mirror the richness and diversity of life. As a field dedicated to citizenship education, this mandate must be taken seriously. While we acknowledge that this book itself is incomplete, we hope that its publication will stimulate further investigation into those women and men who have contributed to citizenship education across a more diverse array of communities and in a broader variety of ways than those represented here.

Contribution History

Social studies scholar Mary Kay Tetreault has called "contribution history" an approach that includes women in the historical narrative when they meet "male standards of greatness."[7] Contribution history has been criticized in some circles as striving to bring women into the historic annals at almost any cost. Furthermore, some scholars undercut women's history generally by dismissing almost any form of it as contribution history. We believe, however, that histories focusing on women's contributions have a foundational role to play in helping to rewrite the history of the field, especially to the degree that they explicitly challenge "male standards of greatness." We see our gambit of broadening social studies to social education in this light. In considering the difference between contribution history and "transformative history," which truly reshapes collective understanding of a field, we wish to make several additional points.

First, it merits notice that the writing of history is a normative enterprise. Cultural values imbricate our understanding of historical significance. In this culture, wealth and power have brought greater opportunity for historical memorialization, while anonymity and conventionality have guaranteed historical obscurity. To the degree that women have been limited in their access to wealth and power, and even to individuality, it is not surprising that such a standard has limited the number of women included in written history, as Mary Beard pointed out over fifty years ago.[8]

When women's history gathered steam thirty years ago as part of the larger movement called "social history," norms related to historical significance shifted.[9] Today, consideration of large-scale cohorts, mass movements, "obscure" individuals, and long forgotten historical episodes has been used to illuminate and even uproot conventional historical narratives. Scholars such as Gerda Lerner, Natalie Zemon Davis, Joan Scott, Joan Kelly, and Laurel Thatcher Ulrich, among others, have demonstrated the capacity of women's history to alter accepted conceptualizations, periodizations, and interpretations of the historical narrative. Some question whether the field has any capacity remaining for the larger, synthetic narratives of earlier epochs of history writing.

The second point to make in this vein is the shift in the kinds of questions that get asked about women's history. In this book, we pose the question about the history of the social studies and women in this manner: "Over our nation's history, how have women's lives and work reflected a concern with citizenship education?" We do not ask the question of traditional historiographers: "Have there been any important women in social studies?"

Asking the former question may yield new information that could be characterized as contribution history, but it could also transform our understanding of the nature, agents, and legacy of the social studies. The

history of the social studies will no longer be apprehended as isomorphic with that of NCSS but will reflect a richer constellation of concerns, approaches, and frameworks that inform but are not limited to the field's institutional expressions. This transformed understanding will also heighten our awareness of a central paradox of our field that has gone without remark for too long: that even as women (and African Americans, Asian Americans, Native Americans, and Hispanic Americans generally) were promoting citizenship education, they were denied the full prerogatives of citizenship. If this book clarifies the work still needing to be done to resolve such contradictions, then readers may judge this book itself a contribution to citizenship education.

Notes
1. Margaret Smith Crocco and O. L. Davis, Jr., eds. *"Bending the Future to Their Will": Civic Women, Social Education, and Democracy* (Lanham, MD: Rowman and Littlefield, 1999).
2. See O. L. Davis Jr., ed., *NCSS in Retrospect* (Washington, DC: NCSS, 1996); "A History of NCSS: Seventy Five Years of Service," a special issue of *Social Education* edited by Ben A. Smith and J. Jesse Palmer, vol. 59, no. 7 (November/December, 1995); Walter Parker, "Advanced Ideas about Democracy," *Teachers College Record* 98, no. 1 (Spring, 1996): 10-25.
3. Crocco and Davis, 1999.
4. Hazel Hertzberg, *Social Studies Reform 1880-1960: A Project SPAN Report* (Boulder, CO: Social Science Education Consortium, 1981).
5. Ellen Condliffe Lagemann discusses this tradition of scholarship in the history of education in her book, *An Elusive Science: The Troubling History of Education Research* (Chicago: University of Chicago Press, 2000), 177-78.
6. Walter Parker, 10-25.
7. Mary Kay Tetreault, "Rethinking Women, Gender, and the Social Studies," *Social Education*, 51, no. 3 (March 1987): 170-80.
8. Margaret Smith Crocco, "Forceful Yet Forgotten: Mary Ritter Beard and the Writing of History," *The History Teacher* 31, no. 1 (November 1997): 9-33.
9. Indeed, neo-liberal historian Gertrude Himmelfarb has lamented in an essay about the state of the historical field that the margin has become center and the center, the margin: "Some Reflections on the New History," *American Historical Review*, 94, no. 3 (1989): 661-670.

1.

Conceptualizing
Social Education
for a Growing Nation:
1784-1919

Introduction

Margaret Smith Crocco

After the birth of the American republic, women helped build a new social order in a manner that reflected the ideals of democracy but was constrained by gender ideology suggesting that women's contributions should be confined to the private sphere of home and family. Abigail Adams and other educated women like Judith Sargent Murray and Mercy Otis Warren hoped the revolutionary principles of the 1760s and 1770s would bring a more equitable society, one that adhered less rigidly to the patriarchal social arrangements of England. While historians have debated the radicalism of the American Revolution,[1] many who supported the patriots' cause found themselves disappointed in 1789 with the limited reach of the democratic changes consolidated under the framework of the United States Constitution.

In a letter written to her husband, Abigail Adams' famous admonition to "remember the ladies" yielded little opportunity for direct political engagement by women citizens. Despite New Jersey's brief experiment with giving women the franchise between 1776 and 1807, women and blacks across the country found themselves in much the same position after the Revolution as they had been before. Citizenship offered women few prerogatives, certainly not the right to vote.[2] Elizabeth Cady Stanton and Lucy Stone pointed out repeatedly during the 19th century women's rights campaign that propertied female citizens suffered the same indignity as the colonists had: taxation without representation. States rarely provided women with economic or legal rights as independent persons apart from their husbands or fathers.

As a result of the ratification of the U.S. Constitution, African Americans suffered under a slave system that was now constitutionally protected. This sanction strengthened slavery's grip across the South. At the same time, the Constitution weakened slavery in the North where the "peculiar institution" was less profitable than in southern economies based on plantation agriculture.

Despite these problems, the builders of the new republic did not entirely forget the ladies. During the fifty years after the ratification of the U.S. Constitution, states dismantled property qualifications for voting. In response to the relatively wide distribution of the franchise, Dr. Benjamin Rush of Philadelphia in the 1790s promoted education for women under the banner of "republican motherhood." Rush believed providing for a literate (white, male) electorate was essential to the democratic experiment. In this context, literacy meant the ability to read, write, and perform simple arithmetic calculations. Such an education wedded to the development of "civic virtue"—reason, integrity, independence, and "manliness," or the willingness to take up arms to defend the nation—would enhance the strength and stability of the new republic, he believed.

As many historians of education have pointed out, the United States' developing interest in education was defined chiefly by the utilitarian principle of building a democratic nation within the context of an agricultural economy. Although a number of colleges were established in the United States during the 18th century, their purposes were closely tied to the preparation of a well-educated ministry. For the rest of the American population, the modest educational goals of literacy, numeracy, and moral education sufficed.

In this enterprise, Rush believed that women could make a unique contribution. He promoted the creation of female schools, such as the Young Ladies Academy in Philadelphia, for educating women who would be pivotal in nurturing republican offspring. Only small numbers of women attended such schools during the late 18th and early 19th century. More typical of the means by which women received educations at this time is the story of Hannah Adams. Her father encouraged Hannah's use of his private library and even provided access to private tutors. In middle class households across the North and South, many daughters gained an education in this manner alongside their brothers. While the content of such education for sons and daughters might be roughly comparable, parents saw the aims of female education as Rush did. Daughters applied their education within the private sphere of the home. Sons took their education into the public sphere of commerce, industry, and agriculture, thus shaping the fortunes of the new nation directly.

As the 19th century unfolded, several individuals, the best known among them Noah Webster and Horace Mann, began to consider more deeply the education demanded by a democratic republic. These men sought to use education to shape a distinctive and self-conscious American culture, defined in large measure by its distance from old world ways. Even earlier than Webster and Mann, Hannah Adams found inspiration in the idea of creating a unique American approach to education. Adams created new approaches to history and geography, especially for the expanding educational marketplace of Massachusetts, a laboratory of public education. Adams' history and geography texts emphasized the stories of common folk alongside those of elites. Although she felt that the study of history should inculcate national pride and serve as moral education, she did not seek to accomplish these ends by mythologizing the nation's leaders. Instead, she stressed the importance of deriving moral lessons from stories grounded in history. Adams also advocated study of the history of the world's religions as a means of promoting religious toleration in a diverse society.

Adams herself was not a teacher. In an unusual move for a woman, she signed her own name to her books in an effort to claim the status of author. Even rarer for a woman, Adams attempted to make a living from her writing. As public education expanded, the rapid development of female literacy closed an earlier gap between the sexes. Many other women became authors, especially of fiction, and made a living from their writing. So many became popular writers in the mid-19th century that Nathaniel Hawthorne expressed his resentment of their success by calling them those "damned female scribblers."

Expanding educational opportunities produced a growing cadre of female teachers as well as female authors. Horace Mann's leadership in establishing public education in Massachusetts spread to other states throughout the 19th century. By 1850, over half the nation's school-age white children were enrolled, although great variation existed from state to state in attendance, funding for public education, and length of the school year.[3] As towns across the country built public schools, a shortage of teachers developed. The low status and poor pay of teaching partially explains why educated young women were given the chance to fill these new jobs.

Emma Willard saw opportunity for women in the growth of public education. Even if a woman taught for only a few years before marrying and tending to her family, as many did, she needed preparation for the work. Willard lobbied the New York state legislature for support of a female academy for the teacher training of women. Although the legislature refused her request, Willard managed to put together private funding to open a school in Troy, New York. With Catharine Beecher, Willard helped to normalize the teaching profession as a hospitable place for women, one consonant with women's duties to home and family. By the mid-19th century, the gender ideology of the day stressed women's moral nature. What has been called "the cult of true womanhood" prescribed purity, piety, domesticity, and submissiveness (to God and man) for middle-class women. Beecher and Willard successfully leveraged these qualities in their bid to have women considered as "natural" candidates for teaching.

Hannah Adams and Emma Willard shared a set of convictions about the nature of education for students and teachers in a democracy. They held that curriculum should build the moral character believed necessary for citizenship. Willard's curriculum at her school in Troy emphasized moral and religious learning, as well as literary, domestic, and artistic pursuits. Like Lucy Salmon later in the 19th century, Willard advocated teaching history in a manner that heightened student interest, avoided rote memorization, and promoted critical engagement with historical materials.

Horace Mann had argued that the form and direction of learning should begin with sympathy for the child. He endorsed women as superior teachers, believing that they generally possessed the tenderness, gentility, and patience necessary for education that was child-oriented. In 1839, the first public normal school for teacher preparation was established in Lexington, Massachusetts.[4] " (*Normal schools* were teacher training institutes designed to serve as a norm, or model, for the profession.)[5] Mann astutely recognized the strain on states' budgets that public education produced. Since towns paid women half or less of a man's salary, Mann's advocacy of women as teachers can be interpreted as both economically motivated and pedagogically justified. By 1860, 80 percent of the teachers in Massachusetts were women. Across the eastern states, the figure was much lower (25 percent), but rose rapidly as cities grew in the last quarter of the century.[6] By 1900, 75 percent of all teachers were women, with that proportion much higher in cities.[7]

Horace Mann's formula for the provision of public education in Massachusetts spread across the country throughout the second half of the 19th century. The cult of true womanhood and doctrine of separate spheres (demarcating the home as the woman's and the rest of the world as the man's) were both justified by cultural understandings of male and female "temperaments" as distinct, if not polar opposites. Woman's lot in life thus lay in creating a home that would serve as refuge for her husband, who required a sanctuary from the hurly-burly world of commerce and industry. To the extent that women wished to or needed to work, they might adopt teaching, a profession for which they were believed uniquely well-suited. For middle-class women, such work would most likely be a temporary transit between the end of their education and the onset of marriage and family life. Only in the case of women willing to forego marriage entirely could lifelong pursuit of a teaching career be entertained as a possibility. As the century proceeded, however, more and more women seemed willing to accept these terms in order to acquire a profession.

Women's rights leader Susan B. Anthony chose this option. From her early teens, Anthony taught school in upstate New York in order to help her father pay the family's bills. She discovered firsthand just how unfairly women were paid. In 1839, she left home to teach and administer at two schools, one a Friends Seminary in New Rochelle, and another near Rochester called the Canajoharie Academy. Eventually Anthony grew dissatisfied with teaching. Not coincidentally, one must assume, she became attracted at about this time to the women's rights movement.[8]

In 1850, Anthony met Elizabeth Cady Stanton. Although Anthony had not attended the famous meeting for women's rights at Seneca Falls, New York, in 1848, her parents and younger sister had. Amelia Bloomer, the advocate of dress reform for women, introduced Anthony to Stanton, launching their lifelong partnership to make the "Declaration of Sentiments," the women's rights platform constructed at Seneca Falls, a reality. Modeled after the Declaration of Independence, this document enumerated the various ways in which men had exercised tyranny over women and usurped their rights. While ownership of property and deprivation of access to employment were major complaints, restriction of access to education also figured centrally in the women's grievances. Suffrage was the only demand not unanimously supported by those convened

for the first women's rights meeting within the United States. Both Stanton and Anthony believed suffrage to be the linchpin for accomplishing everything else and spent their lives working towards this end.

The meeting at Seneca Falls set in motion a series of comparable events across the United States that gradually but fundamentally changed women's status as citizens over the next one hundred years. Stanton and Anthony understood the pivotal nature not only of the ballot but also of education. Without access to higher education, in particular, the professions and pulpit would remain closed to women. In 1860, almost one out of ten women over the age of ten who were not slaves were wage earners. Their options for occupation were severely limited, however—to servants, seamstresses, teachers, or mill operatives. By 1870 close to 14 percent of all women worked for pay; by 1910 that number increased to more than 20 percent of women over sixteen.[9]

Thus, the question of women's access to education, and to higher education especially, became a live and pressing concern during the decades after the Civil War. Public high schools awarded increasingly more diplomas as compared with private academies. By the late 19th century, the enrollment of women in secondary education eclipsed that of men. Normal schools provided an alternative or capstone to the standard high school curriculum for many women, as did the growing number of colleges and universities. In 1870, 11,000 women attended college, comprising 20 percent of the student population. By 1900, this number had grown to 85,000, making women nearly 37 percent of those enrolled.[10] These institutions drew mainly from the expanding middle class and were overwhelmingly limited to white women. Oberlin College was the first to graduate a black woman, Mary Jane Patterson, in 1862. Anna Julia Cooper estimated that by 1891 only thirty black college women could be identified in the entire country.[11] During the 1880s when the first generation of women graduated from college, two-thirds of all those who sought employment became teachers.[12] This group included many black women, like Fannie Jackson Coppin, Lucy Laney, and Nannie Burroughs, who throughout the Jim Crow South helped to staff segregated school systems for black children.

As women seized the opportunity for education in ever increasing numbers, social scientists discovered to their dismay that college-educated women were not marrying at the same rate as other women.[13] At least one-fourth of women graduates never married, a proportion double that for non-college women. Likewise, even those who married produced fewer children. In the "female world of love and ritual" that these women created, individuals like Jane Addams, creator of Hull House, and Lucy Salmon, historian and Vassar professor, found themselves freed from the constraints of Victorian marriage and able to pursue careers demanding intense levels of commitment.[14] Like Addams and Salmon, many of them fought for suffrage. As the life of Mary Sheldon Barnes demonstrates, women who married typically abandoned or compromised their careers to accommodate their husband's career interests. Employment options in college teaching for women were quite limited. Salmon's position at Vassar, a women's college, represented the most common accommodation for women with Ph.D.s. For a married woman like Barnes, following her husband to a coeducational institution meant settling for a position below that of professor.

By the turn of the century, urbanization, industrialization, and massive immigration had created a new national consensus concerning the means and ends of education in a "modern" nation. By 1890, twenty-seven states had enacted compulsory attendance laws.[15] In response to the challenge of compulsory education for a rapidly growing population, educational policy makers established what has been dubbed "the one best system."[16] Centralization and bureaucratization characterized this approach to schooling. As in Mann's time, the educational mandate lay in expanding schooling while keeping costs under control. The "cult of efficiency" applied Frederick W. Taylor's time and motion studies for business to schools.[17]

These realities produced a change in the mission of education. No longer was schooling chiefly about moral or civic virtue, but instead it concerned itself more deliberately with economic betterment and citizenship education. Heightened attention to economic goals reflected educational and civic leaders' desire to fit graduates to the demands of an industrialized workplace and to assimilate immigrants as quickly as possible to the American civic polity.

The progressive period in American politics and education can be thought of as a tree with many branches. Reformist in nature overall, progressivism in practice often split into contradictory directions at the local, state, and national level. In the realm of educa-

tion, historians have identified two distinct categories of progressives: those they call administrative progressives, a more conservative group who promoted the centralization and bureaucratization of schooling, and those considered Deweyan, child-centered, or liberal progressives who wished to use the state and schools as instruments of social justice.[18]

Both camps sought to "help" immigrants adjust to American life, often through the agency of schooling. On the one hand, figures associated with the origins of social studies like Thomas Jesse Jones felt education should override the traditional cultures of African Americans, Native Americans, and immigrants. A report by the Commissioner of Indian Affairs in 1901 maintained that all the federal government money expended had been a waste.[19] The report suggested replacing boarding schools with public day schools on the reservations. In both forms, however, extirpation of the indigenous culture was attempted. Likewise, Booker T. Washington's regimen of industrial, trades-oriented education catapulted him into pre-eminence in national educational circles where white leaders were only too eager to coopt his educational rationale in an attempt to keep blacks in a subjugated position within American society.[20]

By contrast, Jane Addams' settlement in Chicago, Hull House, took a different approach to the education of immigrants and to a lesser extent, African Americans. Addams' educational philosophy called for recognizing the value and preserving aspects of the traditional culture. She hoped Hull House would serve as a model for recreating urban schools according to this ethos. Other progressives like Leonard Covello in New York City thought that schools should become the hearts of their communities, providing an array of social services such as after-school care, medical exams, free lunches, summer recreation programs, speech therapy, vocational counseling, and instruction in English and citizenship.

Schools could thus become broadly socializing agencies, dedicated to bringing marginalized groups into the mainstream, albeit generally on the mainstream's terms. These progressives recognized that occupation was no longer capable of bringing about social cohesion in the face of urbanization, immigration, and industrialization. According to Paula Fass, progressives believed that in this changing environment, formal education ought to serve as "the strategic basis for adult preparation and community survival."[21]

Once again, new goals for education demanded new pedagogical approaches. Social reformer Grace Abbott, like many of the women profiled in this book, disparaged the "steamroller approach" to schooling.[22] One size did not fit all in these educators' judgment; they believed schools run like factories violated sound educational principles. Their child-centered approach has been associated with John Dewey, but took many forms in practice. Salmon demonstrated one application when she began her students' investigation of history by asking them to examine the world around them—the backyard, kitchen, and main street. Barnes's promotion of object-based teaching emanated from this same inclination to begin the educational process with found objects that would lead to students' discovery of the concrete and abstract realities associated with home environments. At once inductive and particularistic, these educational approaches engaged students in analysis of their world, leading them to richer conceptualizations and enhanced powers of inquiry and inference. Like those of Addams, the strategies of Barnes and Salmon reflected openness to the cultures of home and community. Furthermore, in using an inductive approach to learning rooted in students' own life experiences, these scholars trained students to think for themselves in a systematic and empirically oriented fashion, thus subtly undermining the "received wisdom" dominating the classical curriculum of their day.

Addams, Barnes, and Salmon were among the first generation of women to receive a college education. In her biography, Addams acknowledges the paradox produced by this privilege in the lives of her fellow female college graduates. "Well educated with nothing to do" captures the conundrum these women confronted. In establishing Hull House, Addams solved a twin set of problems: her own quandary about what to do with her education, and her desire to be responsive to the needs of immigrants. The solution of the settlement house offered a means for both parties to live in new, creative, and more satisfying ways. As Nancy Woloch put it, Hull House gave Addams a socially sanctioned manner of replacing the "family claim" with a larger, public one that contained both an intellectual challenge and the opportunity to do benevolent work.[23]

While largely satisfying for many women, the college experience also produced difficulties related to the cultural sense that too much education damaged a woman's frail constitution. Many women could recollect an experience like the one described by Lucy Salmon with Woodrow Wilson, who found himself uncomfortable teaching women at Bryn Mawr and let it be known. Likewise, the famous sociologist, Franklin Giddings of Columbia University, told the graduating class at Bryn Mawr that "the social order demanded the subordination of women."[24] Salmon responded to these sorts of experiences not, she said wryly, with "inspiration," but rather with the "courage to disprove the doubts."[25] In these early generations of female college graduates, therefore, was often born a sense of refusal—about marriage, gender ideology, and women's status as citizens. After 1900, college women founded suffrage organizations from campus to campus, organized debates and lectures by suffrage leaders, and like Lucy Salmon at Vassar, often braved administrative disapproval in so doing. As Keith Melder put it, "not every educated woman was a rebel, but nearly every rebel had been educated."[26]

Disciplinary specialization and the development of professional organizations appeared almost in tandem in the early 20th century. The National Council for Teachers of Mathematics and the National Council of Teachers of English were both established by 1920.[27] In 1916, the National Education Association promulgated a report on secondary education that has been seen as a watershed in the history of the social studies.[28] Within five years, the National Council for the Social Studies was launched, establishing an institutional framework for a field that had been evolving for over a century. The 1916 NEA Report had formalized this evolution by establishing a secondary school social studies scope and sequence. The report called for courses in community civics, world history, and modern problems that were new additions to the standard secondary curriculum of the day, alongside perennial course offerings such as American history. In 1920, educators from Teachers College, Columbia University, called for a meeting in Atlantic City the following year that would effectively found the modern social studies movement.

Coincidentally, 1920 also marked ratification of the 19th Amendment to the Constitution, giving women the right to vote. Women's rights leaders such as Alice Paul inveighed against a sense of closure at this moment, lobbying immediately for an equal rights amendment to give fuller expression to women's equality under the law. Still, many women found tremendous satisfaction in the culmination of an effort that had been almost one hundred years in the making. As women began voting and consideration of the next phase of their incorporation into the full life of the republic, many women social studies educators recognized that they were well-situated to deliver citizenship education. In the chapters that follow, their contributions to a richer, more inclusive understanding of citizenship education will be discussed.

Notes

1. See for example, Gordon S. Wood, *Radicalism of the American Revolution*, (New York: Random House, 1993).
2. The question of whether women were, indeed, citizens under the law was formally adjudicated in the Supreme Court case, Minor v. Happersett, in 1874. See Eleanor Flexner, *Century of Struggle: The Woman's Rights Movement in the United States* (Cambridge, MA: Harvard University Press, 1959, rev. 1975), 172.
3. Nancy Woloch, *Women and the American Experience* (New York: Oxford, 1984), 125.
4. Urban and Wagoner, *American Education: A History*, 2nd ed. (Boston, MA: McGraw Hill, 2000), 109.
5. Urban and Wagoner; Joseph Watras, *The Foundations of Educational Curriculum and Diversity: 1565 to the Present* (Boston, MA: Allyn and Bacon, 2002)
6. Woloch, 129.
7 Woloch, 247.
8. Edward James, Janet James, and Paul Boyer, *Notable American Women*, vol. 3 (Cambridge, MA: Belknap Press, 1971), 52.
9. Alice Kessler-Harris, *Women Have Always Worked: A Historical Overview* (New York: Feminist Press, 1981), 73.
10. Barbara Solomon, *In the Company of Educated Women* (New York: Oxford, 1984), 63.
11. Anna Julia Cooper, *A Voice from the South* (New York: Negro Universities Press, 1969; reprint of 1892 edition), 3.
12. Woloch, 247.
13. Carl Degler, *At Odds* (New York: Oxford University Press, 1986), 34.
14. Caroll Smith-Rosenberg, *Disorderly Conduct: Visions of Gender in Victorian America* (New York: Oxford University Press, 1985).
15. Urban and Wagoner, 172.
16. David Tyack, *The One Best System* (Cambridge, MA: Harvard University Press, 1974).
17. Raymond Callahan, *The Cult of Efficiency* (Chicago, IL: University of Chicago Press, 1962).
18. Urban and Wagoner, 200.
19. Vine Deloria, Jr. ed., *American Indian Policy in the Twentieth Century* (Norman, OK: University of Oklahoma Press, 1985), 43-44.
20. Louis R. Harlan, *Booker T. Washington: The Making of a Black Leader 1856-1901* (New York: Oxford University Press, 1972).
21. Paula Fass, *Outside In: Minorities and the Transformation of American Education* (New York: Oxford University Press, 1989), 21.
22. Fass, 31.
23. Woloch, 253.
24. Solomon, 88.
25. Solomon, 89.
26. As quoted in Degler, 34.
27. Wilbur F. Murra, "The Birth of NCSS - As Remembered by Earl U. Rugg," *Social Education* 34, no. 7 (1970): 728-729.
28. Stephen J. Thornton, "NCSS: The Early Years," in O. L. Davis, Jr., ed. *NCSS in Retrospect*, Bulletin No. 92 (Washington, DC: NCSS, 1996):1-7; Murry Nelson ed., *The Social Studies in Secondary Education: A Reprint of the Seminal 1916 Report with Annotations and Commentaries* (Bloomington, IN: ERIC Clearinghouse for the Social Studies, 1994).

Hannah Adams

November, 1755 — December, 1831

SHERRY SCHWARTZ

Hannah Adams arguably was the first American woman to write, sign, and publish history textbooks intended for school-age children. Writing at a time when America was virtually inventing its educational traditions, values, and citizenship roles, she was among the new republic's first educators. Born and raised in Massachusetts, a state with a strong commitment to education, Adams was the fifth generation of an extended American family of successful farmers, merchants, local politicians and United States Presidents. Her birthplace of Medfield, approximately seventeen miles outside of Boston, was one of only seven colonial towns in Massachusetts that admitted girls to primary school. Although colonial boys routinely advanced from primary school to male-run writing schools and to Latin grammar schools prior to college, colonial girls were fortunate even to receive a brief formal education. Hannah Adams, however, learned Latin, Greek, geography, and logic from local college students who tutored her while they boarded in her large family home.

Young Hannah, one of four children, also had the opportunity to use the extensive, personal library of her father Thomas (1725-1809). Thomas reluctantly gave up a coveted college education himself to inherit the family farm. He was an enthusiastic supporter of his daughter's intellectual endeavors. In return, Hannah, whose mother died when she was ten, modeled her father's literary passion. In her autobiography (1832) published shortly after her death at age 76, she wrote, "[a]s I always read with great rapidity, perhaps few of my sex have perused more books at the age of twenty than I had."

Life abruptly changed for Hannah when her father, more a scholar than a businessman, bankrupted the family farm by making the poorly timed economic decision to import and sell British-published books on the eve of the Revolution. The result left the family destitute. Before she reached adulthood, financial circumstances forced Hannah to seek a living outside the home.

Throughout her life, Adams relied solely upon her own extended education and intellectual abilities to succeed. Prior to writing, she undertook several jobs which included school teaching. Unfortunately, the few

teaching positions then available to women were brief, low paying summer sessions. At age 29, Adams made the decision to publish her first work as "the last resort" for income. This book, *Alphabetical Compendium of the Various Sects ...* (1784), later renamed *View of Religions* (1791, 1805), was a compilation of ancient and current beliefs from diverse religious sects. Adams held out the faint hope that her researching "hobby ... might be printed, and afford me some little advantage."

In the publication of this work, Adams took the bold step of signing her own name. Scholars consider her one of the first American women to earn a living from writing. At that time, most women authors wrote as an avocation or to a limited audience of family members. Rare, published writers, like social critic Mercy Otis Warren or women's rights advocate Judith Sargent Murray, were financially secure through marriage. Some hid their gender behind pseudonyms. In the preface of Adams's first publication, Thomas Prentiss, the minister of Medfield's Congregational Church, apologized for Adams's "[having] done violence to her own inclinations, by prefixing her own name."

Choosing to remain single for life, Adams rejected what she herself called "the shackles of matrimony." Unlike most of her married contemporaries, she could sign contracts and own property. To protect her literary property, Adams acquired a state copyright in 1784, and lobbied the United States Congress to pass the first U.S. copyright law in 1790. As a "spinster," however, Adams faced many obstacles in a male-dominated professional world. Most significant of these was her prolonged public battle with powerful minister and textbook writer Jedediah Morse over charges of plagiarism concerning their competing geography textbooks.

The financial success and civic contributions of two editions of her religious history inspired Adams to write a *Summary History of New England* (1799) to "benefit the public" and "be useful to those in early life." No complete New England history existed at the time. Adams's shorter and simplified school text, *An Abridgment of the History of New England* (1805, 1807), specifically addressed the first generation of America's school-age citizens. Adopted in Boston's public schools and elsewhere, Adams's textbooks rejected the strong inherited customs and traditions of a classical European aristocracy and substituted American voices and stories from a diverse array of backgrounds.

Another dimension of Adams's contribution to social education were her efforts to foster civic pride and responsible character traits for all Americans. Her textbooks identified individuals of historic note different from the traditional military or political leaders found almost exclusively at that time in history textbooks. Adams included, for example, the story of Nathan Hale, a relatively unknown (at that time) Revolutionary War captain, who "lamented that he had but one life to lose for his country." She also detailed the contributions of Anne Hutchinson, whom Adams labeled "a very extraordinary woman." At a time when other textbook writers created myths about America's Founding Fathers, such as the famous story by M. L. "Parson" Weems (1810) about George Washington and the cherry tree, Adams perceived no need to whitewash America's heroes.

Adams sought to instill tolerance and understanding concerning diverse beliefs as an important condition for strengthening the country and its citizens. Noting that America was the first nation to be established without a state religion, Adams emphasized religious tolerance in particular. Education was the key to achieving these goals. Quoting her famous cousin John Adams, she believed that the prevention of tyranny necessitated "knowledge diffused generally through the whole body of people."

Despite the challenges of recognition for a woman author, Adams claimed authority as a social educator. Over her lifetime, she published thirteen books, including an autobiography. Adams wished her young readers to realize that "by overcoming difficulty the mind acquires new energy" and that "early habits of preserving diligence" would lead them "from a low situation" towards new possibilities.

References

Adams, Hannah, *An Abridgment of the History of New England for the Use of Young Persons*, 2nd ed. Boston, MA: Etherridge & Bliss, 1807.

Adams, Hannah, *A Memoir of Miss Hannah Adams, Written by Herself with Additional Notices by a Friend*. Boston, MA: Grey Bowen, 1832.

Adams, Hannah. Papers, Massachusetts Historical Society, Boston, MA.

Adams, Hannah. Papers, New England Genealogical Society, Boston, MA.

Tweed, Thomas A., "Hannah Adams, An American Pioneer in the Study of Religion." *Journal of The American Academy of Religion* 60 (1992):437-464.

Vella, Michael W., "Theology, Genre and Gender: The Precarious Place of Hannah Adams in American Literary History." *Early American Literature* 28 (1993): 21-41.

Emma Hart Willard

February 23, 1787 — April 15, 1870

Mary Beth Henning

Emma Hart Willard founded what might be called America's first normal school. Born into a large, patriotic family in Berlin, Connecticut, Emma grew up with a love of reading and history. In 1802-1803, she attended the nearby Berlin Academy. From the age of seventeen to twenty, she taught children or older youth for part of each year in Berlin schools. When she was not teaching, she studied at the Pattens' "dame school" or Lydia Royse's school in Hartford.

In 1807, Emma Hart began to teach and to act as female assistant at the Westfield Academy, in Westfield, Connecticut. Soon afterward, she moved to Middlebury, Vermont, to head an academy there. In 1809, she married Dr. John Willard and, with the birth of her only natural child the following year, devoted herself to domestic motherhood. She continued, however, to read voraciously and to investigate curricula at schools. When her nephew boarded with her during his attendance at Middlebury College, she mastered his textbooks and learned about the college's course of study.

Willard returned to teaching and school administration in 1814 when she opened a boarding school in her own home. Gradually, she introduced "higher subjects" into her curriculum such as history, geography, philosophy, and mathematics. In 1818, she wrote a plan and justification for women's higher education, "An Address to the Public; Particularly to the Members of the Legislature of New York, Proposing a Plan for Improving Female Education," which became her most famous work.

After a year as the principal of the Waterford Academy, Willard moved to Troy, New York, in order to administer a new school, the Troy Female Seminary. From 1821-1838, she acted as principal, mentor, and teacher to the students at this seminary, while also publishing many successful textbooks, as well as letters, poetry, and political appeals. Upon her retirement from school administration, she traveled in Europe and the United States as an advocate for women's education. As superintendent of the common schools of Kensington, Connecticut, she provided in-service training to teachers and continued to write visionary curricula for young women. On April 15, 1870, Willard died in Troy, New York.

In her most eloquent work, the 1819 "Plan for Improving Female Education," Willard argued that women needed to be educated at public expense in order to be prepared for their roles as mothers of the republic. Using frequent references to God, man, and patriotism, Willard argued that what women needed was not the same kind of education that men had, but a better education than was being offered to them. She focused on the role of women's education in the development of character and citizenship. She recognized that contemporary institutions of higher education for women usually depended on parents and pupils for financial support. Consequently, she held that state legislators should financially support women's higher education in order to improve the quality of grade school curricula and of teachers.

One of the chief aims for seminaries, in Willard's view, was to provide qualified teachers to the growing republic. Although the New York legislature never agreed to provide the funding that Willard requested, she used her personal resources to support her vision. She provided approximately seventy-five thousand dollars in scholarships to young women who wanted to become teachers, but could not afford Troy's tuition. The students were obligated to repay the loans gradually after they secured employment, but many of them married and never repaid the loans. Although Willard often spoke to her students about the benefits of teaching for a measure of financial independence, she was also a staunch supporter of marriage and motherhood.

Willard called for instruction in four themes at the Troy Female Seminary: moral/religious, literary, domestic, and arts education. Her own textbooks often provided the progressive curriculum. Her bestseller, *History of the United States or Republic of America*, was reprinted fifty-three times and was translated into German and Spanish. Not only did Willard believe that the study of history was essential to shape character and to preserve national wealth, but she also believed that students should find history relevant to their own lives. In her teaching, she de-emphasized rote memorization and used graphic representations such as maps and charts. End of the year examinations featured students drawing maps of different periods in history in order to illustrate chronology and historical events. Using her own students, Willard tested her theory of an integrated curriculum of history and geography. She then promoted this curriculum through successful textbooks. Her *Ancient Geography* was popular and noteworthy for its use of colored maps and drawings such as "the temple of time." This graphic depicted world history as pillars representing the centuries, battles, nations, and epochs that she considered significant. As a teacher, she also integrated writing and literature into studies of different historical time periods.

Emma Willard was a vocal advocate for early women's education. Through her textbooks and Troy Female Seminary, she taught hundreds of the best-prepared teachers of the nineteenth century. Not only was she instrumental in showing that women's opportunities would be enhanced by a challenging higher education, her textbooks showed how history and geography were complementary studies. She also emphasized critical thinking, graphic organizers, maps, charts, and interdisciplinary curriculum. Willard was thus a notable early practitioner and theorist of social studies education.

References

Baym, Nina. "Women and the Republic: Emma Willard's Rhetoric of History." *American Quarterly* 43, no. 1 (March 1991): 1-23.
Lutz, Alma. *Emma Willard: Daughter of Democracy*. Boston, MA: Houghton Mifflin, 1929.
Goodsell, Willystine, ed. *Pioneers of Women's Education in the United States*. New York: McGraw-Hill, 1931.

Many of Willard's papers may be found in the archives of the Emma Willard School in Troy, New York, and at Smith College in Northampton, Massachusetts.

Mary Downing Sheldon Barnes

September 5, 1850—August 27, 1898

FRANCES E. MONTEVERDE

In the mid-1870s, Mary Sheldon Barnes departed radically from traditional memory-recitation methods for pre-collegiate history classes by pioneering "source method" instruction and materials. Her three landmark texts, published by D. C. Heath in 1885, 1886, and 1891, provoked great debate over the use of primary sources and the role of inductive inquiry in schools.

Mary, the eldest of five siblings, was born at Oswego, New York. She attributed her tenacious inquisitive spirit to her mother, Frances A. B. Stiles Sheldon, a school-teacher born to a prominent Syracuse, New York, family. Her father, Edward A. Sheldon, served as the Superintendent of Schools and founded Oswego State Normal and Training School (OSNTS). His exemplary teacher education program, adapted from Pestalozzian beliefs and practices, earned him lasting recognition in United States educational history.

Rather than rely on abstract lectures and recitations, Pestalozzian teachers conducted active "object lessons" and discussions about concrete realities in the immediate environment. Emphasizing sense perceptions, concepts, reason, and humanistic values, they sought to create a more just society. Teacher education at Oswego required extensive work in classrooms, in which experienced educators served as instructors of learning theory, mentors for criticism and praise, and models to observe and emulate. "Pupil teachers" learned to take responsibility for all classroom teaching tasks. They were expected to know subject matter, write well, adhere to strict rules of comportment, and, at graduation, to demonstrate speaking and teaching skills.

From about ages ten to twenty-one, Mary Sheldon was educated in Pestalozzian methods—as a public school pupil, normal school student, and novice teacher. She finished public high school at age sixteen, and the normal school three years later at age nineteen. She completed the advanced Oswego training program and classical studies, i.e., Greek, Latin, and German. Besides the normal school diploma, she qualified for a state teaching certificate that was conferred only to superior graduates. She taught two years at Oswego before she entered the University of Michigan at Ann Arbor in 1871. Admitted with sophomore standing, she followed

the lure of the sciences, then considered beyond the intellectual grasp of women. She also enrolled in two courses with historian Charles K. Adams, a leading proponent of the "source method" developed by Leopold von Ranke in Germany. A product of the European Enlightment, his "seminary method" formed the second educational pillar upon which Sheldon built her professional and intellectual life.

Rankean scholars separated history from its literary roots in the humanities. They applied scientific principles and philological criticism to primary sources, the grounding for their discourses about the past. They collected, evaluated, and interpreted original documents, as well as artifacts and archival materials. Their classrooms resembled laboratories more than lecture halls. Seminar discussions replaced recitations and dogmatic lectures. These new professional historians fostered objectivity and terse writing styles. They demanded intellectual honesty, independent judgment, and hard work.

From 1874 to 1876, "scientific history" replaced the physical sciences as Sheldon's intellectual passion. After earning an A. B. degree at the University of Michigan in 1874, she returned to OSNTS, where she taught Latin, Greek, botany, and history. A definitive moment occurred in 1876 when she declined a position in chemistry at Wellesley College, but subsequently accepted an invitation to join the history faculty later that year. From the winter of 1877 to spring of 1879, she taught history seminars at Wellesley.

Although her students appreciated her primary source documents and discussion methods, she resigned her position because of deterioration in her health and conflicts with the administration. She returned to Oswego for a year of rest and recuperation. From 1880 to 1882, she traveled in Europe with Dr. Mary Victoria Lee, a feminist friend and Oswego teaching colleague. While in England, Sheldon studied briefly with historian John Seeley of Cambridge University. In the fall of 1882, both women resumed their posts at OSNTS. Sheldon began to assemble and draft materials for her first history textbook.

Two watershed events rendered 1885 a turning point in Sheldon's life. On August 6, she married Earl Barnes, her former student, a graduate of OSNTS, Class of 1884, and eleven years her junior. On September 30, D. C. Heath of Boston published her first textbook, *Studies in General History*, which treated ancient and modern Western history.

For the next 13 years, she became an itinerant scholar, following the vicissitudes of her husband's career. Earl Barnes taught at an academy in Hoboken, New Jersey, until 1886, when he moved to Cornell University. For a year, he studied psychology and history while she conducted historical research with Andrew D. White. After studying "pedagogics" at the University of Zurich, Earl accepted a two-year appointment (1889-1891) in the fledgling history department at Indiana University at Bloomington (IUB). The couple spent 1890-91 on leave from IUB to conduct research at Cornell. In 1891, they moved to California with former IUB President David S. Jordan and a group of IUB professors in order to establish Stanford University. As head of the education department, Earl Barnes employed source methods in his teaching of educational history. With the assistance of his wife, he initiated child development studies and served as a consultant to schools throughout California.

From 1885 to 1891, Mary Sheldon Barnes conducted research, wrote, and lectured. Her overarching project was *Studies in American History*, a textbook for eighth-grade pupils. She became the first female faculty member at Stanford in March 1892 when Jordan appointed her assistant professor of history. She taught 19th century European history and a seminar called "Pacific Slope History." The latter featured artifacts and documents from Native American and early Spanish-speaking communities, as well as from European and U. S. citizens who had settled in the area. Under her guidance, graduate students and teachers investigated history instruction in four local school districts. They tested her assumptions about teaching and contributed chapters to *Studies in Historical Method* (1896), a resource book for preservice and experienced teachers that she edited.

Despite his early success, Earl Barnes lost his position at Stanford due to an extramarital relationship that President Jordan deemed unacceptable for a professor.

In 1897, both Earl and Mary resigned, planning to travel and write in Europe. Shortly before her forty-eighth birthday, she suffered a recurrence of chronic heart disease. On August 27, 1898 she died after an experimental medical procedure in a London hospital.

Following her wishes, Earl Barnes buried her ashes in the Protestant Cemetery in Rome between the plots of the English poets, Shelley and Keats. Two years later, he married Anna Kohler, one of his former students at Stanford University.

Significant for social education, Mary Sheldon Barnes synthesized Enlightenment pedagogy and epistemology to develop distinctive new methods and materials for teaching history. She designed her texts and teachers' manuals to sharpen the thinking and language skills required for participatory citizenship. She incorporated extracts from primary and secondary historical sources and literature, as well as drawings, photographs, maps, and charts to build a credible story about the past.

Interspersed throughout the texts, questions guided students' reading, stirred independent thought, and demanded evidence for opinions. Students had to consider conflicting views, the adequacy of information, and cause-and-effect relationships. Barnes also believed that history needed to relate to students' lives. The historian's methods are as important as, if not more important than, the acquisition of facts, according to Barnes.

As the new approach to teaching history evolved in the 1890s, several national committees met to chart suitable course content, methods, and materials for school history courses. Led by Barnes' Michigan mentor C. K. Adams in 1893, the NEA Committee of Ten championed the source method as the standard to follow in teaching history. Professors Fling and Caldwell at the University of Nebraska successfully spread Barnes' approach to teachers throughout their state. Nevertheless, her methods sparked debate among educators and scholars. Some of those on the American Historical Association's Committee of Seven in 1899 questioned pupils' abilities to understand and interpret primary sources. Other scholars argued that schools should not teach pupils to think for themselves but rather "to learn what is in the book." Ultimately, the AHA Committee rejected the source method as preferred practice. Teachers were urged to use original documents sparingly, in order to illustrate the historical method or lend credibility to a narrative. Reconstruction of the past would remain in the hands of trained scholars, not ordinary citizens.

Subsequent history was not kind to Mary Sheldon Barnes. With few exceptions during the 20th century, she remained invisible. Her achievements, if recognized, were often misunderstood.

References

Keohane, Robert E. "The Great Debate over the Source Method." *Social Education* 13, no. 5 (May 1949): 212-218.

-----. "Mary Sheldon Barnes and the Origin of the Source Method of Teaching History in the American Secondary School, 1885-1896."*American Heritage* 2, no.3 (October 1948):68-72; and no. 4 (December 1948): 109-112.

Monteverde, Frances E. "Considering the Source: Mary Sheldon Barnes," in *"Bending the Future to Their Will": Civic Women, Social Education, and Democracy*, Margaret Smith Crocco and O. L. Davis, Jr., eds. Lanham, MD: Rowman and Littlefield, 1999, 17-46.

The bulk of Mary Sheldon Barnes' and Earl Barnes' papers are at the Sophia Smith Collection, Smith College, Northampton, Massachusetts. Background materials may also be found at the Penfield Library, State University of New York at Oswego. Instructional materials and the scrapbooks of Earl Barnes are located at Stanford University Libraries, Stanford, California.

Jane Addams

September 6, 1860—May 21, 1935

PETRA MUNRO

Jane Addams was a social reformer and philosopher whose analysis of gender, race, and class provided a radical critique of the fundamental assumptions of classical liberal democracy. Her vision of "social democracy," embodied in the settlement house she founded called "Hull House," challenged dominant discourses of political thought by exposing how the political theory of her day that conceptualized rights as universal, individual, natural, and inalienable was nevertheless greatly limited by gender. Addams maintained that recognizing difference, not minimizing it, was essential to democracy. Her work as a social theorist of social education is especially relevant to ongoing discussions of the relationship of democracy and education, as well as the gendered nature of political thought.

Jane was born in 1860 in Cedarville, Illinois, to John and Sarah Addams. The youngest of eight children, Jane was greatly influenced by her father, a mill owner, banker, Quaker, and state senator who was one of the most powerful and respected political figures in Illinois. In 1881, Jane Addams graduated from Rockford Seminary for Females and joined a generation of women who believed that social activism was the special mission of educated women. Opportunities for college-educated women to find work in the public sphere, however, were extremely limited. Addams thus spent the next seven years of her life searching for a way to begin meaningful life work. After she spent a brief time studying medicine, her search took her to Europe. During the winter of 1888 she visited Toynbee Hall settlement in the slums of East London. Here she came to envision a role for herself in addressing social problems. She returned to Chicago and, in 1889 at age 29, opened Hull House with her college classmate, Ellen Starr Gates.

Hull House became part of a larger social movement of progressive reform designed to address the social and economic inequalities of American society in a variety of ways. Addams involved herself in numerous organizations and social movements, including the Immigrants Protective League, the National Association for the Advancement of Colored People, the Chicago Woman's Club, the National Women's Trade Union League, the National American Woman Suffrage Asso-

ciation, the National Educational Association, and the American Sociology Association. In addition, she served as arbitrator of several major labor strikes and was a major force in establishing a juvenile court in Chicago. Under her guidance, Hull House became involved in urban investigation, social work, education, politics, public health, the status of women, industrial reform, labor relations, international relations, and the arts.

Addams saw Hull House as a dynamic social experiment designed to critique the emerging factory model of schooling by providing alternative forms of education designed especially for migrants and immigrants. Hull House embodied Addams' philosophy of education, which maintained that learning must be lifelong, community-oriented, reciprocal, empowering, and addressed at healing social, economic, and ethnic divisions. Central to her notion of a radical democracy was the belief that all people must have a voice in decisions affecting their daily lives and society. By defining a settlement as "an institution attempting to learn from life itself," Addams grounded Hull House in the belief that meaningful learning and social action occurred only when education allowed individuals and communities to define their own needs.

Hull House offered numerous educational activities, including the teaching of English, reading clubs for adults, mothers' clubs, kindergartens, cooking and dressmaking classes, sex education, theater productions, vocational training, an art gallery, public library, music school, and labor museum. The labor museum endeavored to validate the heritage, values, and culture of immigrants. The interactions among academics, women's clubs' members, and immigrants served an important educational function by providing a means for people of different classes to "speak together" in order to facilitate mutual understanding and encourage involvement in the work of social change.

During and after World War I, Addams's focus shifted to the peace movement. First president of the Women's International League for Peace and Freedom and co-recipient of the Nobel Peace Prize in 1931, she was an ardent pacifist. Her dedication to peace lost her much support during World War I when she was targeted by the U.S. government as the most dangerous woman in America. During the 1930's she became spokesperson for many of the values and policies adopted during the New Deal. She and her female colleagues were instrumental in establishing social security and many other government programs that altered the nature of American capitalism. When she died in 1935, she was mourned worldwide as a great leader and interpreter of American thought.

Author of eleven books and hundreds of articles, Addams was a prolific writer. Among her early books were *Democracy and Social Ethics* (1902), *Newer Ideals of Peace* (1907), and the classic *Twenty Years at Hull-House* (1910). In these works Addams articulated her own view of democracy, amending the ideas of universal, individual rights and its corollaries of "natural man" and "inalienable rights." These concepts, as inherited from the classical liberal tradition, tended, she felt, to obscure the experiences of women and immigrants. Likewise, Addams felt that liberal democracy's focus on inalienable rights assumed a static view of the political process and threatened to impose conformity of political behavior. Addams saw democracy as a living, breathing social organism. Its future rested on its ability to respond to social change. Addams believed that classical democracy had focused on political rights at the expense of social and economic considerations. Consequently, liberal democracy was incapable of creating the social equality that, in Addams' judgment, was a prerequisite for the forms of collective interaction that she felt essential to a just society.

References

Deegan. Mary Jo. *Jane Addams and the Men of the Chicago School 1892-1918*. New Brunswick, NJ: Transaction Books, 1990.

Elshtain, Jean Bethke. *Jane Addams and the Dream of American Democracy*. New York: Basic Books, 2001.

Lagemann, Ellen C. *Jane Addams on Education*. New York: Teachers College Press, 1985.

Seigfried, Charlotte Haddock. *Pragmatism and Feminism: Renewing the Social Fabric*. Chicago, IL: University of Chicago Press, 1996.

Lucy Maynard Salmon

July 27, 1853 — February 14, 1927

Chara Haeussler Bohan

Lucy Maynard Salmon, a professor of history at Vassar College for forty years (1887-1927), became the first woman elected to the Executive Council of the American Historical Association in 1915. She was also the founder and first president of the Association of History Teachers of the Middle States and Maryland. Renamed the Middle States Council for the Social Studies, it is the oldest regional council still in existence in the United States. Established in 1902, the Middle States Council preceded the formation of the National Council for the Social Studies by twenty years.

Salmon became a national authority in the field of history. She was particularly interested in social history and in the teaching of history. Earning an A. B. in history from the University of Michigan in 1876, only the second class to admit women, Salmon was a pioneer during the early growth of women's higher education in the United States. Continuing her studies, Salmon earned an A.M. from the University of Michigan in 1883 and later spent a year as a fellow in American history at Bryn Mawr College, at which she studied under Woodrow Wilson, then a young professor. Wilson and Salmon proved to be unsuited for one another and their professional relationship ended after one year.

As a long-time professor at Vassar College, Salmon's work in history and education came into prominence in the 1890s when she served on the American Historical Association's Committee of Seven, which made recommendations for the teaching of history in the nation's secondary schools. Active in numerous organizations, Salmon also served on the Executive Council of the American Association of University Professors, was a founding member of the organization that became the American Association of University Women, and was a leader in the national suffrage movement. Salmon was the Vice-President of the National College Equal Suffrage League, an auxiliary of the National American Woman Suffrage League, and helped organize the Vassar students' suffrage association despite a campus ban on suffrage activities. A progressive educator, she hoped to improve society through education.

In addition to her leadership in several national organizations, Salmon wrote nearly one hundred publications, including several exhaustive works on the history of domestic service, the newspaper, general history, and education. Her most significant publications include *Domestic Service* (1897), *Progress in the Household* (1906), *The Newspaper and Authority* (1923), *The Newspaper and the Historian* (1923), and *Why is History Rewritten?* (1929), published posthumously. Salmon's study of domestic service stands as one of the first modern works of new social history. She conducted surveys and collected data for the study with the assistance of Carroll Wright, the first Commissioner of the U.S. Bureau of Labor. Such methods of research were typical of the new professional social scientists, whose work came into prominence in the early 1900s.

Salmon's legacy is particularly significant in the area of social studies and history education. Not only did she help to found and lead organizations that have been influential in affecting the development of social studies education in the United States, but, in her classroom at Vassar, she employed progressive methods of teaching history. Salmon encouraged students to examine their everyday world in order to observe history. She taught students to broaden their understanding of historical material beyond political and military leaders and events. For Salmon, history could be found in the backyard, kitchen, or main street, and she brought students to these places to discover history. From both her experience and beliefs, she wrote articles for teachers and assembled collections of documents for use by students. Her advice was direct and historical, "Go to the sources."

Salmon's unconventional approach to teaching and learning history garnered pointed criticism from colleagues who favored more traditional methods of teaching. Nonetheless, she earned considerable recognition for her academic accomplishments toward the end of her life. Salmon was awarded honorary doctorates from Colgate University and the University of Michigan, and a research fund was established in her name at Vassar. She died in 1927 from a stroke.

References

Bohan, Chara Haeussler. "Lucy Maynard Salmon: Progressive Historian, Teacher, and Democrat," in *"Bending the Future to Their Will": Civic Women, Social Education and Democracy*, Margaret Smith Crocco and O. L. Davis, Jr., eds. Lanham, MD: Rowman and Littlefield, 1999, 47-72

Brown. Louise Fargo. *Apostle of Democracy: The Life of Lucy Maynard Salmon*. New York: Harper Brothers, 1943.

Salmon, Lucy Maynard. Papers. Special Collections, Vassar College Libraries, Poughkeepsie, New York.

2.

Becoming Partners in Citizenship Education: 1920-1945

Introduction

Margaret Smith Crocco

As the twenties began, two significant events for women working in social education occurred. First, passage of the Nineteenth Amendment in 1920 provided suffrage for women of the country, except in the South where Jim Crow laws prevented Black women and men from voting. This amendment gave most women the opportunity to participate in the prerogatives of citizenship in a wholly new way. In response, the League of Women Voters, which grew out of the National American Woman's Suffrage Association, established "citizenship schools" around the country to acquaint women with the candidates, issues, and procedures involved in the election process.[1]

As we have seen, the first steps toward the long march to victory could be traced back to the 19th-century days of Susan B. Anthony, the most famous schoolteacher-suffragist in the country. Many, though not all, schoolteachers, social educators, and women faculty in the universities supported and participated in the struggle for suffrage. The work they did for suffrage often merged with advocacy for teacher tenure, pensions, equal pay, and greater access to higher education; much of this effort took place in women's clubs and teacher associations.[2] After suffrage was won, women moved slowly to embrace the practice of voting, only gradually reaching men's level of participation in 1980, a lag time that political scientists attribute to the need for political socialization of women to their new situation.[3]

Of all the individuals appearing in this chapter, the one most actively identified with suffrage was Mary Ritter Beard. Beard worked closely with the radical wing of the suffrage movement represented by Alice Paul's National Women's Party. Beard also blazed trails in terms of social education. While not a teacher herself, she influenced teachers and scholars through her writing, archival efforts on behalf of women's history, public speaking engagements, and radio addresses.[4] Along with her husband, Charles, she wrote groundbreaking and best-selling textbooks for school children. These works contain a good deal of social and women's history, which was quite unusual for the time. Using the concept of "civilization" as a springboard, the Beards wrote about a broad range of topics in what today would be considered an interdisciplinary, as opposed to conventionally historical, treatment of America's past.

The twenties also represent the heyday of the "flapper" and the "New Woman," as the independent working woman of the twenties was called. These years saw fractious debates between women's rights advocates over the wisdom of "protective legislation" that treated women workers as a separate category of employees whose health and well-being demanded special protection from long hours and poor working conditions. As a result of such disagreements, the Equal Rights Amendment proposed by Alice Paul soon after passage of the 19th Amendment made little headway.

Historians emphasize a number of developments in education during these decades: the cult of efficiency as evidenced by centralization and bureaucratization of schooling,[5] the rise of progressive education in several forms,[6] the push for restriction and Americanization of immigrants,[7] and by the end of the period, retrenchment in terms of the resources and aspirations for education as a result of the Depression and World War II.[8]

The second significant event for social educators was the founding of the National Council for the Social Studies (NCSS) in 1921, an event with which Charles Beard was closely connected. The causes and influences behind formation of this organization have been richly chronicled elsewhere.[9] In addition to Bessie Pierce, the first female president of NCSS in 1926, four other women served on the NCSS Board of Directors: Nellie Jackson (corresponding secretary in 1923); Mary Carney (corresponding secretary from 1925-1927); Edna Stone (vice-president in 1927); and Ruth West (vice-president in 1938 and the second woman to become NCSS president in 1939).[10]

In looking through the NCSS archives concerning these years, one recognizes immediately that women played a role in the organization, although not always a prominent or highly visible one. Virtually every NCSS committee at the national level had at least one female member during these decades. At the regional and state level, women were probably represented in equal or even greater numbers. This situation roughly approximates the kind of imbalance that also existed at the time within the National Education Association and its state affiliates. Leadership was almost exclusively male, despite the fact that women constituted a significant, and growing, proportion of the membership.[11]

The imbalance of men in leadership positions within NCSS had more to do with academic status hierarchies within education than with the number of women working as social educators. While it is perhaps less surprising that the leaders of the American Historical Association or the American Political Science Association were almost exclusively male, NCSS was a hybrid organization, a mix of educators and disciplinary specialists. As a result, social studies mimicked the academic professional organizations in its effort to establish itself on an equal footing with the APSA and the AHA, producing its own "great man era," represented by, among others, Charles Beard, Harold Rugg, Edgar Wesley, Henry Johnson, and Rolla Tryon. These individuals were responsible for producing the series of commission reports, textbooks, and foundational publications geared towards defining the "what" and "how"—and, by extension, the "who"—of the social studies.

A small but telling example of this dynamic can be seen in one piece of evidence from the NCSS archives. In 1923, Edgar Dawson, the first NCSS secretary, sent out a letter to potential participants in a series of summer conferences on the social studies. In this correspondence, he described the value of the conference as proceeding from the opportunity for "spontaneous and informal conversation among virile people about their own experience and difficulties." Characterizations such as these served to delimit quite vividly the population seen as appropriate to the work at hand.[12]

While the names of Beard, Johnson, Rugg, and Tryon have all endured, that of a woman among the "founding fathers" is a rare occurrence. Jessie Campbell Evans, chronicled here, was one of two women (the other was Lucy Salmon) to contribute to the 1916 Report on the Social Studies. Like Salmon and Bessie Pierce, Evans has gained historical recognition, in part, because she participated in what has been one of the central preoccupations of social studies historians to date: analyses of the commission work and report writing that helped produce the field.

Given the social and educational context in which the social studies as school subject began, it is probably not surprising that so few women were present at the creation. As historians have noted about women's low status within educational hierarchies at this time, even "women's institutions faltered in their commitment to female professors by the 1930s, when a male faculty was assumed to signal quality."[13]

During the first decade of the 20th century, Lucy Sprague Mitchell's position as Dean of Women at the University of California at Berkeley allowed her to critique women's treatment as second-class citizens (both as students and faculty) on coeducational campuses and the narrow professional options open to female graduates of these institutions. As a result of dissatisfaction with her own career choices, she used a move to New York City in 1913 with her husband, the economist Wesley Clair Mitchell, as an opportunity to pursue social work, progressive education, and geography, thus transcending the conventional gender boundaries of her day.

Doing citizenship education in this climate presented challenges for women, who may have been widely respected within the culture as teachers, but little considered as conceptualists, theorists, or experts within education in general or social studies in particular. All the women profiled in this chapter struggled against the odds to become educational leaders. In the years between 1920 and 1950, women held the NCSS presidency only three times, once each decade. In 1939, when Ruth West became NCSS president, she was the second woman and the first teacher to hold this position. The following year, she worked closely with Merle Curti on the first Academic Freedom Committee, called into existence to deal with attacks on social studies educators like George Counts and Harold Rugg whose work was criticized as too radical for the schools.[14]

Women married to famous husbands, like Mary Beard, Helen Merrell Lynd, Lucy Sprague Mitchell, and Eleanor Roosevelt, struggled for recognition as independent thinkers and creative scholars who did not exist merely as acolytes, appendages, or imitators of their spouses and their work. During these years, perhaps only single or divorced women, such as Rachel Davis DuBois, or women with life long female companions, such as Helen Heffernan, could lay full public claim to their professional accomplishments. Even Hilda Taba was rarely credited with an idea that was not considered derivative of those of her mentor, Ralph Tyler.

As a result of these difficulties, women intellectuals often were sensitive to the social construction of identities, matters of difference, and how unfavorably deviations from the male norm were construed within the hierarchical, racist, and sexist educational and social climate of this period.[15] Whether or not women professionals articulated these sentiments publicly, however, was another issue. Negotiating academic and professional environments characterized by such conditions produced variable responses from the women included in this chapter. Some elected to identify openly with other women, women's interests, and women's rights, such as Mary Beard, Helen Heffernan, Lucy Sprague Mitchell, and Eleanor Roosevelt. Others, such as Bessie Pierce and Mary Kelty, did not marry or, from what can be gleaned from the available evidence, call attention to their status as women, or support women's issues vocally.[16]

Several women profiled here spent a good portion of their lives working for disenfranchised groups. Eleanor Roosevelt's advocacy for the rights of African Americans and the poor during her husband's four terms in office and her visionary leadership in creating the United Nation's Universal Declaration of Human Rights suggest a woman attuned to the plight of the powerless.[17] Likewise, Helen Heffernan and Emma Neal both fought strenuously for the educational rights of children of Mexican American migrant workers. Their actions made them vulnerable to right-wing criticisms of their "progressive educational" methods. Hilda Taba and Rachel Davis DuBois labored within and beyond the social studies for the intercultural education movement. Taba's career concerns in the United States clearly were affected by her own experiences of gender discrimination in Estonia. DuBois' commitments owed much to her background as a Quaker, but also to disputes with school administrators who resisted her outspoken efforts on behalf of introducing Black history into her high school's assembly program.

These women stand out among their contemporaries because they recognized that the prerogatives they enjoyed as white women rested on the denial of rights to women of color.[18] Silence on matters of social justice does not exempt individuals, especially well educated ones, from being implicated in systems that oppress others, although it was not until the decades after World War II, when the horrors of the Nazi atrocities had become widely known, that many other social educators and historians recognized this principle unmistakably.[19]

By the end of this period, the disruptions of war had affected all aspects of life on the domestic front, including the schools and social studies. Within NCSS, official documents suggest a growing commitment to equality, reflecting developments within the broader society and education in general. In 1940, the board of directors questioned whether the NCSS should appoint a standing committee on civil rights as well as academic freedom.[20] A confidential report filed with NCSS by Howard Wilson in January 1943 about his trip south commented on the "reports on rising race conflicts which came to me all over the South and illustrate the wave of disturbing rumor and uncertainty heralding in a new adjustment of race relations in this country."[21] Perhaps due to the divisive nature of this issue, NCSS chose, like women suffragists decades before, to satisfy southern whites by ignoring blacks' calls for justice.

The darker aspects of these decades can be captured in moments like this, as well as in the images associated with militarism and war making their way to the United States in the thirties and forties, or the homegrown horrors of lynching and cross-burning by the Ku Klux Klan that surfaced out of states from Texas to Illinois and from Mississippi to New Jersey during the twenties and thirties. Further, Walker Evans' dust-bowl photographs gave poignant visual memorialization to a malaise that had been felt on the farms since the end of World War I.[22] As World War II ended, social educators increasingly understood the urgency of civic and social education to the task of rebuilding a world now threatened by nuclear annihilation.

The complex and contradictory nature of these times can be captured, to some extent, in the career of Mary Kelty. In 1945, when Kelty took over as president of NCSS, she was a popular writer, whose engaging prose and nicely illustrated textbooks drew a broad audience of readers. Nevertheless, her schoolbooks in world history also reflect racist attitudes toward "primitive" countries outside the United States. An American history textbook she authored for elementary school children blithely presents slavery as simply another labor option, failing to make any comment about the denials of freedom, much less the physical, mental, and social cruelties meted out on slaves.[23]

Nevertheless, a sense of the urgency of change in a shattered, yet hopeful, world permeated official social studies documents at the time. In 1945, the board of directors, on which Kelty still served, pledged its "support during the difficult postwar years to the further advancement of equality of opportunity for all youth and all groups in our nation."[24] In 1946, Kelty was on the NCSS publications committee, which sponsored the 16th NCSS Yearbook, *Democratic Human Relations*, on which Hilda Taba and William Van Til, among others, worked. This yearbook was perhaps the most famous one that NCSS had ever published. It was supported by the National Council of Christians and Jews and the Bureau for Intercultural Education. Advance publicity on the book led to expressions of interest from the American Council on Race Relations, the Anti-Defamation League, and the American Jewish Committee, as well as predictions that the book would sell at least twice the normal number of yearbooks sold.[25] By 1948, the Board of Directors passed another resolution on the subject of equality of opportunity, urging "social studies teachers to support civil rights, guaranteed in the Constitution and defined by the President's Commission for Americans of all races, creeds, and nationality backgrounds."[26] Clearly, many social educators, including Kelty, had come to recognize the degree to which the events of the past decades had changed the world. Subsequent decades would, to an unprecedented degree, both witness and accelerate the pace of changes altering women's place in that world.

Notes

1. One analysis of the evolution in citizenship status of women over the course of U.S. history and its implications for the social studies can be seen in Margaret Smith Crocco, "Citizenship, Women, and the Social Studies," *Educational Forum* 65, no. 1 (Fall, 2000): 52-59.
2. See, for example, the career of Elizabeth Almira Allen, the first female president of the New Jersey Education Association, as described by Crocco in Margaret Smith Crocco, Petra Munro, and Kathleen Weiler, *Pedagogies of Resistance: Women Educator Activists, 1880-1960* (New York: Teachers College Press, 1999): 47-61.
3. On the political socialization process, see Margaret Smith Crocco and Della Barr Brooks, "19th Amendment: Reform or Revolution?" *Social Education* 59, no. 5 (September 1995): 279-283.
4. Gerda Lerner, who some consider the "mother of all women's historians," credits Mary Beard as inspiration for her own career as a women's historian in *The Creation of Patriarchy* (New York: Oxford University Press, 1987).
5. Raymond Callahan, *Education and the Cult of Efficiency* (Chicago, IL: University of Chicago Press, 1962).
6. Arthur Zilversmit, *Changing Schools: Progressive Education in Theory and Practice, 1930-1960* (Chicago, IL: University of Chicago Press, 1993).
7. On the issue of immigrants and schooling, see, as only two examples in a growing body of literature: Nicholas Montalto, *A History of the Intercultural Education Movement, 1924-1941* (New York: Garland, 1982) and Paula Fass, *Outside In: Minorities and the Transformation of American Education* (New York: Oxford University Press, 1989).
8. Wayne Urban and Jennings Wagoner, *American Education: A History* (New York: McGraw Hill, 2000), 255ff.
9. See, for example, Stephen J. Thornton, "NCSS: The Early Years," in *NCSS in Retrospect*, O. L. Davis, Jr. ed. (Washington, DC: NCSS, 1996), 1-7 and Murry R. Nelson, "The Early Years, 1921-1937," *Social Education* 59, no. 7 (November/December 1995): 399-407.
10. Nelson, 403.
11. See Crocco, *Pedagogies of Resistance*, 47-61.
12. Edgar Dawson, "Summer Conferences on the Social Studies," Letter dated May, 1923, NCSS Archives, Box 1, Series 1, Folder 9, Milbank Library, Teachers College, Columbia University, New York.
13. Linda Eisenmann, "Reconsidering a Classic: Assessing the History of Women's Higher Education a Dozen Years after Barbara Solomon," *Harvard Education Review* 67, no. 4 (Winter 1997): 1-26.
14. Merle Curti, Ruth West, and Howard E. Wilson, The NCSS Academic Freedom Committee, "Statement of NCSS on Academic Freedom," NCSS Archives, Series II-B, Box 10, Milbank Library, Teachers College, Columbia University. This statement was published in the *Christian Science Monitor*, the *New York Times*, and *Social Education* in 1941.
15. For fuller treatment of the intersections of gender, race, and class, and the consideration of these categories with national imperialism, see: Glenda Elizabeth Gilmore, *Gender and Jim Crow: Women and the Politics of White Supremacy in North Carolina, 1896-1920* (Chapel Hill, NC: University of North Carolina Press, 1996); Louise Michelle Newman, *White Women's Rights: The Racial Origins of Feminism in the United States* (New York: Oxford University Press, 1999); and Laura Wexler, *Tender Violence: Domestic Visions in the Age of U.S. Imperialism* (Chapel Hill, NC: University of North Carolina Press, 2000). These works owe much to Gail Bederman, *Manliness and Civilization: A Cultural History of Gender and Race in the United States, 1880-1917* (Chicago, IL: University of Chicago Press, 1996).
16. For a discussion of the phenomenon of "unsexing" in relation to the career of Mary G. Kelty, see the three treatments of her career by Keith C. Barton, Linda Levstik, and Margaret Smith Crocco in Sherry Field and Lynn Burlbaw, eds., *Explorations in Curriculum History* (Greenwich, CT: Information Age Publishers, in press). For a fuller analysis of women educators' identification with the rights of the marginalized and disenfranchised, see the introductory essay by Margaret Smith Crocco and the concluding essay by Andra Makler in M. S. Crocco and O. L. Davis, Jr., eds., *"Bending the Future to Their Will": Civic Women, Social Education, and Democracy* (Lanham, MD: Rowman and Littlefield, 1999).
17. Mary Ann Glendon, *A World Made New: Eleanor Roosevelt and the Universal Declaration of Human Rights* (New York: Random House, 2001).
18. See Gilmore, Newman, and Wexler for a complete explication of these interrelationships.
19. For a comprehensive treatment of what was known and when it was known in the United States about these Nazi atrocities, see David Wyman, *Abandonment of the Jews: America and the Holocaust, 1941-1945* (New York: Pantheon, 1984).
20. Agenda for annual meeting of the NCSS Board of Directors, November 21-23, 1940, NCSS Archives, Series 2B, Box 1, Folder 5, Milbank Library, Teachers College, Columbia University, New York.
21. Log of the National Council Trip of Howard Wilson in January, 1943, NCSS Archives, Series II-B, Box 10, Milbank Library, Teachers College, Columbia University.
22. James Agee and Walker Evans, *Let Us Now Praise Famous Men: Three Tenant Farmers*, reprint (New York: Houghton Mifflin, 1989)
23. Mary G. Kelty, *The American Colonies* (Boston, MA: Ginn, 1932).
24. Resolutions adopted by NCSS at the Twenty-Fifth Annual Meeting in Milwaukee, Wisconsin, November 22-24, 1945, NCSS Archives, Series II D, Box 1, Milbank Library, Teachers College Columbia University.
25. Merrill Hartshorn, NCSS Executive Secretary, Memo to the Executive Committee dated January 28, 1946, NCSS Archives, Series 3A, Box 1, Folder 3, Milbank Library, Teachers College, Columbia University.

26. Resolution adopted by unanimous vote at the Annual Meeting of the National Council for the Social Studies in Chicago, November 26, 1948, NCSS Archives Series II D, Box I, Milbank Library, Teachers College, Columbia University, New York.

Mary Ritter Beard

August 7, 1876 — August 14, 1958

SARA BAIR

Mary Ritter Beard was a pioneering scholar in women's history and a social reformer during the Progressive Era. She campaigned for women's suffrage, advocated improved conditions for the working class, and critiqued women's education, but it was her vision of women's history that most vividly shaped her life and work. It is primarily in this context that she made her contribution to the dialogue on social education.

Mary was born on August 7, 1876, near Indianapolis, Indiana, to Eli Foster Ritter and Narcissa Lockwood. The fourth of seven children, Mary grew up in what appears to be a traditional mid-western environment. Always a strong student, she graduated valedictorian of her high school class and then, like her father and siblings, attended De Pauw University. She was recognized for her leadership there and upon graduation became a member of Phi Delta Kappa.

It was also at De Pauw that Mary Ritter met the future historian Charles Austin Beard, whom she married in 1900. By all accounts, theirs was a strong and supportive partnership in which they raised two children and wrote seven books.

Shortly after their wedding, the Beards moved to Manchester, England, where Charles helped to develop Ruskin Hall, a college for working class men, and where their first child, a daughter, was born in 1901. Over the next three years, Mary Ritter Beard's interest in women's history and working class issues intensified. Under the influence of British socialists and radical suffragists like Emmeline and Christabel Pankhurst, Beard adopted a feminist perspective and concern for social justice that remained throughout her life.

In 1902 the Beards returned to the United States and settled in New York City, close to Columbia University, where she and Charles both enrolled in graduate school. Though her husband earned his doctorate at Columbia and then taught on the faculty there until 1917, Mary Beard left the program in 1904. By 1910 she was devoting much of her time and energy to raising her two children and to working for women's suffrage and various labor causes. She aligned herself with Alice Paul's radical wing of the woman's suffrage movement and became a leader in the Congressional Union, which later became the Woman's Party.

With the passage of the Nineteenth Amendment in 1920, many leaders in the suffrage movement, including Alice Paul, turned their attention to passage of the Equal Rights Amendment, a measure designed to provide legal equality for women. Beard, however, never supported the Equal Rights Amendment because she believed it would negatively impact working class women by dismantling the protective legislation they had worked so hard to attain. Beard believed that developing equality in an unjust capitalist system was not in the interests of women and that, instead, women should use their talents to reshape the system itself.

Partly as a result of the conflict over the Equal Rights Amendment and her growing belief in the creative power of women, particularly those in the working class, in the 1920s Beard began to attend less to social activism and more to writing and promoting women's history. Like other early 20th-century New Historians, Beard called for a broader, more inclusive history that would encompass social and economic themes and would serve as a vehicle for dealing more effectively with contemporary problems. Unlike other historians, however, Beard emphasized the role of women in history.

She wrote and edited numerous books on the topic, including *On Understanding Women* (1931); *America Through Women's Eyes* (ed., 1933); and her best known work, *Women as Force in History: A Study in Traditions and Realities* (1946), in which she argues that, contrary to popular belief, women had, from the beginning, been active agents in history, not merely passive victims. The fact that the rich history of women had been largely written out of the record did not negate its existence. History, Beard argued, could not be whole without the story of women who had always been at the center of developing civilization. She believed that once modern women appreciated their own historical significance, they would no longer strive for incorporation into the male world, but would try to reshape the world to their own uniquely female vision. The series of highly successful textbooks that Beard wrote with her husband on American civilization also reflect this inclusive perspective.

As a writer of women's history, Beard's most productive years were the 1930s and 1940s , but these decades also brought her a series of disappointments. She spent the years from 1935 to 1940 in an ill-fated effort to create the Women's Center for World Archives, a project she hoped would restore women to the historical record and provide contemporary women with an intellectual center for research, education, and political initiatives. Though this project never came to fruition, Beard is credited with a role in the development of women's archives at both Radcliffe and Smith Colleges. In 1941 Beard began an eighteen-month project that critiqued the male bias in the *Encyclopedia Britannica* and provided suggestions for its improvement. Despite assurances from *Britannica*'s editor, few of the suggestions were ever implemented.

Beard demonstrated remarkable good health, energy, and productivity well into her seventies. Charles Beard died in 1948. In 1953, Mary Beard published *The Force of Women in Japanese History* and in 1955, *The Making of Charles Beard*. She spent the last few years of her life living with her son and died on August 14, 1958 at the age of eighty-two.

Mary Ritter Beard's life and work contributed to the development of social education in the United States in both direct and indirect ways. The widely used textbooks written by the Beards were innovative in their approach to social and economic history and in their treatment of the role of women in civilization. Mary Beard also left an indirect legacy that includes women's studies programs as well as high school and college courses on the history of women, both of which she strongly promoted in the first half of the 20th century.

References

Cott, Nancy F., ed. *A Woman Making History: Mary Ritter Beard Through her Letters,* New Haven, CT: Yale University Press, 1991.

Crocco, Margaret Smith. "Forceful Yet Forgotten: Mary Ritter Beard and the Writing of History." *History Teacher* 31, no. 1 (November, 1997): 9-33.

Crocco, Margaret Smith. "Shaping Inclusive Social Education: Mary Ritter Beard and Marion Thompson Wright," in Margaret Smith Crocco and O. L. Davis, Jr., eds. *"Bending the Future To Their Will": Civic Women, Social Education and Democracy*. Lanham, MD: Rowman and Littlefield, 1999: 93-123.

Lane, Ann J., ed. *Mary Ritter Beard: A Sourcebook* (New York: Schocken Books, 1977).

Mary Ritter Beard's papers are located at the Sophia Smith Collection, Smith College; Arthur and Elizabeth Schlesinger Library, Radcliffe College; and De Pauw University.

Bessie Louise Pierce

April 20, 1888—October 3, 1974

Murry R. Nelson

Bessie Louise Pierce was the first female president of the National Council for the Social Studies. In a professional career that stretched from 1910 to her death in 1974, Pierce distinguished herself as a teacher and historian. These two words, more than anything else, sum up Pierce's view of herself and the way she presented herself professionally. Adding her strong sense of family to those terms provides a succinct description of Pierce and her life.

Bessie Pierce was born in 1888 in Caro, Michigan, but grew up in north central Fona, near Waverly, where her family moved shortly after her birth. In 1910, Pierce graduated from the University of Iowa with a degree in history. Immediately, she began her teaching career in Sanborn, Iowa, and later moved to Mason City (the locale for Meredith Wilson's musical, *The Music Man*). In 1916, she returned to the University of Iowa as the head of the social studies department at the University's laboratory high school. In addition, she was granted the rank of instructor in the department of history.

In the summer of 1918, Bessie Pierce began her more than forty-year relationship with the University of Chicago by enrolling in its graduate program in history. There, she first became acquainted with Professor Rolla Tryon, one of two celebrated mentors in her career (the other being Arthur M. Schlesinger). Pierce's A.M. in history was granted in 1918 and she then pursued her doctoral degree in history under Professor Schlesinger's guidance at the University of Iowa.

Both Schlesinger and Tryon were active members of the American Historical Association, which Pierce joined in 1918. From 1916 to 1921, Pierce continued to teach history and social studies at the University of Iowa High School. She also began synthesizing her teaching and her graduate studies into professional writings, most notably in *The Historical Outlook*, an official AHA publication that focused on history teaching. In 1919 and 1920, Pierce published articles in that journal addressing questions of methodology in history teaching.

Pierce shifted to the history department of the University of Iowa in 1921 and became a full-time instructor. Upon completion of her Ph.D. degree in 1923, she

was promoted to assistant professor, then to associate professor three years later.

Through her early involvement with the AHA, Pierce joined NCSS in 1921, and the next year became a member of the NCSS Executive Committee. The influence of Rolla Tryon, NCSS's initial vice-president, surely was important in Pierce's swift rise to prominence in NCSS. Her continued success, however, clearly was due to her own diligence, competence, and intelligence.

Pierce became a regular attendee at both AHA and NCSS meetings, and she continued to publish articles in *The Historical Outlook*, and elsewhere. In 1925, NCSS members elected Pierce vice-president, and the next year president, the first woman to hold that office.

After this service to NCSS, Pierce became less interested in the teaching aspects of history, devoting herself increasingly to historical research and the AHA. She served as a member of the AHA Program Committee for both the 1926 and 1927 annual meetings held in Rochester, New York, and Washington, D.C., respectively.

In 1926, Pierce published *Public Opinion and the Teaching of History*, a revision of her dissertation that focused on uses made of the school curriculum. After writing mostly about teaching methodology in history, Pierce now shifted her research emphasis to larger issues of policy, ideology, and power. Pierce displayed a commitment to academic freedom and went to great lengths not to judge the "integrity" of any of the propagandist agencies that she examined.

Her *Civic Attitudes in American School Textbooks* appeared in 1930, and Pierce once again presented her analyses without prejudice (although she did speak forcefully against the pre-censorship of textbooks, a position consistent with that of the AHA). This volume was part of a massive (seventeen-volume) endeavor undertaken by AHA's Commission on the Social Studies under the general title "Investigation of the Social Studies in the Schools."

In 1929, Pierce accepted a position at the University of Chicago as associate professor of history and head of the History of Chicago Project, a task that she continued to direct even after her official retirement in 1953. This effort, funded largely by the Social Science

Research Committee, yielded a three-volume *History of Chicago from 1673 to 1915*. The first two volumes were published between 1937 and 1940, but volume three did not appear until 1957, four years after Pierce's retirement. An intended fourth volume remains unpublished.

Pierce was extremely close to her sister, Anne, a music educator. In the later years of her career Bessie Pierce spent a great deal of time writing and attempting to get published a manuscript on music that she and her sister authored. Neither this nor a number of other co-authored manuscripts on American and world history were published, however. This failed investment of time and lack of return seriously disappointed her.

After her retirement, Pierce frequently commuted from Chicago to Iowa City to spend more time with her sister. In 1972, she moved to Iowa City and died there on October 3, 1974.

References

Nelson, Murry R. "Bessie Louise Pierce and Her Contributions to the Social Studies," in Margaret Smith Crocco and O. L. Davis, Jr., eds. *"Bending the Future to Their Will": Civic Women, Social Education, and Democracy*. Lanham, MD: Rowman and Littlefield, 1999, 149-69.

Pierce has not been the subject of a biography or dissertation, to our knowledge. The Pierce Papers are located in the Department of Special Collections, The Regenstein Library at the University of Chicago.

Ruth West

October 30, 1882 — October 29, 1960

PAUL ROBINSON

Ruth West was the first practicing classroom teacher and second woman (after Bessie Pierce, thirteen years earlier) to serve as the president of the National Council for the Social Studies.

Ruth was born in Faribault, Minnesota, the eldest of fourteen children born to Willis Mason and Melissa (Mott) West. Hers was an academically inclined family: Her father, Willis Mason West, was head of the Department of History at the University of Minnesota for many years. Several of her brothers and sisters followed varied academic careers.

In 1903, West received her bachelor's degree in history from the University of Minnesota. She then taught at various high schools in the vicinity of Minneapolis for nearly a decade: two years in Stillwater (1907-09) teaching English and German, a year in Winona (1910), a year or two at LaSalle in north central Illinois (1912-13), and several years in Minneapolis (1915-18), interspersed with a year of study at the Sorbonne in Paris on a Grace Whitney Hoff Fellowship (1910-11). For an undetermined reason, she made the leap from her Midwestern roots to the Northwest in 1913 and taught at Lewis and Clark High School in Spokane, Washington, from 1913 to 1916. She rejoined the Lewis and Clark faculty in 1921, the same year NCSS was established, after several years of worldwide adventures, including a year with the Red Cross in France just after World War I.

For the next twenty-eight years, West taught at Lewis and Clark high school, becoming head of its history/social studies department in 1925. During that period she achieved such a notable reputation as a teacher throughout the area that she was awarded an honorary doctor of education degree by Reed College, Portland, in 1937. Becoming active in NCSS, she moved through the leadership ranks to its presidency in 1939. In the course of her service she edited the ninth NCSS yearbook, *The Utilization of Community Resources in the Social Studies* (1938), and wrote the foreword for what was to become the first volume in the NCSS curriculum series, *The Future of the Social Studies: Proposals for an Experimental Social-Studies Curriculum*, edited by James A. Michener (1939).

Her presidential address, "The National Council and the Social Studies Teacher," (1940) began with recognition of her place as the first classroom teacher to become president of NCSS: "Once in a while even so important and imposing a body as the National Council for the Social Studies goes democratic in the old American tradition and chooses a 'log cabin president.'" She went on to describe the "lifelong task of preparing ourselves for social studies teaching."

This task involved developing (1) a "broad sweep of human interests," (2) the "narrow discipline of a specialized field" (for West, of course, the discipline was history which she offhandedly portrayed as currently "the lowly handmaid of the social studies, but to which I still hold my allegiance"), and (3) civic participation (She herself was active in civic affairs and international meetings, and also found time to write school history texts, several in collaboration with her father.) The second half of the address was a "promotion talk" on the assistance NCSS could provide teachers in that lifelong task of preparation. She had surprisingly little to say about the looming war, but concluded with her response to the then-burning question of whether social studies teachers could "save democracy": "Not alone, of course, although ... we ... have a crucial part to play in that challenging task. ... One thing we know: we can not accomplish our aim by talking about democracy. ... Practice in democratic living both in and out of school will be the only way."

By all accounts West was highly regarded in Spokane and throughout the Northwest. Reflecting on her long career, she said, "Teaching is a wonderful opportunity for anyone who is interested in people and who has faith in the improvability of mankind. It is difficult, especially in history and the social studies, because subject matter changes so rapidly. Classes are always new and challenging."

West is now a rather obscure figure in the history of the social studies. She is easily confused with the better known Edith West, a professor who shared her Minnesota roots. In their article on the history of NCSS between 1937 and 1947, Field and Burlbaw (1995) make no reference to her, although they include a list of "noted names" of editors and chapter authors of NCSS year-books during this period. They mention fourteen individuals—all university-based (with the exception of one publishing executive) and all men (with the exception of Hilda Taba). Ruth West carved out a notable career as both a teacher and an educational leader in the years between the world wars. She taught well and provided dedicated service to NCSS.

References

Field, Sherry L. and Lynn Burlbaw. "A Time for Growth, A Time for War, A Time for Leadership: 1937-1947," *Social Education* 59, no. 7 (November/December 1995): 408-416.

Michener, James A., ed. *The Future of the Social Studies: Proposals for an Experimental Social-Studies Curriculum. Curriculum Series: No. One*. Cambridge, MA: NCSS, 1939.

West, Ruth. "The National Council and the Social Studies Teachers," *Social Education* 4, no. 2 (February 1940), 81-84.

West, Ruth, ed. *Utilization of Community Resources in the Social Studies*. 9th Yearbook. Cambridge, MA: NCSS, 1938.

Jessie Campbell Evans

January 5, 1874—April 13, 1956

Ashley G. DeWaal-Lucas

Jessie C. Evans, a Philadelphia teacher, was one of two women members of the National Education Association committee that produced the seminal *1916 Report on Social Studies Education*. A social studies teacher for forty-five years, Evans was active in the international relations department of the American Association of University Women, participated in the American Academy of Politics and Social Science, founded the History Teacher's Club of Philadelphia, was president of the Middle States Association of Social Studies Teachers, and co-authored three social studies textbooks.

Evans was born and reared in Philadelphia. She attended Wellesley College and, after receiving her B. A. in 1896, embarked on a teaching career that lasted until she retired in 1941. As a Philadelphia teacher, she organized the social studies department at William Penn High School (1901-1927) and subsequently chaired the history department at Simon Gratz High School (1927-1941). She obtained her master's degree in history and economics from the University of Pennsylvania in 1914. While studying there, Evans joined the Committee on the Social Studies and participated in its work. In addition to the 1916 publication, Evans contributed to four other works, one of which she authored herself.

She was a major although unacknowledged contributor to *The Course of Study in Civics for the Public Schools of Philadelphia* (Garber, 1916, 1917). Wellesley College holds one copy of the second volume of the book with the following remark penciled on its cover: "Jessie Evans is responsible for about one third of this."

Evans' best-known work is *Citizenship in Philadelphia*, written with J. L. Barnard (1918), which details community civics in Philadelphia. The book espouses the authors' belief that community life can be improved by schools teaching good citizenship. This viewpoint flowed from the 1916 Committee's recommendation that Community Civics, a new course, be added to the social studies offerings in the schools.

"Teaching International Relations through the Social Studies" was Evans' only independent writing. In this 1923 article, she stressed that teaching world citizenship requires an appreciation for (1) international interest, (2) the contributions of other nations to our common heritage, (3) humanity regardless of race or color, (4) the essential unity of human history, and (5) pride in national achievement.

Years later, Evans and her much younger collaborator, Suzanne Sankowsky, wrote *Graphic World History* (1942). The book is in many ways a conventional history textbook, but it also seeks to connect history with civics. For example, the book discusses the importance to people and workers of industrial invention. The book also reprises several suggestions that were made in the *1916 Report*, such as an emphasis on history as a part of students' lives.

Evans' contributions to the *1916 Report* are not easily determined, but it does contain two explicit references to her. An endnote acknowledged the 1915 bulletin on "The Teaching of Community Civics" from which much of the *1916 Report's* section on community civics was based. Evans, along with Thomas Jesse Jones and David Snedden, had provided accounts of school offerings to that bulletin. The second reference is a quotation in which she expresses concern that not every student will enroll in the social studies curriculum.

In her collaboration with Barnard, she likely wrote the book's section on community civics. Notable similarities are apparent between the sections on community civics in the *Citizenship in Philadelphia* and the *1916 Report*. For example, the suggested themes in the *1916 Report* for teaching community civics (e.g., health and education) appear as chapters in *Citizenship in Philadelphia*.

Evans' written work certainly exerted influence on the education community. *Citizenship in Philadelphia* had two editions, as did *Graphic World History*. In addition, the latter was included in a U.S. government-sponsored traveling library during World War II, which reached allied countries where citizens were interested in learning more about the United States. In sum, Evans played a role in developing the field of social studies, marking it with her own vision, and extending its influence beyond the boundaries of the United States.

References

Barnard, J. Lynn, F. W. Carrier, Arthur William Dunn, and Clarence D. Kingsley: Special Committee of the Commission on the Reorganization of Secondary Education, National Education Association. "The Teaching of Community Civics." *United States Bureau of Education Bulletin No. 23*, Washington, DC, 1915.

Barnard, J. Lynn and Jessie C. Evans. *Citizenship in Philadelphia*. Philadelphia, PA: John Winston, 1918.

Evans, Jessie C. and Suzanne Sankowsky. *Graphic World History*. Boston, MA: D. C. Heath, 1942.

Evans, Jessie C. "Teaching International Relations Through the Social Studies." *The Historical Outlook* 7, no. 14 (1923): 251-253.

Garber, John P., *The Course of Study in Civics for the Public Schools of Philadelphia*. Philadelphia, PA: Century Printing Concern, 1916,1917).

Nelson, Murry, ed. *The Social Studies in Secondary Education: A Reprint of the Seminal 1916 Report with Annotations and Commentaries*. Bloomington, IN: ERIC Clearinghouse for Social Studies, 1994.

Saxe, David. *Social Studies in Schools: A History of the Early Years*. Albany, NY: State University of New York Press, 1991.

United States Bureau of Education. Bulletin No. 23, Whole No. 650: *The Teaching of Community Civics*. Prepared by a special committee of the Commission on the Reorganization of Secondary Education and the National Education Association, Washington, DC, 1915.

Lucy Sprague Mitchell

July 2, 1878—October 15, 1967

SHERRY L. FIELD

Lucy Sprague Mitchell founded Bank Street College of Education in New York City. She authored numerous scholarly papers and books for children, parents, and teachers. Born in Chicago, Illinois, to wealthy parents, Lucy was tutored at home prior to attending the Marlborough School in California at the age of sixteen. She graduated from Radcliffe with honors in 1900 and began work at the University of California, Berkeley, where she became Dean of Women in 1906 and remained until 1913. Upon her marriage to Wesley Clair Mitchell, a noted economist at Berkeley and Columbia, she moved to New York City, where she spent the remainder of her impressive career and long life as a teacher of young children, author, curriculum developer, and teacher educator.

Several people who were forces in the growing fields of social work and education influenced Mitchell's work, including Jane Addams, social reformer and founder of Hull House in Chicago; John Dewey, educational theorist, philosopher, and teacher educator at the University of Chicago; Alice Freeman Palmer, Dean of Women at Wellesley and the University of Chicago; and Lillian Wald, founder of the Henry Street Settlement. Mitchell's work as a teacher and researcher of young children grew partly out of her interest in the new scientific focus on children's psychological and educational development during the early 1900's. In her 1953 memoir, *Two Lives: The Story of Wesley Clair Mitchell and Myself* (1953), Mitchell noted that she "began seeking some practical job with children in New York public schools—for public education was then, and has been ever since, the goal of my efforts."

Mitchell spent several years developing her theories about children's learning. She formed the Bureau of Educational Experiments (which later became Bank Street College of Education) in 1916, and spent intermittent years, until 1929, working at the Play School (later named City and Country School) and at the Little Red Schoolhouse, where she could try out her theories about appropriate curriculum for young children. During this time, she wrote *The Here and Now Storybook* (1921), the first of her many popular books for parents and teachers. It was a departure from typical storybooks

of traditional tales for children in that it contained stories about the lives and familiar social worlds of children in comfortable language designed for them. Equally successful storybooks written by Mitchell during her career included *Here and Now Primer* (1924); *Horses, Now and Long Ago* (1926), *Manhattan, Now and Long Ago* (1926); *North America: The Land They Live In for the Children Who Live There* (1931); and *Another Here and Now Storybook* (1937).

Mitchell made several impressive contributions to elementary social studies during her career. After working for the National Geographic Society for a year, she became interested in children's spatial awareness and how they learn about their surroundings. She began to write about methods for teaching about related concepts, believing that "the more he [the child] knows [about people and places] through personal contact, the better for his social growth." Important, sustained work grew out of her conviction that geography education, and especially human geography, which she described as "what the earth does to people, and what people do to the earth," should be an integral component of social studies and of the everyday school curriculum. *Young Geographers: How They Explore the World and How They Map the World* was published in 1934 and is still found on the reading lists of many elementary social studies methods courses today. In it, Mitchell theorized that children experienced various stages in their development of geographical knowledge and skills. She also provided meaningful procedures by which teachers could introduce map making and develop those skills in children. Among the teaching strategies that Mitchell continued to promote throughout her career were the consideration of relationships among the social studies subjects, especially geography and history, and the use of frequent field trips during the school year so that children could explore their local and larger community and return to school to recreate scenes with materials readily available, such as blocks, modeling clay, and boxes. She continued to value the effects of field trips on students' thinking. Years later, at Bank Street College of Education, she required that preservice and inservice teachers participate in longer, exploratory field trips.

As Mitchell's thoughts about exploring communities expanded, she developed her ideas about intercultural education, even as World War II began. In *The People of the U.S.A.: Their Place in the School Curriculum* (1942), she offered ideas for urban, rural, and suburban field trips as well as an extensive reading list concerning people of various cultural groups.

Linking teachers with research-enriched pedagogy always played a prominent role in Mitchell's work. She felt that the emerging field of teacher education deserved as much attention as the field of child development. By 1930, the Bureau of Educational Experiments, which by then had become a cooperative school and routine meeting place for experimental teachers, moved to a larger site, 69 Bank Street. In its newly remodeled factory building, the Bank Street's School for Teachers became a place where innovative teacher education theories could be shared and tested. In 1950, the name was changed to Bank Street College of Education; Mitchell chaired its Working Council and served as acting president until her retirement in 1956. Throughout her life, she wished to be remembered simply as "teacher." Her legacy remains, however, as a remarkable educator who provided illuminating ideas about how children can learn.

References

Antler, Joyce. *Lucy Sprague Mitchell: The Making of a Modern Woman.* New Haven, CT, 1987.

Field, Sherry L. "Lucy Sprague Mitchell: Teacher, Geographer, and Teacher Educator," in *"Bending the Future to Their Will": Civic Women, Social Education, and Democracy*, Margaret Smith Crocco and O. L. Davis, Jr., eds. Lanham, MD: Rowman and Littlefield, 1999: 125-147.

Mitchell, Lucy Sprague. Papers, Rare Book and Manuscript Library, Columbia University, New York.

Rachel Davis DuBois

January 25, 1892—March 30, 1993

O. L. DAVIS, JR.

Rachel Davis DuBois pioneered intercultural education in American schools. She insisted that schools must work to develop students' knowledge about and positive attitudes toward peoples of all cultures. Consequently, she sought both to devise achievable projects and to develop among teachers the experiential background and sensitivity that would support these purposes. A major American progressive, DuBois laid some of the important foundational elements of contemporary multicultural education.

Born into a Quaker family that farmed in southern New Jersey, Rachel Davis grew to maturity intimately aware of the cultural conflicts that were a part of her community and region. Institutional segregation in local schooling, for example, divided her and other white children from their black friends and neighbors. Such practices clearly were at odds with both her developing understandings of the ideals of political democracy and of the tenets of her faith community. For example, she early accepted the understanding of "God in every man." The life of Quaker meetings nourished the seeds of her lifetime commitments to social justice as well as to personal responsibility for social action.

She began her education in a rural common school near her home and completed an unremarkable secondary education at nearby Pilesgrove High School. Although graduates of her school routinely did not attend college, Davis developed a hesitant interest in obtaining further education. Admitted to Bucknell University, she pursued a major in natural science. She participated in several campus groups, but did not feel accepted socially. Upon her graduation in June, 1914, and unable to enter a career in science because of her gender, she took a position at Glassboro High School in New Jersey and taught algebra, biology, and American history. Although she was poorly prepared in history, she worked diligently to increase her knowledge and to enliven her students' engagement with historical matters. Davis married Nathan Steward DuBois on June 19, 1915, but continued to teach at Glassboro.

As the "Great War" in Europe devoured populations and resources, Rachel DuBois recognized that American preparation for war would test her political and religious convictions. In 1917, soon after U. S. entry into the war, she refused to sell war savings stamps to her pupils. Many American school officials dismissed or disciplined teachers who opposed the war, but DuBois' superintendent understood her position. He also appointed her acting principal of the high school when he departed for military service.

DuBois experienced a turning point in her life through her attendance at the First International Conference of Friends in London in 1920. The conference sessions about the conditions of the world's societies and peace in the postwar world were grim. She heard especially of the brutalizing conditions of wartime on civilians and of paternalism and other injustices imposed on colonial subjects by imperial nations. She became increasingly concerned by the reports of violence meted on black Americans by white Americans. Confessing that she knew too little about social problems in her own country, DuBois resigned her teaching position and volunteered for service with groups concerned with these social problems. For the next four years, she worked particularly in efforts to eliminate or reduce discrimination against blacks. She joined the NAACP and was an activist in its causes for the rest of her life. In 1924, she returned to teaching as a social studies teacher at Woodbury High School in New Jersey.

Her first deliberate attention to programs of intercultural education occurred the following year. Her committee of teachers proposed two assembly programs each month. One would feature speakers, musicians, or artists of different cultures; the second would be planned and presented by an ethnically mixed group of students. This "Woodbury Plan" enjoyed general community acceptance. The one dramatic exception occurred when the school board, under immense pressure by local "patriotic" groups, cancelled one month's programs on black culture and requested DuBois' resignation. She refused to leave her position; she continued to teach at Woodbury for several years. Not only did the program of intercultural assemblies continue, a comparative study revealed that Woodbury students were more tolerant on international and racial topics than were students at a nearby high school.

DuBois' local successes, however, only demonstrated to her that she needed to know more. Thus, she resigned her teaching post and enrolled for graduate study at Teachers College, Columbia University. Pursuing a graduate degree, however, was insufficient involvement for this committed interculturalist. Consequently, she worked with teachers and administrators in high schools of several states to extend the Woodbury Plan to the commonplace school assembly programs of the era. She recognized, however, that these good programs were not powerful enough to fully meet students' needs. With colleagues, she wrote a series of curriculum materials, pamphlets that were among the first materials explicitly intended for use in ethnic studies programs in American schools. Some critics have labeled these pamphlets "sanitized ethnicity" because they did not include aspects of cultural life that divided Americans. She offered the first university course in intercultural education at Boston University in 1933.

In 1934, she founded the Service Bureau for Intercultural Education to provide services to teachers rather than to advocate a particular vision of intercultural education. It quickly developed an extensive publications program, offered consultative services to area schools, and embarked on a large-scale research and demonstration program in fifteen New York City high schools. Focused specifically on the development of a generalized social harmony, the program attained success, but it attracted challenges from others committed to other purposes. Faced with diminished financial support for the Bureau by 1936, DuBois merged its operations with the Progressive Education Association's Commission on Intercultural Education. The relationship was not satisfactory and, two years later, the PEA board dismissed DuBois. She rebounded by reconstituting the Service Bureau and quickly becoming involved in a high visibility, federally sponsored radio project, "Americans All—Immigrants All" (1938-39). This twenty-six program series was quite popular, receiving a number of prestigious awards. During this pre-war period, DuBois continued to focus attention to separate ethnic groups, but some supporters and critics misunderstood her principled focus as contrary to the need for national unity. Also, some members of the Bureau's board became convinced that she was not a satisfactory administrator. Once again confronted with a request that she resign, in May 1941, she silently left the bureau that she had brought into existence.

Not one to succumb to despair, DuBois recreated her life. Within a year, she completed her long-delayed doctorate at New York University. She also formed the Workshop for Cultural Democracy, an enterprise that mainly worked to improve the relationships of adults, and she popularized her new Group Conversation Method. Importantly, she labored actively for civil rights and social justice throughout the remainder of her life. She died, aged 101, in Woodstown, New Jersey, on March 30, 1993.

References

Covello, Leonard. *The Heart is the Teacher*. New York: McGraw-Hill, 1958.

Davis, O. L., Jr. "Rachel Davis DuBois: Intercultural Education Pioneer," in *"Bending the Future to Their Will": Civic Women, Social Education, and Democracy*, Margaret Smith Crocco and O. L. Davis, Jr., eds. Lanham, MD: Rowman and Littlefield, 1999: 169-184.

DuBois, Rachel Davis. *All This and Something More: Pioneering in Intercultural Education*. Bryn Mawr, PA: Dorrance, 1984.

Montalto, Nicholas V. A *History of the Intercultural Education Movement, 1924-1941*. New York: Garland, 1982.

Savage, Barbara Dianne. *Broadcasting Freedom: Radio, War, and the Politics of Race, 1938-1948*. Chapel Hill, University of North Carolina Press, 1999: 21-62.

Helen Heffernan

January 25, 1896—August 30, 1987

KATHLEEN WEILER

Helen Heffernan was born in Massachusetts in 1896, the youngest of nine children, and moved to Goldfield, Nevada, with her family by the time she was in the eighth grade. She attended high school in Goldfield and later the Nevada Normal School, from which she graduated in 1915. She then held a series of positions as a teacher and principal in Nevada, Idaho, and Utah. From an early age, she was a supporter of women's rights and an advocate of women's suffrage.

In 1923, Heffernan received a B.A. from the University of California, and in 1925, she received her M.A., having studied during the summers. From 1923 to 1926, she worked as a rural supervisor in Kings County. She became active in the state Rural Supervisors Association and spoke frequently about her work. In 1926, she was invited by the State Board of Education to apply for the vacant position of commissioner of elementary schools. She was only thirty years old.

The early focus of Heffernan's work was on rural education, particularly after 1927, when the State Department of Education was organized and Heffernan became chief of the Division of Rural Education. Heffernan was concerned with supporting and strengthening the work of rural elementary school teachers, many of whom still worked in small one-, two-, or three-room schools. She became involved with rural education at a national level as well. In 1920 she was elected president of the Rural Supervisors Section of the National Education Association and worked to encourage a Deweyan approach to rural schools.

Heffernan used a variety of methods to bring progressive educational approaches to rural schools: She visited schools and spoke at institutes and conferences; created state demonstration schools; encouraged and guided the work of rural school supervisors; and organized the publication of state educational journals. Throughout the 1930s, Heffernan argued for progressive education, not only for rural schools, but for urban ones as well. In 1931, she established *The California Journal of Elementary Education*, which was published through 1963, showcasing the ideas of John Dewey, William Kilpatrick, and other progressive educators. Heffernan's influence was felt by elementary teachers

and supervisors throughout the state of California. With Corinne Seeds, the head of the University of California at Los Angeles laboratory school, she led a network of like-minded teachers and administrators, most of whom were women.

By the mid-1930s Heffernan's progressive vision increasingly incited conservative educators and local communities. The animosity of local communities to Heffernan's progressive ideas was heightened in the tense political climate of the 1930s, shaped in part by the influx of families of migrant farm workers and the need to provide schooling for their children. In the 1920s Mexican families had been recruited to work in expanding California agribusiness, replacing single, male migrant workers. In the 1930s the "dust bowl" migrants arrived in California from southwestern states. In response to this new population of school-age children, California established and supported migratory or emergency schools. Heffernan organized conferences and published state pamphlets and articles on the education of migrant children and on the need to provide health and family services through the schools.

With the outbreak of World War II, Heffernan became involved with the movement to provide day care and services to war workers and to provide adequate support for the rapidly expanding urban schools. She also faced the moral issue of the forced removal of Japanese-American families, including school-age children, to camps in 1942. Heffernan was not as public in her sympathy for the Japanese-American internees as was her friend Seeds, who received death threats after organizing a drive to bring food and blankets to the Japanese-Americans being held at the internment center at Santa Ana. But Heffernan did remain in contact with the superintendent of education at the Manzanar Camp, Dr. Genevieve Carter. In a letter to Dr. Carter on November 23, 1943, she raised the issue of trying to educate against prejudice and racial hatreds, citing favorably Carey McWilliams's talk on "the problem of education of minority groups" at an earlier state education conference.

As the progressive education movement became associated with more critical and politically radical ideas during the 1940s, all aspects of progressive education came under attack. For example, Heffernan was involved in defending curricular materials deemed unsuitable by conservative groups. In California, as was true elsewhere, social studies materials influenced by George Counts and Harold Rugg from Teachers College, Columbia, were attacked as biased and "socialistic," and Heffernan came to their defense. In 1946 her pamphlet *Framework for Social Studies* was attacked by the California Society of the Sons of the American Revolution as injecting "political propaganda" and teaching "international socialism." This pamphlet remained in use, but the social studies series *Building of America*, a series of photographic texts on social problems in America, was not so fortunate. Although defended by Heffernan and others, *Building of America* became the target of a number of right-wing groups in the 1940s, who eventually succeeded in having it removed from the schools.

Nevertheless, Heffernan retained strong support from liberal groups and local educators and continued a wide range of activities in California, nationally, and internationally. In the early 1960s she traveled widely, visiting schools throughout the world. In 1961, she conducted workshops in Kenya and Nigeria for African educators on the importance of providing equal educational opportunity for girls and women.

In the face of increasing criticism of progressive education in the McCarthy and cold war years, Heffernan remained steadfast in her commitment to child-centered and democratic education. After conservative Max Rafferty's successful campaign for state superintendent of public instruction, Heffernan, protected by civil service regulations, remained in office until 1965, but her influence declined. She retired without public announcement or ceremony at the age of sixty-nine. In 1966, her supporters raised funds to dedicate in her honor a redwood grove on the northern California coast. She lived quietly in Sacramento until her death in 1987 at the age of ninety-one.

References

Heffernan, Helen. *Building of America: A Textbook Series*. (1938) Helen Heffernan Collection, University of California, Riverside.
-----. "Democratic Living and Classroom Control." Unpublished manuscript. Helen Heffernan Collection, University of California, Riverside.
-----. Letter to Dr. Genevieve W. Carter, November 23, 1943, Bureau of Elementary Education files, California State Archives, Sacramento.
-----. *Framework for Social Studies*. Helen Heffernan Collection, University of California, Riverside.
-----. *Suggested Course of Study in the Social Studies for Elementary Schools*. Sacramento, CA: California State Printing Office, 1932.
"Helen Heffernan Retires from Education Bureau," *The Sacramento Bee*, September 2, 1965, D4.
Weiler, Kathleen. "Helen Heffernan," in Seller, Maxine, Ed. *Women Educators in the United States, 1820-1993* (Westport, CT: Greenwood Press, 1994), 238-247.
Weiler, Kathleen, "The Struggle for Democratic Public Schools in California: Helen Heffernan and Corinne Seeds," in Margaret Smith Crocco, Petra Munro, and Kathleen Weiler, *Pedagogies of Resistance: Women Educator Activists 1880-1960* (New York: Teachers College Press, 1999): 83-104.

This chapter was based on the author's piece on Helen Heffernan in Women Educators in the United States, 1820-1993, *edited by Maxine Seller. Used with permission of Greenwood Publishing Group, Inc., Westport, Connecticut.*

Elma Alva Neal

November 3, 1883—June 15, 1957

Matthew D. Davis

Elma Alva Neal served as a catalyst in changing professional opinions in Texas about educating Mexican and Mexican American pupils. Her pioneering efforts to provide instructional materials for and significantly increasing academic achievement of these "others" in the classrooms of San Antonio, Texas, mark her as an exemplary social educator. Elma Neal was a consummate "progressive" educator during the early 20th century.

Elma was born on November 3, 1883 near San Antonio, Texas, to James Polk Neal and Julia Virginia Neal. Her father had settled in the San Antonio area with other Missouri Mormons, including his subsequent bride's parents, during the years just prior to the American Civil War. The extended Neal family eschewed north or "white" San Antonio and made their home southwest of the San Antonio city limit, an area coterminous with the "Mexican" part of town. Thus, Elma grew up among Mexican American children and, likely, was bilingual on entering the San Antonio public schools. Just as surely, this intimate knowledge of Mexican American life inspired her eventual work as a progressive schoolteacher and administrator.

San Antonio and its culture nourished Neal throughout her life-long residence. The city, long misunderstood within Texas and elsewhere as a "Mexican" town, was an early Spanish colonial center of population. Throughout its long history, San Antonio's residents have been subject to Spanish, Mexican, and American rule. By the late 1920s, more Mexicans and Mexican Americans lived in San Antonio than in any other American city, but they still comprised about one third of the total population in that city. The San Antonio public schools, in which Neal was educated as a child and which employed her through most of her adulthood, were marginally more welcome to Mexican and Mexican American children and youth in the early 20th century than were other Texas schools. For example, William J. Knox, a long time San Antonio school administrator and Neal's eventual supervisor, allowed Mexican pupils at Navarro School during his time as principal to sing the Mexican national anthem in their native language. However, by the xenophobic years of World War I, this practice apparently was discontin-

ued. Knox's courageous act, during a time when Mexican pupils regularly were punished when they used their home language, must have inspired Neal and her subsequent work on behalf of these children.

Elma Neal graduated from San Antonio High School in 1901 and began teaching in the city's public schools in 1907. The intervening six years of her life are lost to history. Neal likely worked on the family farm; like countless other young adult females, she was missed by the local directory publisher when canvassing the area. By 1918, Neal had progressed to the position of principal of Green Elementary School at which presumably she had been teaching for the preceding ten years. Two years later she was selected to fill the post of Supervisor of Primary Grades. In subsequent school district reorganizations, this post's description changed to Director of Elementary Education (1923) and subsequently to Assistant Supervisor of Elementary Education (1929). Neal held the last title until she retired in 1948.

Neal, in an uncharacteristic move for a young Texas female teacher, continued her education at Teachers College, Columbia University, in New York City. Likely attending during the summers, she earned a diploma in supervision in 1922, an A. B. in 1923, and an A. M. in 1926. Elma, unsurprisingly for an individual with this educational background, was a prominent southwestern member of the Progressive Education Association, rising to become a member of its advisory board. She garnered numerous other national distinctions in the field; for example, Neal chaired the National Education Association's Fifth Yearbook on Creative Teaching (1932).

San Antonio's Mexican and Mexican American pupils came under Elma Neal's purview. A survey undertaken by University of Texas professor Herschel T. Manuel in the late 1920s revealed that more than 90 percent of such students attending the state's public schools languished in the lower elementary grades. Similarly, the University of Chicago educator Franklin Bobbitt, in his 1915 survey of San Antonio public schools, reported that nearly 80 percent of that city's Mexican and Mexican American students were over age for their class. Neal endeavored to change the dismal educational circumstances for these students. By 1932, Neal had made impressive strides at increasing educational attainment for these students: the number reported to be over age had been reduced to between 8 and 11 percent and, increasingly, the upper elementary grades were being opened to these students. No other Texas educator of the period could point to such progressive practical results for Mexican and Mexican American children and youth.

Neal's accomplishments can be attributed, at least partially, to her authorship, with her assistant for elementary schools Ollie Storm, of the *Open Door* (1929) series of readers (Primer, First Reader, Second Reader). The readers served as the centerpiece of a newly implemented course of study for Mexican and Mexican American students in San Antonio. They represented several years of research in which teachers used mimeographed early drafts with students at the Margill School. Neal was a staunch supporter of the direct method of language instruction. For example, following state law, students learned to say "pencil" without first saying "*lapiz*." All of the children in Neal's readers, however, were addressed by their Spanish language names, complete with accents and tildes. Thus, such students in the public elementary classrooms of San Antonio and other southwestern American school districts may have claimed a modicum of relationship between school and home. Her pedagogical material and techniques for Mexican American students garnered wide appeal, both within Texas and across the nation, as evidenced by laudatory accounts in the *Christian Science Monitor* and *School and Society*.

The recognition of Neal as a progressive educator of Mexican and Mexican American children and youth must be understood within the racialized context of the time and place in which she worked. For example, the boys depicted in Neal's readers wore sailor suits, an unlikely choice of clothing. Similarly, the children's mother baked bread instead of tortillas, and the family engaged in stereotypic Anglo activities.

Also, in line with contemporary professional sentiment, Neal wrote of using the readers in ways to capitalize on the Mexican singing and dramatic talent; an ability that she understood to be inherited from Aztec artistry. Presumably, her observation of Mexican pageantry in her hometown reinforced her impression of collective talent.

Despite these contextual caveats, Elma Neal left an indelible legacy on the dialogue about improving Mexican and Mexican American education. Her ministrations with regard to Mexican American children and youth reserve for her a place among the nation's most progressive social educators. A San Antonio elementary school was named in Neal's honor on her retirement in 1948. Neal, a long-time resident at 510 E. Dewey Place in San Antonio, died on June 15, 1957, at age seventy-three.

References

Hanus, Charles Eugene, "That All May Learn: A History of Curriculum in the San Antonio Public Schools to 1925," Ph.D. dissertation, The University of Texas at Austin, 1997.

Manuel, Herschel T. *The Education of Mexican and Spanish-Speaking Children in Texas.* Austin, TX: The Fund for Research in Social Sciences at the University of Texas, 1930.

Neal, Elma A., "Adapting the Curriculum to Non-English Speaking Children," *Elementary English Review* 6, no. 7 (April, 1929): 183-185.

-----. The Development of a Social Studies Curriculum in San Antonio, *Educational Method* 10, no. 5 (February 1931): 268-273.

-----. *Leaders in Education*, 2nd ed. Lancaster, PA: Science Press, 1942: 745.

-----. and Ollie Storm, *The Open Door: Primer; First Reader; Second Reader; Teacher's Manual.* New York: MacMillan, 1929.

Other primary sources used were various San Antonio City Directories and city maps at the Center for American History and the Perry-Castaneda Library, The University of Texas at Austin.

Hilda Taba

December 7, 1902—July 6, 1967

JANE BERNARD-POWERS

Hilda Taba was a curriculum theorist, curriculum reformer, and teacher educator whose work provided a theoretical and pedagogical foundation for concept development and critical thinking in the social studies. Taba was an architect and participant in three major curriculum events of the twentieth century: the "Eight Year Study," in which she evaluated progressive student-centered curricula in terms that included critical thinking abilities; the Intergroup Education in Cooperating Schools Project, which anticipated the multicultural education movement of the nineteen seventies; and the productive collaboration between San Francisco State University and the Contra Costa County schools, which resulted in the "spiral of curriculum development" in elementary social studies curriculum.

Hilda was born in Kooraste, a small village in South Eastern Estonia, into the family of Liisa Leht and Robert Taba, a "schoolmaster." She attended Kanepi Parish School, Voru's Girls' Grammar School, and earned an undergraduate degree in English and Philosophy at Tartu University. Taba was introduced to Progressive Education ideas at Tartu University, and she pursued this interest in the United States when the opportunity to do master's degree work at Bryn Mawr College in Pennsylvania arose in 1926. After earning a master's degree there, she went on to Teachers College, Columbia University where her interest in progressive education gave rise to her career in curriculum theory, curriculum development, and teacher education. Taba studied with William Kilpatrick, Boyd H. Bode, and John Dewey, and her dissertation entitled "Dynamics of Education: A Methodology of Progressive Educational Thought" (1932) acknowledges her gratitude to these progressive education pioneers.

Taba's dissertation established a foundation for much of her subsequent work, and in it she drew on a wide range of academic disciplines. Three key ideas in the work are particularly important for curriculum history. First, she argued that learning and the study of learning should be modeled after contemporary physics in that the processes are dynamic, interrelated, and interdependent. Thus, she established a paradigm that was radically different from a simple transmission model of education. Second, she argued that education for democracy was at the heart of education, and that it had to be based on rich experiences where children learned to live together in democratic relationships. Third, she argued that educators must deliver substantial curriculum, not slogans, and that they are accountable in both the delivery and the evaluation of the work. Parenthetically, she eschewed objective testing as the primary method of evaluation.

Taba returned to Estonia in 1931 just prior to the publication of her dissertation with hopes of taking a position at Tartu University, but the hiring committee turned her down despite her impressive credentials because she was female. Male candidates were preferred at that time, according to Edgar Krull, a Taba scholar from Tartu University. Deeply disappointed, she came back to the United States, where she became curriculum director at the Dalton School in New York City.

Following her return to the United States, the political tides of repression returned to Estonia, and she could not go back for many years because her ideas about democracy were considered dangerous. Her rejection from the job may have saved her life.

Over the next four decades, Taba's career and work as a curriculum theorist flourished. The particular combination of her towering energetic intellect, her deep appreciation for democracy (which developed out of Estonia's political repression in the twentieth century), her belief in the power of individuals and groups in educational contexts to realize significant social goals, and her commitment to demonstrate empirically the effects of social education fueled her leadership in curriculum generally and in three major twentieth century projects specifically.

The Eight Year Study, also known as the Commission on the Relation of School and College, or the Thirty Schools Project, was an ambitious research project that was to evaluate how students from progressive secondary schools would fare in colleges. Ralph Tyler, at the University of Chicago, was responsible for the overall evaluations in the Eight Year Study, and he invited Hilda Taba to join him following a meeting at the Dalton School in New York.

Taba's contribution to the study was evaluation of "social sensitivity," which was related to the general goal of preparing students for effective democratic participation. Taba measured social sensitivity by multiple means, including group activities, informal conversations, anecdotal accounts, and students' book reviews and other writings. Taba delved under the surfaces of social phenomena to discover the attitudes and problems in student social life. She tackled two challenging areas of social studies pedagogy: the measurement of attitudes about race, class, and ethnicity and the development of authentic alternatives to paper and pencil assessment.

Taba's work on evaluation led to a productive collaboration with Ralph Tyler and the design of a general framework for developing curriculum. It also led to a position as director of the Curriculum Laboratory at the University of Chicago in 1938 and her subsequent leadership in intergroup education in the 1940s.

Racism, anti-semitism, and perceived threats to national unity gave rise to a collaboration between the National Conference of Christians and Jews and the American Council on Education. This collaboration, focused on the reduction of prejudice and conflict through education, was known as the Intergroup Education in Cooperating Schools Project. Taba developed an association with the project in 1944 when she headed up a summer workshop at Harvard, which resulted in the 1945 yearbook for NCSS, *Democratic Human Relations*. She assumed the directorship of the project in 1945, then served as director of the Center for Intergroup Education at the University of Chicago until 1951.

Taba brought a staff of eight educators together who fanned out across eighteen sites and seventy-two schools over a period of two years to work with local site faculty on issues of prejudice and discrimination. The Intergroup Education Project tackled issues related to newcomers, economic instability, housing patterns, and community relations using interactive curriculum and processes such as literature groups, conflict resolution, and role playing.

In 1951 Taba left the Intergroup Education Center to take a position at San Francisco State College, where she developed a major curriculum reform project. Working collaboratively with teachers and administrators in Contra Costa County, California, Taba formulated, researched, and wrote about the foundations of curriculum development. Taba and her colleagues explicated and documented the complex processes that children use to form concepts. They also organized and implemented staff development for teachers, documenting this work for research. Mary Durkin, a teacher and curriculum specialist from the Contra Costa County Schools, was a close associate who anchored the critical bridge between Taba's theoretical work and the practice of classroom teachers who spent summers and weekends learning about concept attainment and writing social studies curriculum.

The Taba Spiral of Curriculum Development is a graphic organizer designed to illustrate concept development in children as it relates to the elementary social studies curriculum. The Taba Spiral was used by teachers in workshops in the nineteen-sixties, and it is found in curriculum texts today.

Taba's theorizing and curriculum development were unusual for her day. She understood and articulated the deep connections between culture, politics, and social change; cognition and learning; experience and evaluation; and the significance of all three for teacher preparation and civic education. As an educator, her work was profoundly optimistic and democratic. She believed that teachers should be the curriculum designers and that all children could learn to think critically about complex ideas.

Hilda Taba died in Burlingame, California, on July 6, 1967. Her curriculum theory and project work was captured in publications that are still available today, including *Curriculum Development: Theory and Practice* (1962), *Teacher's Handbook for Elementary Social Studies* (1967), and an elementary textbook series published posthumously (1970).

References

Bernard-Powers, Jane. "Composing Her Life: Hilda Taba and Social Studies History," in *"Bending the Future to Their Will": Civic Women, Social Education, and Democracy*, Margaret Smith Crocco and O. L. Davis Jr., eds. Lanham, MD: Rowman and Littlefield, 1999): 185-206.

Taba, Hilda. *Curriculum Development: Theory and Practice*. New York: Harcourt, Brace and World, 1962.

Taba, Hilda, Mary Durkin, Jack Fraenkel, and Anthony McNaughton. *A Teachers' Handbook to Elementary Social Studies: An Inductive Approach*. Reading, MA: Addison Wesley, 1970.

Taba, Hilda and William Van Til, eds. *Democratic Human Relations*. 16th Yearbook. Washington, DC: NCSS, 1945.

Helen Merrell Lynd

March 17, 1896—January 30, 1982

JAMES WESLEY NULL

One of Helen Merrell Lynd's major contributions to the fields of sociology and social education was her groundbreaking work, *Middletown: A Study in Contemporary American Culture* (1929). In this work, she and her husband, Robert Staughton Lynd, studied a small midwestern town in order to uncover the everyday lives of American citizens in one particular region of the country. They dedicated a sizeable portion of this study to the education of Middletown's children and youth. In a relatively short time, the book became a standard sociology text throughout the country.

Helen Merrell was born March 17, 1896, in La Grange, Illinois, to Edward Tracy Merrell and Mabel Waite. Her father was editor of *The Advance*, a Congregationalist publication, and her mother taught school prior to marriage, after which she remained at home with her daughters. With her two sisters, Helen grew up in a suburb of Chicago and was brought up in a family environment that was religiously strict and modestly wealthy. She attended Lyons Township High School and planned to enroll at Northwestern University, but her family's relocation to Framingham, Massachusetts, led her to choose Wellesley College. As a student there, she worked in a local restaurant to help support herself and pay for college expenses.

Helen Merrell's academic interests flourished at Wellesley, where she majored in philosophy, English, and history, and participated in numerous extracurricular activities such as student government and the debate team. At Wellesley, Mary S. Case was one of her most important teachers, encouraging her to study the idealism and the dialectics of Hegel. She graduated in 1919 as a member of Phi Beta Kappa.

Soon after her Wellesley years, Helen met Robert Staughton Lynd during a vacation trip with her family in Randolph, New Hampshire. For the 1919-1920 school year, Helen Lynd taught eight courses at Ossining (New York) School for Girls. During the following school year, she served as a secondary teacher at Miss Master's School in Dobbs Ferry, New York. She married Robert Lynd, moved to New York City, and lived with Robert's parents. During these years , she studied history at Columbia University, earning an M.A. there in 1922.

In 1924, with support from the Rockefeller Foundation, Robert began to study small town religious life. For the next two years, the Lynds lived, worked, and studied in Muncie, Indiana, which they called "Middletown." Their book on life there was published in 1929. During this period, Lynd mothered two children, Staughton and Andrea.

After a brief association with Vassar College as a lecturer, Helen Lynd accepted an academic position at Sarah Lawrence College and taught there for the next thirty-five years. While a teacher at Sarah Lawrence, she continued her personal academic pursuits at Columbia University. As a mother, a faculty member, and a doctoral student at Columbia, Lynd's time was certainly stretched, but she persevered and completed her Ph.D. in the history of ideas in 1944. In 1945, Oxford University Press published her dissertation as a book, *England in the Eighteen Eighties: Toward a Social Basis for Freedom*.

Also in 1945, Lynd published her first major work on education, *Field Work in College Education*. This book described her early work at Sarah Lawrence and her efforts to build a community of learners, to base her courses on the interests of her students, and to interest college students in sociology. During this time, many teachers at Sarah Lawrence emphasized the necessity for students to assist their instructors in the development of course content and curriculum. Lynd's teaching constantly improved in this environment as collegiality between faculty members and students assumed top priority. She also worked closely with her Sarah Lawrence colleagues to develop and teach courses together in their overall efforts to further the advancement of liberal ideas. Also, while in New York City, Lynd joined the American Federation of Teachers and the American Civil Liberties Union, both of which she supported for many years. She also served on the Board of the New York Teachers Union.

During the McCarthy era of the early 1950s, numerous faculty members at Sarah Lawrence were suspected of communist activities, a situation that furthered Lynd's insistence upon academic freedom. Notably, when asked to submit her "political history" to the

59

president of Sarah Lawrence, Harold A. Taylor, she refused to comply with his request. In the early 1950s, Lynd's commitment to liberal ideas and leftist causes drew suspicion from several ideologically driven members of the U.S. Senate. Eventually, she was called before the Senate Internal Security Subcommittee, chaired by William Jenner, to be questioned about her political affiliation and the activities of her colleagues at Sarah Lawrence College. Later, Lynd regretted that she had answered "No" to Jenner's question about whether or not she had ever been a member of the Communist party. She wished that she had taken the Fifth Amendment and stayed to challenge publicly Jenner and the rest of the committee.

Lynd officially retired from Sarah Lawrence in 1964, but she continued her work by teaching a reduced load. She also authored several publications. Lynd lived in New York City until 1981, at which time she relocated to Ohio where she died of a heart attack in 1982.

References

Deegan, Mary J. "Helen Merrell Lynd," in *Women in Sociology: A Bio-Bibliographical Sourcebook*. New York: Greenwood Press, 1991.

Dinneen, Marcia B. "Lynd, Helen Merrell." *The Scribner Encyclopedia of American Lives*, Vol. 1, 1981-1985. New York: Charles Scribners, 1998.

Lynd, Helen M. *England in the Eighteen-Eighties: Toward a Social Basis for Freedom*. London: Oxford University Press, 1945.

-----. *Field Work in College Education*. New York: Columbia University Press, 1945.

Lynd, Robert S., and Helen M. Lynd. *Middletown: A Study in Contemporary American Culture*. New York: Harcourt, Brace, 1929.

The Esther Rauschenbush Library of Sarah Lawrence College houses a collection of the Helen Merrell Lynd papers. A photograph of Lynd is also available at the Sarah Lawrence College Archives.

Eleanor Roosevelt

October 11, 1885 — November 7, 1962

DANIEL PERLSTEIN

Few Americans are more fully identified with liberal reform than Eleanor Roosevelt, and few reformers have more consistently placed education at the center of their activism. Eleanor's career epitomized efforts to democratize both American politics and civic education.

Born into a family touched in equal measure by extraordinary wealth, appalling misfortune, and astonishing cruelty, Eleanor was rescued from the barrenness and casual bigotry of her class when, at age fifteen, she enrolled at Allenswood, an elite girls school in England. Marie Souvestre, the school's headmistress and dominant personality, repudiated notions of women's intellectual inferiority, and the girls and women of Allenswood offered Eleanor deep emotional bonds, access to a sophisticated, liberal political world, and a rich intellectual life. She traced the synthesis of affect, intellect, and political engagement in her own thought and work to her time at Allenswood.

When Eleanor returned to the United States and married her cousin Franklin Delano Roosevelt (FDR), the claustrophobic world of her childhood once again closed in around her. Slowly, however, she began to redefine her place in the world. In 1922, Eleanor began a close relationship with educator Marion Dickerman and Nancy Cook, and the lesbian couple introduced her to networks of women activists. Led by Dickerman, Eleanor helped establish evening classes for the Women's Trade Union League. By 1927, Eleanor joined Dickerman as co-owner of New York City's fashionable Todhunter School for Girls. For the next four years, while FDR was governor, Eleanor divided her week between her official duties in Albany and her New York career as Todhunter's history/civics teacher and vice principal.

Todhunter combined a moderately progressive pedagogy with the reinforcement of students' social privilege. The pedagogy was derived from the "project method." Teaching, Eleanor believed, needed to progress from students' interests to a broad understanding of history and social life, and "to develop in students...the ability to find out things for themselves and a curiosity to know more in whatever line they are studying." Eleanor later remembered: "Our history and English and crafts activities are all correlated about a single period or theme."

Eleanor stressed the value of "contact with big people and remarkable personalities, whether obtained through books, or through actual action." Todhunter students, she wrote novelist Dorothy Canfield Fisher, "should see a little more of the world than their own surroundings, with an understanding eye and heart." Still, Eleanor had firm ideas about the need to inculcate intellectual and moral dispositions. "The most important thing for a child," Eleanor believed, "is to acquire an attitude of responsibility .... Following rules like others is the real character building of schools." Todhunter's curriculum also included "strict accountability" through "frequent tests...for we believe that the girls will have to take certain hurdles in life, and that hurdles in school are an important preparation."

Gradually, as FDR's rise in national politics expanded her own horizons, Eleanor became increasingly disenchanted with Todhunter's commitment to social privilege. "The point of real education," she came to believe, "is an ability to recognize the spirit that is in a real human being, even though it may be obscured for a time by lack of education or opportunity." Abandoning Todhunter, Eleanor turned her interests to less elitist forms of schooling and adult education.

No New Deal program occupied more of Eleanor's attention than the attempt to create a new homestead community in Arthurdale, West Virginia, an area marked by extraordinary human misery. Inhabitants of the mining camps, Eleanor would recollect at a 1939 press conference, "were like people walking around dead. They were alive, but they were dead as far as any real living was concerned." She was convinced that conditions in the camps had rendered residents so despondent that they had lost the capacity to direct their own lives. She expected Arthurdale to refashion the lives of the poor and at the same time to establish conditions in which people profoundly scarred by privation could begin to direct their own lives. Because she simultaneously understood the incapacitating injuries of misery and held to the democratic belief that the poor could learn to participate fully in

American life, Eleanor placed education at the center of Arthurdale's community revitalization.

Envisioning Arthurdale as "a social experiment in community life which centers around its school," Eleanor was convinced that the homestead could serve as a national research and exhibition center, displaying methods of social reconstruction in much the way that agricultural extension stations demonstrated efficient farming practices. She took an active interest in every aspect of community life, and recruited such noted educators as John Dewey, Lucy Sprague Mitchell, Progressive Education Association President Carson Ryan, Dean William Russell of Teachers College, and John Dewey protégée Elsie Clapp to join her in planning the community's educational program.

Eleanor worked to bring to Arthurdale the elements of domestic grace and beauty that other Americans enjoyed, but newspapermen and politicians ridiculed her for wasting tax dollars on such "trivial" matters. Community revitalization in Arthurdale was based on the impractical notion that subsistence homestead farms would allow miners to escape the ravages of industrial society. Arthurdale's schools, while being models of progressive pedagogy, contained a strain of sentimentalism common in progressivism of that era. Students learned square dances and traditional ballads rather than union songs; they studied the process of spinning wool, but not the brutalization of the extraction industries; they learned of West Virginia's pioneer heritage, but not of the slave plantation that constituted the area's first non-native settlement. A quarter of those individuals who applied to move to Arthurdale were black, but not one was admitted to the community, despite black protests and Eleanor's efforts to win whites over to racial tolerance.

The failures of the Arthurdale experiment led Eleanor to confront more fully racial inequality. Just as Eleanor had gained much from the mentoring of Dickerman and others in the 1920s, she also learned much from Mary McLeod Bethune, Walter White, and other black leaders in the 1930s. For two decades beginning in the 1940s, she actively supported a school that challenged the racial inequalities that Arthurdale reproduced. Wiltwyck, an integrated residential school for troubled New York City boys, was created because existing programs excluded blacks. Celebrated for its efforts to apply progressive pedagogy to the treatment of delinquent youths, Wiltwyck's bucolic Hudson River Valley campus embodied the rehabilitative possibilities of rural life. Frequent visits by Eleanor during the school's early years and annual school picnics at Hyde Park contributed much to the school's fame. The notion that all children shared similar needs and that professionals could address them, beliefs at the heart of elite liberal reform, suffused Eleanor's support for Wiltwyck. The school, she liked to say, demonstrated that all children share the need "to feel that they are known, that they are distinct individuals. It is not enough to be part of a group."

Even military preparation for World War II was, for Eleanor, an occasion for civic education and community revitalization. In 1941, she served as co-director of the Office of Civilian Defense. Challenged by conservatives who sought to limit OCD to military and police matters, Eleanor argued, "this is no time to overstress the importance of personal safety against token bombing, rather than developing fortitude in the people for whatever they must face as citizens of a country at war." In order for Americans "to have confidence in themselves, to feel secure in their way of life, to have high moral codes," she urged that OCD foster "the knowledge that daily conditions can be met, that you have a say in meeting them, and that you have a part in the defense of your community and the country."

The ideas and ideals that shaped Eleanor's work in the heyday of American liberalism differ in several respects from those of today's liberal thinkers. She had a much greater faith in the possibility of discovering a progressive science of education and much less interest in cultural diversity. Excluded from the inner circle of New Deal policy-making, Eleanor was forced to seek change through the slower and more ephemeral process of transforming Americans' minds and hearts, including her own. As Eleanor transcended her origins, her own political understanding deepened, broadening her educational goals.

A vision of civic education and democratic life unites Eleanor's work with Arthurdale, Wiltwyck, and the OCD, along with such activities as her daily syndicated newspaper column, "My Day," and her involvement in the Works Progress Administration theater and the She-She-She Camps. For Eleanor, education and democracy were ongoing, unfinished projects. Her career demonstrates the utility of seeing democratic education, like democracy itself, as a developmental, often rehabilitative, process for citizens and teachers as well as students.

References

Bernard, Eunice Fuller, "Mrs. Roosevelt in the Classroom," *New York Times Magazine* December 4, 1932.

Perlstein, Daniel. "Eleanor Roosevelt: The Schooling of An American Liberal." Paper presented at the Annual Meeting of the American Educational Research Association, New Orleans, LA, April, 2000.

-----. "Community and Democracy in American Schools: Arthurdale and the Fate of Progressive Education," *Teachers College Record* 97, no. 4 (Summer 1996): 625-650.

The papers of Eleanor Roosevelt are archived at the Franklin D. Roosevelt Library in Hyde Park, New York.

Mary Gertrude Kelty

February 15, 1890 — April 13, 1964

KEITH C. BARTON

Mary Gertrude Kelty served as president of the National Council for the Social Studies in 1945. She was the author of numerous scholarly works and elementary school history textbooks. Born in Midland, Michigan, she taught in the state's public elementary and secondary schools and later received bachelor's (1915) and master's (1924) degrees from the University of Chicago. She worked as a supervising teacher (1915-1918), faculty member (1921-1924), and later chair (1925-1926) of the Department of Social Studies at the Wisconsin State Teachers College, Oshkosh. She also served on the faculty of the University of Puerto Rico from 1918-1920.

As a single woman with no children, Kelty had the freedom of professional and geographic mobility. Beginning in 1927, she abandoned her full-time academic appointment and began work as a writer, consultant, and visiting lecturer. From 1929 to 1931, she and Nelle E. Moore co-edited *News-Outline*, a nationally circulated current events newspaper for use in the upper elementary grades. Between 1930 and 1937, Kelty authored seven elementary school history textbooks (along with supplementary materials) in Ginn & Company's Tryon-Lingley Series; titles included *The Old World Beginnings of America, The American Colonies, The Beginnings of the American People and Nation*, and *The Growth of the American People and Nation*.

In 1938, Kelty began twelve years of service on the NCSS board of directors. She moved from Chicago to Washington, D.C. in 1941, and later worked as a consultant for the Office of Price Administration (1942) and the Office of Military Government in Germany (1947-1948). In this latter capacity, she assisted in the preparation of postwar textbooks on German history for use in West Germany's schools and, in 1950, she chaired the U.S. delegation to the Brussels UNESCO seminar on the improvement of history textbooks. Through the 1930s and 1940s, Kelty also held positions as a visiting lecturer at Minnesota, Chicago, Nebraska, Syracuse, Colorado State, Emory, and Harvard. She retired from active professional life in 1953 and was later killed in an automobile accident near Lake Wales, Florida, in 1964.

Kelty published throughout her career, beginning with the results of her M.A. thesis on children's understanding of time expressions, which she published in two articles in *Elementary School Journal* in 1925. In addition to authoring school textbooks, she published more than thirty scholarly books, chapters, and journal articles. Her best known professional work, *Learning and Teaching History in the Middle Grades*, was a methods textbook for teachers in the upper elementary grades. Her writings are particularly notable for their extensive citation of the contemporary scholarship on children's thinking and reasoning.

Kelty labored to develop a coherent and empirically grounded social studies program for grades four through six. This attempt placed her at the intersection of competing educational philosophies and, in many of her writings, she sought to mediate the claims of rival approaches by adapting their recommendations to the needs and interests of children situated between the primary and junior high school levels. Her early work reflected the scientific curriculum-making associated with educators at the University of Chicago; these early writings emphasized a carefully planned procedure for covering material, a continual process of assessment and remediation, and a concern for establishing lists of the specific individuals, terms, and dates that she believed students needed to learn. The influence of this approach on Kelty's later career may be found in her abiding interest in curricular alignment, thoughtful lesson planning, and empirical verification of effectiveness.

However, Kelty also focused attention on children's comprehension of content, rather than simple memorization or verbal mastery. This emphasis led her early on to emphasize pupils' active involvement through stimulating questions, research projects, presentations, and the reading of well-written narratives. By the mid-1930s, she abandoned much of the regimentation of her earlier recommendations and sought, instead, to position her work in relation to philosophies centered on children's development and interests, on the one hand, and those stressing social needs and values on the other. She considered the activity approach of the period's developmentalists to be a crucial component of meaningful learning at all ages. She argued, however, that pupils' immediate interests no longer could be the focus of the curriculum by the fourth grade; the purpose of social studies at that level, Kelty maintained, was to provide vicarious experiences of other times and places. She also praised Harold Rugg and other educators who sought to engage students in reflective consideration of broad social issues, but she considered this approach beyond the ability of most children before junior high years.

Kelty attempted to resolve the demands of these competing philosophies by centering the fourth to sixth grade social studies curriculum on history. This focus, she argued, provided a more coherent and compelling framework than any other means of organization. Pupils would continue to engage in interesting mental and physical activities, as they had during their primary grades, but they would do so mainly through learning about historical developments and the origins of modern life. Their familiarity with history, meanwhile, would provide the foundation for their deliberations about societal issues later in their schooling. She also was concerned to distinguish instruction at this level from the kind of historical study that focused on chronology, biography, or political and military events.

For Kelty, the chief goal of studying history was the ability to comprehend a coherent narrative of successive events, and this aim required the use of units organized around broad movements, particularly from U.S. history (such as why English people came to live in the New World and how the United States became a Great Industrial Nation). Such an approach called for pupils' deliberate attention to social and economic context. These principles underlay most of Kelty's historical writings for children. Her chief influence on social education probably lies in her popular textbooks, which introduced generations of elementary children to a history curriculum based in narratives of national history.

References

Hartshorn, Merrill. "Mary G. Kelty (1890-1964)," *Social Education* 28, no. 6 (October 1964): 349.

Kelty, Mary G. *Learning and Teaching History in the Middle Grades*. New York: Ginn, 1936.

Kelty, Mary G. "Curriculum Development in Social Studies for the Middle Grades: Differing Factors During the Past Twenty-five Years which have Led to the Present Confusion in Social Studies for Older Children: Programs for Grades Four, Five, and Six," in Loretta E. Klee, ed. *NCSS Curriculum Series No. 5*. Washington, DC: NCSS, 1953: 2-15.

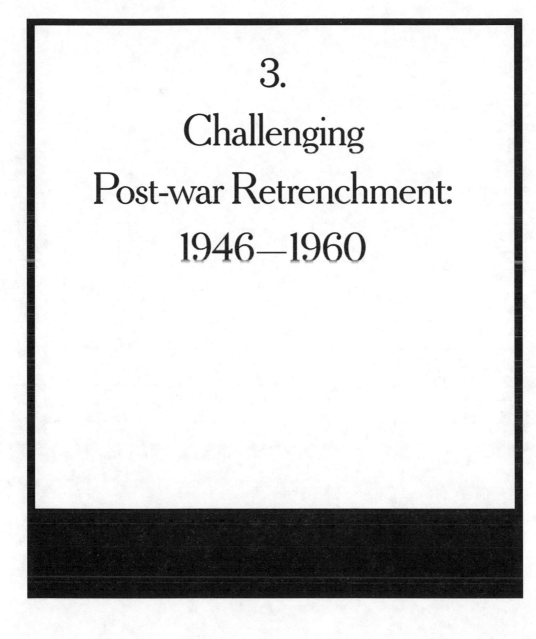

3.

Challenging Post-war Retrenchment: 1946–1960

Introduction

Margaret Smith Crocco

In her book *The Home Front and Beyond: American Women in the 1940s* Susan Hartmann concludes her discussion of women and education with these words:

> The brief promise of greater educational equity which surfaced amidst the imperatives of war vanished as another imperative, the need to compensate those who had defended the nation, increased the distance between women's and men's opportunities.[1]

In terms of sheer numbers of women going to college, progress had been made: In 1940, just over 600,000 had been enrolled; by 1950, that number had swelled to over 805,000. The more telling statistic, however, charts the reduced proportion pursuing higher education: In 1940, women were 40% of the total number of college graduates; by 1950, they were only 25%.

One of the reasons for this downward shift was the enormous number of male students returning to college under the auspices of the GI Bill of Rights, passed by Congress as the Servicemen's Readjustment Act in 1944.[2] Women veterans were also eligible for benefits from this bill, and according to historian Linda Eisenmann, used the bill in proportion to their military participation, or about 3 percent. Of interest here, Hunter College, where Dorothy Fraser taught during the sixties and early seventies, had been the largest women's college in the country during the thirties, but decided to become a coeducational college after experimenting with male students enrolling under the GI Bill after the war.[3]

As a result of the legislation:

> This flood of returnees entering schools and colleges brought new meaning to the notion of equal educational opportunity. Mass education now had to be planned and implemented at both the high school and post-secondary levels, since school success was seen increasingly as being essential to one's success in life. The activities of black and women teachers seeking single salary scales were also part of the new thrust for more equality in American life. The pursuit of equal opportunity in and through education came to be a dominant theme in the decades following World War II.[4]

Concerns with equality in education served as an important focus of Lavone Hanna's life and work. Hanna was professor of education at San Francisco State University from 1947 to 1961. Like many progressive educators, Hanna stressed the importance of aligning curriculum with the needs of children. Ahead of many other progressive educators, Hanna was explicit about the need for teachers to make curriculum responsive to students of diverse ethnic and racial backgrounds. In her later writing, she called for curriculum development and educational equality for students from low-income families and for those with physical, emotional, and intellectual handicaps. Like Alice Miel (who is also discussed in this chapter), she believed strongly that schools in general and social education in particular should work to expand educational equality for all the nation's children.

Fulfilling this obligation fell chiefly to women, since the teaching profession remained overwhelmingly a woman's field during the post-war years, despite a widespread teacher shortage and renewed efforts to attract men into teaching. Numerous life stories could be assembled matching, at least in part, that of Myrtle Roberts who, for 52 years, served as a public school teacher in Dallas, Texas. However, few teachers matched Roberts' professional attainment as president of NCSS in 1951. As we have seen with Ruth West, and find here again with the cases of Myrtle Roberts and Eunice Johns, women teachers did become NCSS presidents, just not very many of them.

Slippage in the attainment of advanced degrees during these decades clearly affected women's ability to attain leadership, school administration, and college teaching positions.[5] In 1950, women held fewer than 10 percent of high-school principals' positions, about the same as they had in 1900. In 1950, only one woman served as superintendent in the largest 360 school districts of the nation.[6] Furthermore, federal aid to education, which began to increase toward the end of this period, had the perverse effect of expanding women's access to higher education while excluding or limiting women's access to funds and fellowships that were essential to becoming a scholar.[7] Rare, indeed, were women like Wilhelmina Hill, who served as a member of MacArthur's transitional government in Japan and went on to work as a social science specialist in the Department of Health, Education, and Welfare during the fifties and sixties; Dorothy McClure Fraser, who became a senior specialist for social studies in the U.S. Office of Education in 1948; or Alice Spieseke, a faculty member at an elite institution, Teachers College, Columbia University from the 1930s to the 1960s.

The post-war decline of women in leadership and non-traditional roles can be attributed, to some degree, to a public relations effort to get women out of factories, offices, and classrooms and back into the home. Besides making way for veterans to take over the positions women had held during the war, social scientists and social welfare experts "routinely included working mothers among the causes of family instability," which was identified as a growing social problem before the war began.[8]

For many women who pursued higher education at this time, a primary goal was making an educationally compatible match for the husband they hoped to find at college. Women, including well-educated women, married at an earlier age; a greater proportion married than before; and the birth rate increased substantially. Somewhat paradoxically perhaps, the proportion of working women continued to climb after briefly faltering in the late forties. Whatever their reasons for seeking employment, working women bucked a national public-relations effort that promoted marriage and stay-at-home motherhood to a degree unparalleled in our nation's history.[9]

Just how confining the domestic sphere was, however, for some women can be seen in the popularity of Betty Friedan's *The Feminine Mystique*, published in 1963. Calling domestic unhappiness "the problem that has no name," Friedan's book catapulted into women's consciousness the perceived disconnection between their college educations and their lives rearing children, what one historian has described as "a malaise affecting educated middle-class women, frustrated and bored, kept in suburban homes in a false round of busyness, and denied the place in the world for which their education had prepared them."[10]

Suburbanization was an important demographic development within post-World War II society, with a host of ramifications for the environment, race relations, politics, the economy, and education.[11] The phenom-enon, according to Alice Miel, produced negative effects on children as well as women. In *The Shortchanged Children of Suburbia*, Miel laid out her concerns that the newly emerging, largely white and middle class residential patterns found in the suburbs harmed children in the United States by robbing them of the experience of human diversity. While deeply committed to helping children who experienced poverty or other forms of deprivation, Miel recognized well that even in a "culture of affluence," certain forms of impoverishment could undermine the nation's democratic project.

The impact of the social history described above affected different groups differently, of course. For black women, postwar developments reflect the more limited occupational opportunities open to them than were available to white women. In 1940, black women took more college degrees than black men from the black colleges. As a result of the GI Bill, however, by 1950 black men received about half of all college degrees conferred by these colleges. In the forties and fifties, just as before the war, more black men took advanced degrees.

During these years, black women retained their dominance of teaching positions at the primary and secondary levels as well as holding two out of five teaching positions at black colleges.[12] Nevertheless, black female leaders like Lucy Diggs Slowe, the first Dean of Women at Howard University, found the concentration of black women in teaching deeply disturbing and counseled her students as early as the twenties to consider other options. In the 1950s, Jeanne Noble surveyed black female college graduates and reported what she clearly considered positive news: that young black women were now pursuing other career fields, a reaction echoed by numerous other black commentators on women and education during subsequent years.[13]

World War II had a profound impact on black social, educational, and political aspirations. Well before the war began, the National Association for the Advancement of Colored People, with the involvement of many black teachers, had begun its efforts at challenging Jim Crow and gaining the full prerogatives of citizenship for blacks.[14] Still, the war gave major impetus to these efforts. Two women profiled in this chapter, Septima Clark and Ella Baker, worked closely with the leaders of the NAACP and the Southern Christian Leadership Conference on educational activism involving black citizens.[15] Clark pursued preparation as a teacher while Baker disparaged such preparation, in keeping with the views of Lucy Diggs Slowe. In the end, however, both recognized the centrality of education and leadership at the grass-roots level to citizenship efforts among blacks and devoted their lives to these goals.

In 1950 the glaring injustices associated with segregation and discrimination against black veterans and other black citizens compelled President Harry Truman to issue an executive order desegregating the armed forces. One of the women included in this chapter, Marion Thompson Wright, played a central role in bringing about this change with her work on New Jersey's third constitution, which in 1947 ended all forms of de jure segregation in the state.[16] Through her work as a professor of education at Howard University, Wright also researched, wrote, and taught about the importance of black history to the preparation of teachers. Wright's dissertation on the resegregation of schools in New Jersey, along with the work of many other black scholars, contributed to the social science research cited during the trial of *Brown v. Board of Education* in 1954. This Supreme Court decision overturned the "separate but equal" doctrine with regard to public schooling.

Anti-Communist hysteria, fomented by Senator Joseph McCarthy during the 1950s, challenged or damaged the careers of many of the progressive educators profiled in this chapter. One of the major hurdles the NAACP had to overcome was various allegations that its members and leaders were Communists.[17] The press trumpeted such accusations, especially in the rural South.[18] Such accusations damaged relationships even within the Black community.

As early as 1940, NCSS had organized a Committee on Academic Freedom. During the McCarthy era, Helen McCracken Carpenter, elected NCSS president in 1956, felt the need to strengthen the organization's efforts on behalf of social studies teachers. The Committee on Academic Freedom promulgated a series of statements emphasizing the role of schools, teachers, and social studies in a free society.[19]

Allegations of "Un-Americanism" linked to school de-segregation efforts in Houston during the fifties figured prominently in the resignation of Nelda Mae Davis from her position as teacher and supervisor with the Houston Independent School District. Since many of these women worked not only for social education but for social change, their efforts were suspect in a society clinging, in certain quarters, to established patterns of power, dominance, and subordination.

Finally, it should be noted that a number of women included in this chapter are associated with elementary education. During this period and since, elementary education has been the most "feminized" enclave within education. Not surprisingly, therefore, this arena has been the most deeply devalued sphere within education. The field of social studies is no exception to this pattern. As Ruth Ellsworth noted in her interview for this book, "Elementary social studies was the underdog." Furthermore, Ellsworth remembers NCSS as a conservative organization during the fifties and sixties: NCSS neither embraced international and global education (to the extent that she and others like Maxine Dunfee or Alice Miel proposed) nor challenged the status hierarchies of either the broader society or the profession.

What emerges from this chapter's profiles of women social educators is a portrait of a group deeply concerned with matters of social justice, diversity, citizenship education, and human relationships, both as subject, context, and norm for work in social studies. Whether they worked in Trenton, New Jersey or Dallas, Texas, these women practiced progressive education long after it was fashionable to do so.

Notes

1. Susan M. Hartmann, *The Home Front and Beyond: American Women in the 1940s* (Boston: Twayne Publishers, 1982), 116.
2. Wayne J. Urban and Jennings L. Wagoner, *American Education: A History*, 2nd ed. (New York: McGraw Hill, 2000), 282.
3. Linda Eisenmann, "Reconsidering a Classic: Assessing the History of Women's Higher Education a Dozen Years after Barbara Solomon," *Harvard Educational Review* 67, no. 4 (Winter 1997): 1-26.
4. Urban and Wagoner, 282.
5. Hartmann, 107.
6. Hartmann, 103.
7. Eisenmann, 11.
8. Hartmann, 21.
9. Hartmann, 112.
10. Blanche Linden-Ward and Carol Hurd Green, *Changing the Future: American Women in the 1960s* (Boston: Twayne Publishers, 1993), 382; Betty Friedan, *The Feminine Mistique* (New York: Norton, 1963).
11. On this subject, see Kenneth T. Jackson, *Crabgrass Frontier: The Suburbanization of the United States* (New York: Oxford University Press, 1985).
12. Hartmann, 108.
13. Linda Perkins, "The History of Blacks in Teaching," in Donald Warren, ed., *American Teachers: Histories of a Profession at Work* (New York: Macmillan, 1989): 340-370.
14. See Mark Tushnet, *The NAACP's Legal Strategy against Segregated Education, 1925-1950* (Chapel Hill, NC: University of North Carolina Press, 1987) for greater consideration of these efforts.
15. For an analysis of Clark's and Baker's roles as leaders who clearly understood the importance of education to the civil rights movement, see Belinda Robnett, *How Long? How Long? African American Women in the Struggle for Civil Rights* (New York: Oxford

University Press, 1997).

16. Margaret Smith Crocco, Petra Munro, and Kathleen Weiler, *Pedagogies of Resistance: Women Educator Activists, 1880-1960* (New York: Teachers College Press, 1999), 71.

17. Robnett, 16

18. For more on the effects of McCarthyism on academic life, see Ellen Schrecker, *No Ivory Tower: McCarthyism and the Universities* (New York: Oxford University Press, 1986).

19. Bessie Pierce was instrumental in the thirties in raising the issue of teacher freedom, but the first NCSS Committee on Academic Freedom, chaired by historian Merle Curti, was established in 1940, according to Jack L. Nelson and William R. Fernekes, "NCSS and Social Crises," in O. L. Davis, Jr., ed., *NCSS in Retrospect*, Bulletin No. 92 (Washington, DC: NCSS, 1996): 89-101.

Lavone A. Hanna

October 8, 1895—November 5, 1982

Tyrone C. Howard

Lavone A. Hanna was born in Clay Center, Kansas, and spent her life committed to public education and the social studies. She authored many books, articles, chapters, and reports that were concerned with social education and curriculum development. Throughout her academic career, Hanna was active in a number of professional organizations, including the National Council for the Social Studies, the Association for Supervision and Curriculum Development (for which she served on the organization's executive committee from 1957-1960), the National Council of Christians and Jews, the National Society for the Study of Education, and National Education Association. She was President of the California School Supervisors Association. Although Hanna wrote many journal articles across fields, her most significant contributions were in the social studies. In this area, she authored or co-authored several books that addressed the social nature of education and the improvement of elementary and secondary school curriculum and instruction.

Hanna received a bachelor's degree (1919) from the University of Wisconsin, a master's degree (1927) from the University of Chicago, and doctoral degree (1943) from Stanford University. She taught history at Clay County High School in Kansas (1920-23) before moving onto similar stints in Oklahoma at Bartlesville High School and Junior College (1923-31), and Tulsa Central High School (1931-39). Her professional career included service as director of general education for the Tulsa Secondary Schools (1938-39); research associate and assistant professor of education at Stanford University (1939-44); director of curriculum for Long Beach, California, public schools (1944-47); and associate professor, professor, and professor emeritus, San Francisco State College (1947-61). Hanna also lectured at Mills College (1947-51), the University of Chicago, and Claremont College.

In 1948, with I. James Quillen, Hanna co-authored *Education for Social Competence*, a book that grew out of their joint work on the Stanford Social Education Investigation. Established in 1939 at Stanford University, this project acquainted educators with the purposes and characteristics of a good program in social education. Moreover, the text served as a methods book on problems of curriculum and instruction in high school social studies in grades seven through twelve.

Hanna maintained a high level of scholarly productivity during a professional career spanning more than four decades. Particularly impressive is her wide range of topics. In her publications during the thirties and forties, Hanna wrote about the nature of effective evaluation program development, value patterns in school instruction, and the problems approach to social education. One of Hanna's significant contributions was *Unit Teaching in the Elementary School*, co-authored with Gladys Potter and Neva Hagaman (1955). This book provided in-service and pre-service teachers with a practical guide to the development of unit teaching that integrates various subject matter with students' lived experiences. Moreover, Hanna and colleagues stressed the importance of how unit teaching should be organized in line with four key criteria: (1) the needs of children; (2) the growth characteristics of children; (3) the nature of the learning sequence; and (4) the values inherent in a democratic society. This work is notable because it attempted to move unit teaching away from simple scope and sequence arrangements to increased student- and society-centered matters. Hanna helped teachers understand the importance of structuring curriculum so that it would be consistent with students' developmental needs and social and cultural demands. Subsequent editions of the book (1963 and 1973) maintained this focus, but also stressed how interdisciplinary, developmentally appropriate, problem-oriented social studies programs could contribute to democratic ideals within a changing society.

Other works of Hanna's had similar themes. *Facing Life's Problems* (1955) was a problem-oriented high school text that stressed skills and strategies in dealing with complex personal and social problems. Hanna addressed topics such as personality development, making and maintaining friendships, establishing a successful marriage, acquiring an education, and developing a philosophy of life. Subsequent works such as *Challenge for a Free People* (1964) also stressed the teaching of core social studies concepts designed to promote effective and responsible citizenship.

Hanna spent much of her career articulating why and how classroom teachers should contribute to students' values, insights, and skills within a democracy. However, Hanna problematized the extent to which all students reap the benefit of democracy. One of the central themes of her work was the gross inequities that existed in urban and rural school settings. Conscious of the contradictions between the democratic ideals of freedom and equality and the harsh realities of poor and minority students, Hanna repeatedly called for educators to take additional measures through curriculum development and instructional practices that would help to ensure equality for all students. To reach this end, Hanna suggested that teachers structure content in ways that made it relevant to the concerns and culture of the students and with a special emphasis on the communication skills and social development that students bring to the classroom. Moreover, Hanna called on school leaders to understand the social and psychological dynamics of students who grow up in poverty and to translate this understanding into what today would be called "culturally responsive" educational programming. She stressed that a curriculum for low-income and minority students should not stress memorizing meaningless facts, but provide first-hand experiences requiring students to act, feel, and think intelligently about their daily social encounters and decision-making. Hanna also called for educational equality for students with physical, emotional, and intellectual handicaps. In many of her later writings, she consistently called for students not to be discriminated against because of their race, creed, or socioeconomic status. She viewed educators and schooling institutions as important for creating a more humane and open society. Hanna's lasting legacy rests upon her advocacy of the social studies as an interdisciplinary, problem-solving, and student-centered format that can help all students reach their full potential.

References

Hanna, Lavone A. "An Educational Imperative: Commitment to a Humane and Open Society," in Mary-Margaret Scobey and Grace Graham, eds. *To Nurture Humaneness: Commitment for the 70s,* Association for Supervision and Curriculum Development Yearbook, Washington, DC: ASCD, 1970, 212-230.

Foremost Women In Communication. New York: Foremost American Publishers Corporation, 1973, 77-78.

Who's Who of American Women. Chicago, IL: Marquis Publishers, 1975, 61-62.

The author would like to acknowledge assistance from the archives of Stanford University, San Francisco State University, Mills College, the University of Chicago, and Claremont College.

Alice Miel

February 21, 1906—February 1, 1998

ELIZABETH ANNE YEAGER

Alice Marie Miel was a nationally prominent scholar-practitioner in the field of curriculum development at Teachers College, Columbia University, for some three decades (1944-1971). She contributed substantially to the practice and theory of children's democratic social learning through numerous books and articles, through supervision of approximately 140 doctoral students from around the world, through national leadership as president of the Association for Supervision and Curriculum Development (1953-54), and as a founder of the World Council on Curriculum and Instruction in the early 1970s. Born on a farm near Six Lakes, Michigan, she graduated from Central Michigan Normal School in 1924, worked as a teacher, supervisor, and principal in the state's public elementary and secondary schools, and received bachelor's (1928) and master's (1931) degrees from the University of Michigan

The progressive movement in education emerged as the strong undercurrent in Miel's life. As a teacher at Tappan Junior High School in Ann Arbor during the Great Depression, Miel collaborated with her principal, G. Robert Koopman, and other colleagues on a curriculum guide that incorporated the ideas of John Dewey, Harold Rugg, Ann Shumaker, and William Heard Kilpatrick. Miel and her colleagues demonstrated their conviction that the school curriculum must be modified to emphasize the effects of contemporary social problems on the schools.

Miel received her doctorate from Teachers College in 1942, joined its faculty in 1944, and later became a professor in the Department of Curriculum and Teaching. She served as chair of that department from 1960-1967. Her career at Teachers College spanned the latter years of the college's preeminence in the progressive education movement. Her career also spanned the movement's alleged decline and disarray in the 1950s as the main target of conservatives such as Arthur Bestor and Hyman Rickover who attacked progressive philosophy and demanded a return to the "basics" of schooling. During the late 1940s and 1950s, Teachers College also experienced a number of internal struggles as the progressive movement splintered. Miel maintained her strong progressive convictions, while acknowledging

problems within the progressive movement and criticizing its lack of a unified base of support as well as its lack of new ideas. In 1971, she retired from Teachers College, but occasionally wrote and taught both in the United States and abroad. She died of natural causes in Gainesville, Florida, in 1998.

Several themes emerge readily in Miel's body of work. First, Miel advocated democratic ideals and the development of democratic behavior as the ultimate goal of schooling. Miel did not adhere dogmatically to a precise definition of democracy. She believed that, although certain fundamental ideas were embedded in the term, its meaning must be developed and continually nurtured by the people who profess it. Like Dewey, she conceived of democracy as more than a system of government; it was a unique way of being, thinking, and living with others.

Miel believed that the school was democracy's proving ground because it bore a large share of the responsibility for socializing the nation's young people into participation in democracy. She viewed the school as a society in microcosm from which individuals from many backgrounds learned about freedom and responsibility, individuality and cooperation. For Miel, the citizen's overarching responsibility in a democratic society was to know how democracy worked and how to maintain it through changing conditions.

Second, Miel focused on the social learning environment of children in schools and articulated aspects of cooperative learning and other democratic procedures available to teachers.

Her work expressed fundamental ideas about what she considered to be appropriate democratic social learnings for children. In her 1957 book with Peggy Brogan, *More Than Social Studies,* Miel described social learnings for which the schools should share responsibility: bearing a friendly feeling; having concern for all mankind; valuing difference; being a contributing member of a group; seeing the necessity of a cooperative search for conditions guaranteeing maximum freedom for all; taking responsibility for a share of a common enterprise; problem-solving and working for consensus; evaluating and cooperating with authority; refining constantly one's conception of the "good society"; and learning effective communication and research skills. Miel particularly emphasized her theme of cooperative learning to build good relationships—what she called the "fourth R" in schools—as an essential component of democratic social learning. Miel recommended three approaches to help children improve human relationships: creating a friendly, respectful atmosphere in the classroom; teaching ways of managing group endeavors; and teaching about peoples' commonalities and differences. Miel also advocated social learning opportunities for world understanding, and she criticized "culture units" commonly taught in the elementary schools for encouraging unhealthy stereotypes of cultural and ethnic groups.

Miel strongly believed that no single school subject, including the social studies, could be expected to carry the full load of children's social education. However, in terms of the unique contribution of the social studies to children's learning experiences and to their democratic socialization, the book *More Than Social Studies* by Miel and Brogan pointed to the field's capacity to place social learning at the center of the curriculum. They argued that teachers could provide opportunities designed to develop children's interpersonal and intergroup relationships through solving problems of daily living; to satisfy children's curiosities about the world; to solve problems of understanding and community action; and to build positive attitudes toward others through organized individual and group studies. Most importantly, teachers could help children to develop socially useful concepts, generalizations, and skills so that children could organize their experiences.

Third, Miel was especially concerned about meanings of American democracy and democratic citizenship for the diversity of American society. In particular, she focused on problems of children who experienced intellectual, economic, or cultural deprivation because of their ethnicity and/or socioeconomic background. She viewed the solution of such problems as central to the mission of American democracy, and she saw schools as places where these children could have, among other things, positive social learning experiences. These concerns emerged fully in Miel's book, co-authored with journalist Edwin Kiester, *The Shortchanged Children of Suburbia* (1967), for which the authors received the National Education Association's Human Rights Award in 1968. Miel believed that this book best represented her research efforts. Its groundbreaking thesis was that in affluent, homogeneous suburban schools, students were failing to learn about human differences and cultural diversity. The authors made numerous, specific recommendations for the study of race, religion, and socioeconomic status—all aimed at dismantling stereotypes, avoiding facile generalizations, studying different groups in their appropriate cultural and historical contexts, and understanding the concerns and struggles faced by particular groups in American society. Miel was able to reassert her conviction that human diversity was a proper subject for the school curriculum in a democratic society. She firmly believed that children should be educated to deal fairly and realistically with questions of social justice, civil rights, national unity, and international peace.

Alice Miel, in many ways, embraced and encouraged what Walter Parker has referred to as "advanced" ideas about democracy and democratic citizenship education. That is, she raised issues related to human social and cultural diversity and saw these as central to the ongoing development and "deepening" of American democracy. She also viewed democracy as a way of life that citizens undertake together through deliberation, reflection, and civic action. For Miel, education for democratic citizenship necessarily begins early in school, where children can acquire a sense of altruism, civic responsibility, community, and connection to other living beings. She claimed that the educational process, and the curriculum itself, should help children understand social problems and feel responsible for striving to solve them.

References

Miel, Alice. Papers. Museum of Education, University of South Carolina, Columbia, South Carolina.
-----. "Toward Democratic Socialization," *Childhood Education* 26, no.1 (September 1949): 4-5.
-----. "Social Studies for Understanding, Caring, Acting," in W. L. Marks and R. O. Nystrand, eds. *Strategies for Educational Change: Recognizing the Gifts and Talents of All Children*, New York: Macmillan, 1981, 257-268.
----- and Peggy Brogan, *More Than Social Studies: A View of Social Learning in the Elementary School.* Englewood Cliffs, NJ: Prentice-Hall, 1957.
----- and Edwin Kiester, *The Shortchanged Children of Suburbia.* New York: Institute of Human Relations Press, The American Jewish Committee, 1967.
Yeager, Elizabeth. "Alice Miel: Progressive Advocate of Democratic Social Learning for Children," in Margaret S. Crocco and O. L. Davis, Jr. eds. *"Bending the Future to Their Will": Civic Women, Social Education, and Democracy.* Lanham, MD: Rowman and Littlefield, 1999, 207-233.

Myrtle Roberts

1893—May 11, 1968

MARY BLACK

Myrtle Roberts was a true champion of social studies education at the national level as well as in her home state of Texas. She was elected president of the National Council for the Social Studies in 1951 after serving on the board of directors from 1945-47. A decade earlier, she inspired history teachers in Dallas to organize the Dallas District Council for the Social Studies in 1936, later serving as its president. The Dallas council, in turn, sponsored establishment of the Texas Council for the Social Studies and its affiliation with the National Council for the Social Studies.

Roberts earned A.B., B.S., and B.L. degrees from East Texas State University and an M.A. degree from the University of Texas at Austin. Except for one year of full-time study, her college work was completed during summer terms while she taught school during academic years. Later, she taught summer session courses at both Southern Methodist University and Southwest Texas State College.

Roberts was a public school teacher for fifty-two years, thirty-five of which she taught American history at Woodrow Wilson High School in Dallas, Texas. She also sponsored the high school's Historical Society, which numbered more than 200 members by 1951. In order for her to have time to serve as NCSS president, the principal of Woodrow Wilson High School relieved her of two classes as well as responsibilities for the Historical Society.

Roberts dedicated her life to improving social studies teaching during the critical years of the Great Depression, World War II, and the Cold War. "Never before in the history of mankind is the domestic and world situation so complex, perplexing, and difficult as it is today," she said in her NCSS Presidential Address in November 1951. Largely due to her influence, NCSS held its 1952 annual conference in Dallas. One of her colleagues has noted that Roberts "brought the National Council to Texas and Texas to the National Council." She continued to attend annual meetings until her retirement in 1963.

Roberts firmly believed that teachers' participation in local social studies councils and teacher organizations was vital to both individual growth and development of the profession overall. She believed that the best way for teachers to meet their responsibility to improve social studies teaching and democratic education was to participate in professional organizations. "In these complex times," she commented, "an individual social studies teacher working alone would find it very difficult, if not impossible, to meet the ever increasing burden and challenge [that we face]." She found great personal satisfaction from service to her profession and students.

Roberts helped edit the *Social Studies Texan*, the journal of the Texas Council for the Social Studies. She also served as regional co-chair of the NCSS Committee on Professional Relations. As a member of the Texas State Teachers Association sub-committee on social studies, she wrote a handbook on teaching methods for grades 1-12. She also wrote a textbook entitled *Patterns of Freedom: A History of the United States* (1953) and various journal articles.

The Dallas Council for the Social Studies honored "Miss Myrtle," as she was affectionately called, at their annual meeting in 1963, upon her retirement from teaching. In 1966, the Dallas Council established the "Myrtle Roberts Award," a plaque and a savings bond to be presented annually to an outstanding teacher who had contributed to the advancement of social studies.

References

Hartshorn, Merrill F. "Notes and News: Myrtle Roberts, 1893-1968." *Social Education* 32, no.5 (May 1968): 583.

"Myrtle Roberts: Obituary." *The Dallas Morning News*, May 12, 1968. A29.

Roberts, Myrtle. Letter to Merrill F. Hartshorn, Executive Secretary, NCSS. NCSS Archives. Milbank Library, Teachers College, Columbia University.

-----. "Social Studies Leadership through Cooperation: NCSS Presidential Address." November 23, 1951. NCSS Archives, Milbank Library, Teachers College, Columbia University.

-----. *Patterns of Freedom: A History of the United States* (New York: Winston, 1953).

"Social Studies Council to Honor Miss Roberts." *The Dallas Morning News*, March 24, 1963: B4.

Eunice I. Johns

September 18, 1902—June 29, 2000

Keith C. Barton

Eunice Irene Johns taught secondary social studies for over thirty years, served as president of the National Council for the Social Studies in 1960, developed a variety of instructional materials for the field, and worked as a consultant to curriculum development projects from the 1940s through the 1970s. Much of her published work consisted of instructional resources or teachers' guides, many of them emphasizing the use of problem-solving activities to teach social science concepts.

Johns was born in Grubville, Missouri, and received her undergraduate degree from the University of Missouri in 1926. She began teaching secondary social studies at the Horace Mann School in Gary, Indiana, in 1927, later becoming chair of the department, and continuing in that position until 1957. Johns also served as a trustee of the Gary Public Library and as a member of the executive boards of the Women's Citizens Committee and the Crime Commission in Gary. Her colleague, Dorothy Fraser Hemenway, later described these civic activities as "typical of her energetic participation in the life of her community, wherever she lived." Johns completed a master's degree from Teachers College, Columbia University, in 1934, and her first known publication was in the journal *The Platoon School* in 1939. In that article, she lamented the practice of ending the study of modern history with World War I and called for greater attention to post-war developments, so that students might make intelligent choices as citizens.

In 1944, Johns co-authored *Meet the Soviet Russians: A Study Guide to the Soviet Union for Teachers in Secondary Schools*, which was an outgrowth of her participation in the 1944 Summer Session of the Harvard Workshop in the Social Studies, sponsored by the National Council of American-Soviet Friendship. She and her coauthors described the Soviet Union as one of the most neglected regions in the secondary curriculum, and this resource guide was designed to provide background material on the people, culture, geography, and politics of that country. Although they noted that teaching about the Soviet Union could be controversial, Johns and her colleagues wrote from the benign perspective of wartime cooperation, with an explicit avoidance of negative judgments (particularly of the Soviet government) and an avowed goal of "learning to work together in harmony."

Johns was most active in the National Council for the Social Studies during the 1950s and 1960s. She served as editor of the organization's *Social Studies in the Senior High School: Programs for Grades Ten, Eleven, and Twelve* (1953), which included sections that analyzed the current status of social studies in secondary schools, described selected programs throughout the country, and made recommendations for improvements. Her chapter in the 33rd Yearbook of NCSS, co-authored with Dorothy McClure Fraser, presented a rationale and procedure for developing a coordinated and integrated program for teaching social studies skills. The appendix (which she wrote) in the same volume described what such a program might look like. During this period Johns served on several NCSS committees, including curriculum, finance, and publications. She was a member of the board of directors, and in 1954, she chaired an ad-hoc committee on improving election procedures within NCSS. In 1957, Johns left Indianapolis to become supervisor of the secondary social studies program for the Wilmington, Delaware, public schools.

Beginning in the mid-1950s, several of Johns' professional activities revolved around economics education. In 1955, she received a doctorate from New York University; her dissertation focused on the programs of the Joint Council on Economic Education (now the National Council on Economic Education), particularly its teacher workshops. She reviewed the current status of economic education in schools and the rationale for increasing its extent and quality, chronicled the creation and development of the Joint Council, described the planning and implementation of the organization's workshops, and evaluated their effectiveness in meeting their stated aims. Although Johns did not attempt to situate her analysis in a wider body of theory or research (nor to reflect critically on the nature or purpose of the Joint Council's efforts), her carefully documented and clearly written dissertation is an invaluable resource for understanding the development of economic education in the United States.

Johns also wrote the "Teaching Aids" section of the NCSS publication *A Teacher's Guide to Money, Banking, and Credit* (1955). Her suggested activities—geared toward the inclusion of economic concepts in secondary courses on U.S. history—emphasized a problem-solving approach in which students collected, evaluated, and interpreted information; developed generalizations and conclusions; and formulated actions consistent with those conclusions. Much later, in 1975, Johns coauthored two volumes in the "Concepts for Social Studies" series, developed by the Social Studies Curriculum Center at Syracuse University and published by Macmillan. The first, *Decisions! Decisions! Comparative Advantage: A Concept Study*, described the application of the concept of comparative advantage to a variety of problems (related to personal choices, community issues, public policy, and foreign relations) and engaged students in identifying and weighing alternative courses of action. Johns' second contribution to the series, *Ahead of Us ... The Past: History and the Historian*, focused on the interpretive nature of historical research, particularly the ways in which primary sources can be analyzed and the factors that influence historians' perspectives. She also co-authored, with James Quillen, an extensive series of U.S. history maps and overhead transparencies, published by Nystrom in the late 1960s and early 1970s.

Eunice Johns passed away on June 29, 2000, at the age of 97, in Kennett Square, Pennsylvania.

References

Ames, Dora A., Katrina B. Anderson, Eunice Johns, et al. *Meet the Soviet Russians: A Study Guide to the Soviet Union for Teachers in Secondary Schools*. Cambridge, MA: Graduate School of Education, Harvard University, 1944.

Fraser, Dorothy M., and Eunice Johns. "Developing a Program for the Effective Learning," in Helen McCracken Carpenter, ed. *Skill Development in Social Studies*, 33rd Yearbook. Washington, DC: NCSS, 1963, 310-327.

Johns, Eunice, and Dorothy M. Fraser. "Social Studies Skills: A Guide to Analysis and Grade Placement," in Helen McCracken Carpenter, ed. *Skill Development in Social Studies*, 33rd Yearbook. Washington, DC: NCSS, 1963, 296-309.

Johns, Eunice, and Warren L. Hickman. *Ahead of Us...The Past: History and the Historian: A Concept Study*. New York: Macmillan, 1975.

Wilhelmina Hill

August 29, 1902—July 8, 1979

Dawn M. Shinew

Wilhelmina Hill was instrumental in shaping social studies education through her publications, professional affiliations, and position as Specialist for Social Science and Environmental Education in the U.S. Department of Health, Education, and Welfare, Office of Education.

Born in Fisher's Island, New York, Wilhelmina spent her early childhood in the hotel that was managed by her parents. While she was still quite young, her father passed away. Her mother, a teacher, became the sole supporter for the family. After living for a short time in Tennessee, the family moved to Kansas City, where Wilhelmina spent most of her adolescence and early adulthood.

Hill served as an elementary and secondary school teacher in the Kansas City, Kansas, Public School District from 1923 through 1937. As a teacher, Hill carried out early experiments in the correlation and integration of subjects. During this period, Hill also continued her education. She completed her bachelor of science degree in English from University of Kansas in 1930. Three years later, she earned a masters degree in geography from Teachers College, Columbia University. In 1939, Hill became among the first to receive a Doctorate of Education degree (Ed.D., which was then a new degree) from Teachers College. Her dissertation was entitled "A Bulletin for Curriculum Suggestions and Materials for Maryland Educators." Hill's graduate advisor was Professor Herbert B. Bruner, a specialist in curriculum.

Upon receipt of her doctorate, she became the associate editor for *Scholastic* magazine, with major responsibility for the high school teacher edition. Subsequently, she assumed a faculty position at the University of Denver, at which she taught from 1939-1949, earning the rank of associate professor. Her responsibilities as a faculty member included establishment of a doctoral program in the School of Education, development of courses for the teacher preparation program, and direction of workshops in elementary education, reading clinics, and a curriculum laboratory. During this time, Hill was also active in curriculum development. In 1946, she wrote a series of elementary social studies textbooks that were published in 1946 by Follett Press. The series laid a foundation for an integrated curriculum in social studies for young learners and was adopted by California, Texas, as well as many other states and districts. Hill's series included a heavy emphasis on the role of the citizen in democratic societies and established explicit connections between children's lives and subject matter. The series was revised and reissued until 1968.

In 1949, Hill joined the staff of the Civil Information and Education (CIE) Division of General MacArthur's transitional government in Japan. In this capacity, she developed a curriculum for Japanese junior high schools. Her work in Japan led to a position with the United States' Office of Education in 1949. In this position, she was responsible for development of initiatives in leadership of the social studies. Her position later was expanded to include an emphasis in environmental education. Her interests in international issues continued, and from 1955 until 1958, she served as a consultant on rural elementary schools in Haiti.

During her tenure with the Office of Education, Hill continued to be a prolific writer and editor. The scope of her work is evident in the titles of just a few of her more notable publications: *How Children Can Be Creative* (1954), authored in collaboration with colleagues Helen Mackintosh and Arne Randall; "New Horizons for Environmental Education" (1969); and *Selected Resource Units for Elementary Social Studies* (1961). Hill also collaborated in the development of educational films for elementary and middle grade social studies that focused on helping students understand their environment.

Hill's position in the Office of Education made her a valuable resource to other government agencies. She served as a consultative assistant to the Education Section of the Department of Public Information at the United Nations. In addition, she worked with UNESCO and its relations staff, as well as the U.S. Department of State. In these capacities, Hill provided guidance on the creation of curriculum materials and instruction for children in the United States and around the world that sought to promote understanding of human rights and cooperation.

Throughout her career, Hill was an active member and leader of numerous professional organizations. She served as a board member for the National League of American Penwomen and the National Council for Geographic Education. She was heavily involved in the National Council for the Social Studies and served as the chair of several of its committees, participated on programs of annual conventions, and wrote articles and yearbook sections for NCSS publications. In addition, Hill served as President of the District of Columbia's Council of Administrative Women in Education. She was a contributing member of the Society of Women Geographers, the National Education Association, the Association for Supervision and Curriculum Development, and numerous other organizations. Hill also served on the President's Council for Recreation and Natural Beauty from 1967-1968.

In 1972, Hill retired from the United States Office of Education. After almost fifty years in education, Hill left a legacy for women in social studies education. Known as "Willie" to her friends and colleagues, Hill's work in social studies education helped to define the field. As a teacher educator, she emphasized the importance of practical experiences in the preparation of teachers. As a curriculum developer, Hill became a leader in the movement for integrated approaches to learning. As a woman in a profession dominated by men, Hill was a pioneer leader.

Wilhelmina Hill died of natural causes at the age of seventy-seven. Garney Darrin, her long-time friend and colleague, established a scholarship in her honor at James Madison University. Each year, an outstanding student in Early Childhood and Middle Education at that university receives financial support to continue the mission to which Hill dedicated her life.

References

Hill, Wilhelmina, Helen Mackintosh, and Arne Randall. *How Children Can Be Creative*. Washington DC: United States Government Printing Office, 1954,

-----. *Selected Resource Units: Elementary Social Studies: Kindergarten-Grade Six*. Washington, DC: NCSS, 1961.

-----. "New Horizons for Environmental Education," *Journal of Environmental Education* 1, no. 2 (Winter 1969): page 10-14.

Hug, William E. *Forty Years of Research in Curriculum and Teaching*. New York: Teachers College, Columbia University, 1979.

The papers of Wilhelmina Hill are kept by Professor Garney Darrin, Washington, DC.

Dorothy McClure Fraser

January 1, 1913—

STEPHANIE D. VAN HOVER

Dorothy McClure Fraser Hemenway served as president of the National Council for the Social Studies in 1954. Born in Columbia, Missouri, Dorothy McClure received a bachelor's degree in education from Northeast Missouri State Teachers College (1930), a master's degree in history from the University of Missouri (1939), and a Ph.D. in history from the University of Minnesota (1947). Her dissertation focused on the social origins of humanist schools in Renaissance Italy. Fraser taught secondary social studies and supervised student teachers at the Demonstration School at Northeast Missouri State College (1930-1933), the University High School of the University of Minnesota (1940-1945), and the Laboratory School of the University of Chicago (1945-1948).

Dorothy McClure moved from Chicago to Washington, DC in 1948 to work as the senior specialist for social studies at the U.S. Office of Education (1948-1950). In this position, she researched current trends in social studies education; served as a consultant to schools and universities; and conducted field research, workshops, institutes, and curriculum development programs in order to introduce new curricular concepts and teaching methods to classroom teachers. She also administered federal funds available for social studies and conducted several funded research studies.

In 1950, Dorothy McClure married Russell Fraser and moved to New York City. There, she worked as a professor of social studies education and supervisor of student teachers at Adelphi College (1951-1953), City College of New York (1953-1958), and Hunter College, City College of New York (1962-1973). She also worked as an assistant for the dean of education, City College of New York (1958-1962). While at Hunter College, Fraser worked on Project #120, a field-based program designed to recruit and encourage social studies students to teach in Harlem schools while also providing in-service education for classroom teachers. The program held classes in Harlem, performed outreach services in the community, provided student teachers with extra experiences in Harlem outside of the schools, and encouraged professors and students to spend large amounts of time working in Harlem classrooms. Most

Project #120 graduates subsequently taught in Harlem schools. Fraser also helped develop a Masters of Arts in social studies education program at Hunter and coordinated the social sciences teacher education program. She retired in 1973 and, several years after Russell Fraser's death, she married Horace Hemenway in 1993.

Throughout her career, Fraser actively served in numerous organizations, including the National Council for Social Studies, the Association for Supervision and Curriculum Development, the American Educational Research Association, the American Association of University Professors, the American Political Science Association, Kappa Delta Pi, the American History Association, and Phi Alpha Theta. Fraser held leadership positions in several of these organizations. In NCSS, she served on the board of directors for several years, acted as the annual meeting program chairman in 1953 and as president in 1954, during the height of the McCarthy Era.

Fraser wrote, edited, and contributed to more than seventy books, textbooks, curriculum guides, newsletters, journal articles, and yearbooks during her prolific career. Fraser's writings focused on the social studies curriculum and effective teaching methods for social studies teachers. Fraser collaborated with Edith West in writing *Social Studies in the Secondary Schools: Curriculum and Methods* (1961), a methods textbook for secondary teachers. She co-authored with Harry Hoy an elementary textbook series entitled *Social Studies Series* (1961), and a secondary history textbook series, *The Adventure of America* (1966). Fraser and Hoy organized the elementary series around the expanding community model; titles included *Our Homes and our Schools*, *Our Neighborhood*, *Our Community*, *Our State*, *Our Hemisphere*, and *Our World Neighbors*. In other writings, Fraser focused on specific issues in the social studies, such as the need to teach skills and values and to incorporate current controversial, multicultural, and global issues into the social studies curriculum.

Fraser argued that the major purposes of the social studies were to prepare students for life in a democracy and to be intelligent, understanding citizens who recognize the human element in social policy and practice. She asserted that students need to develop the attitudes and skills that lead to constructive citizenship and that maintain and improve democratic society. According to Fraser, the social studies curriculum should emphasize human relationships and help students develop attitudes of tolerance and acceptance of change through exposure to controversial, multicultural, and global issues.

Fraser urged the social studies field to resist the temptation to teach more and more about less in order to "cover" information on a list. She highlighted the need to engage in dialogue about what material to include, how to organize that material, and how to teach the information most effectively. Fraser argued that the social studies curriculum could not remain static. Rather, as this society is a dynamic and continually evolving one, the field of social studies must address current issues and topics and utilize the latest, most appropriate materials and teaching methods. Additionally, Fraser contended that the social studies curriculum should strive to engage and interest people rather than emphasize memorization of facts and dates. To this end, in the field of history, Fraser advocated teaching social and economic history.

Fraser maintained the importance of effective teaching methods within the social studies. She encouraged teachers to learn about and understand the community surrounding their school; to utilize recent, effective, appropriate learning materials; to develop students' skills and interests; to individualize instruction; and to dedicate time to professional growth as a social studies teacher. Fraser emphasized the need to develop reading, writing, listening, oral expression, and critical thinking skills in students.

References

Boedeker, Louise. Telephone interview with author, June 26, 2000.
Fraser, Dorothy and Edith West. *Social Studies in Secondary Schools* (New York: Ronald Press Company, 1961).
Fraser, Dorothy. "The NCSS at Work," *Social Education* 14, no. 3 (March 1955): 104-106
-----. "The Organization of the Elementary Social Studies Program," in *Social Studies in the Elementary School: 56th Yearbook of the National Society for the Study of Education*, Part II. Nelson B. Henry, ed., Chicago, IL: NSSE, 1957: 129-162.
Gould, Milton. Telephone interview with author, June 26, 2000.
Hemenway, Dorothy Fraser. Telephone interview with author, July 1, 2000.

Alice Winifred Spieseke

December 28, 1899—November 2, 1991

MICHAEL P. MARINO

Alice Winifred Spieseke, a longtime professor of social studies education at Teachers College, Columbia University, was born in Seattle, Washington in 1899. She came from working class roots: Her father, a German immigrant, worked as an engineer on merchant ships, and her mother came from a family of Canadian farmers. Her mother was also a normal school graduate and had taught in Kansas schools. Growing up, Spieseke was a successful and active student who was valedictorian of her high school class and captain of the girl's basketball team. Historical awareness came early to her, and she credited her grandfather (who had a keen appreciation of history) as well as influential teachers in middle and high school as mentors who steered her toward her chosen career.

Upon graduation from high school in 1919, Spieseke aspired to attend Stanford, but enrolled at the State Normal School located in Bellingham, Washington (now Western Washington University). A year later, she taught the middle grades in eastern Washington. She then enrolled at the University of Washington, completing her bachelor's degree in 1923 and receiving her master's degree in history a year later. While at Washington, Spieseke also played on the basketball team and worked as a coach. When she finished her master's, Spieseke returned to secondary teaching in Kahlotus, Washington, where she taught high school history and civics in addition to coaching and working as a librarian. She perceived the assignment as a difficult one and referred to an element of "lawlessness" among a populace accustomed to cattle rustling. Later, she taught sixth and seventh grade at Bellingham's laboratory school and subsequently moved on to teach at a high school in Seattle. While there, Spieseke was influenced by Henry Johnson's book *Teaching of History in Elementary and Secondary Schools* and incorporated his ideas into her teaching. In 1929, Spieseke taught a summer session at the Normal School at Bellingham. Realizing an affinity for college teaching, she decided to pursue further study so she could increase her career choices in higher education. That decision brought her to Columbia University.

Spieseke came to Columbia in 1933, attracted by the eminence and influence of Henry Johnson as well as the more diverse course offerings at Columbia. Previously, she had complained that the University of Washington was dominated by Europeanists and did not offer courses in Latin American or Canadian history. She spent a year in Columbia's Department of History before transferring to Teachers College in 1934. At that time, Teachers College offered undergraduate degrees and, while a graduate student, Spieseke also taught American history to undergraduates in the nursing program, often on site at various New York City hospitals in which the students were interning. In 1938, she received her Ph.D. and was appointed to the Teachers College faculty. Her dissertation was a study of early American textbooks. Promotions came fairly regularly, and she was made associate in 1944 and professor in 1952. Describing teaching as "long, exhausting work," her last years at the college were spent as the director of the Office of Doctoral Studies. Spieseke was also instrumental in securing the space and funding necessary to establish a Women's Faculty Club at Columbia, for which she also served as president. The club's success under her stewardship was evidently a major reason why the separate men's and women's clubs eventually merged into a single entity. Spieseke retired in 1965, moved to Seattle, and taught occasionally at the University of Washington. She died in 1991.

During her tenure at Teachers College, Spieseke routinely taught courses in American history and in methods of teaching history. Further, she assigned and observed all student teachers in history. Although Henry Johnson was an important factor in bringing her to New York, Spieseke's primary colleague during her career was Erling Hunt, a lifelong friend and mentor, as was Hazel Hertzberg. Spieseke was prominent in NCSS, although she did not serve as president. Her contributions to the organization came mainly in the form of committee participation and as an editor of various NCSS publications. Spieseke considered herself a teacher first and foremost.

References

Alice Spieseke. *The First Textbooks in American History and Their
    Compiler, John M'Culloch*. New York: AMS Press, 1972.
-----. Interview by Hazel Hertzberg. 1978.

Septima Poinsette Clark

May 3, 1898—December 15, 1987

Andra Makler

Septima Poinsette Clark, the "grand lady of the Civil Rights Movement," created the citizenship schools that qualified thousands of disenfranchised African Americans to sign voting registers in the deep South nearly a century after passage of the 13th, 14th, and 15th Amendments. Born and reared in Charleston, South Carolina, Clark transcended the rigid social code of her city: She integrated the executive board of the Young Women's Christian Association (YWCA), forced the city to hire black teachers for black children, and successfully petitioned the State of South Carolina to equalize the pay of black and white teachers with comparable qualifications. She become, at age 78, the first black woman to serve on the Charleston, South Carolina, County School Board.

Young Septima Poinsette grew up aware of class divisions within the black community. Her father, Peter Porcher Poinsette, a former slave who learned to read while Septima was in elementary school, was a caterer. Her mother, Victoria Warren Anderson, who claimed "free issue" status and was educated in British schools in Haiti, took in laundry. Schooled in a private home by two African American women who nurtured her sense of pride and high standards, Septima returned to public school in the fourth grade at a time when Charleston still hired only white teachers, white and black children went to separate schools, and black students were whipped for talking to their white teachers outside of school.

In 1916, Septima Poinsette graduated from Avery Normal Institute and passed the state exam for a Licentiate of Instruction (valid only in rural black schools). She took her first teaching job on isolated John's Island, where she boarded with families, shared a bed with her host's children, and co-taught 132 students in a creosote-tarred log cabin school that was heated only by two open fireplaces and lacked indoor water and plumbing. A teaching principal from 1916-1919, Clark shared a monthly salary of $60 with another black teacher, while the lone white teacher across the road with three pupils received $85. The illiterate black community kept no birth, health, or death records and had no access to medical care. Mothers brought their babies to the plantation fields. Malaria was endemic. The total absence of medical care motivated Clark to work for health reform in the Sea Islands and to include health issues as part of her citizenship education curricula.

She left John's Island to teach at Avery Institute (1919-1921) and joined a signature-gathering drive to petition the Charleston School Board to hire black teachers in the public schools. The change was effected in 1919, which established her reputation as an activist. Against her parents' wishes, she married Nerie Clark in May, 1920. He was a Navy cook whom she met during her wartime canteen work. Widowed in 1925 with a ten-month-old son, she briefly took a job in North Carolina to be near her in-laws; in 1935, she sent her son to live with them permanently.

From 1929-1947, Clark taught elementary school in Columbia, South Carolina, where she also took courses, attended inter-racial lectures, and mixed socially with middle class blacks, which would have been an impossibility in class-conscious Charleston. Propelled by a strong desire to earn a college degree and better serve the needs of black children who were poor readers, she enrolled in summer courses in mathematics and curriculum building at Teachers College, Columbia University, in 1930. Subsequently, she studied with W. E. B. DuBois at Atlanta College (1937) and earned an A.B. degree from Benedict College in Columbia, South Carolina (1942), and an M.A. degree from Hampton Institute in Virginia (1947). Active in her Methodist Church, Clark also participated in the National Federation of Women's Clubs and numerous civic organizations including the NAACP, the Teacher's Association of South Carolina, National Council for Negro Women, the Tuberculosis Association, and the Negro YWCA. In 1945, she worked with NAACP lawyer (and later Supreme Court Justice) Thurgood Marshall on a federal suit to equalize the pay of black and white teachers in South Carolina with equal credentials.

In 1947, with segregation and Jim Crow laws still in full force, Clark returned to Charleston to teach. She continued to break racial barriers, eating dinner at the home of a white judge and inviting his wife to address the Negro YWCA despite strong disapproval from the

Y's executive board, her principal, and fellow teachers. Her activism made her a target for the Ku Klux Klan and white racist threats. When white nurses refused to vaccinate black children, Clark initiated a drive through her sorority, Alpha Kappa Alpha, to eliminate diphtheria among the black children in Charleston and John's Island.

In response to the *Brown v. Board of Education* decision, the state of South Carolina listed the NAACP as a subversive organization in 1956. Clark, then sixty, subsequently lost her teaching job and pension. She became a full-time staff member at Highlander Folk School in Tennessee and led inter-racial workshops that prepared participants to be activists in their communities. Clark wrote pamphlets (*A Guide to Action for Public School Desegregation; What Is a Workshop;* and *How to Become a Community Leader*) and study materials with chapters on political parties, taxes, how to address officials, and the southern states' voting regulations and constitutions.

Clark designed a four-month curriculum to teach illiterate black adults to read and write well enough to pass voter registration literacy tests, sign checks, and purchase goods from mail order catalogs. Her course also taught adults how to organize in order to obtain sorely needed basic health and community services. In 1957, she organized the first citizenship school in a grocery store on John's Island with help from Esau Jenkins and Bernice Robinson.

As director of education and teaching for the Southern Christian Leadership Conference (1961-1976), Clark traveled throughout the South teaching tactics of non-violent civil disobedience. Under her leadership, the citizenship schools, which educated more than 1,000 people, hired only "non-regular" teachers who spoke the local dialect, respected local folk ways and knowledge, and involved the adult students in co-constructing the curriculum. She described her work in her autobiography, *Echo in My Soul* (1962), and in an extended oral history interview, *Ready from Within* (1986).

Although she sat on the dais with Martin Luther King, Jr., when he received the Nobel Peace Prize in 1964, her contributions were not otherwise widely acknowledged. Openly feminist in later interviews, Clark criticized male Civil Rights leaders for devaluing women as sex objects and ignoring their contributions to the movement. She received many honors, including an honorary doctorate from the College of Charleston in 1978, a Living Legacy Award from President Carter in 1979, and South Carolina's highest award, the Order of the Palmetto, in 1982.

References

Brown, Cynthia Stokes with Septima Poinsette Clark. *Ready From Within: Septima Clark and the Civil Rights Movement. A First Person Narrative* (Navarro, CA: Wild Trees Press, 1986).

Brown-Nagin, Tomiko. "The Transformation of a Social Movement into Law? The SCLC and NAACP's Campaigns for Civil Rights Reconsidered in Light of the Educational Activism of Septima Clark," *Women's History Review* 8, no. 1 (January 1999): 81-136.

Clark, Septima Poinsette with LeGette Blythe. *Echo in My Soul.* New York: E. P. Dutton, 1962.

Horton, Myles with Judith Kohl and Herbert Kohl. *The Long Haul: An Autobiography.* New York: Doubleday, 1990.

Ling, Peter. "Local Leadership in the Early Civil Rights Movement: The South Carolina Citizenship Education Program of the Highlander Folk School," *Journal of American Studies* 29, no. 3 (December 1995): 399-422.

McFadden, Grace Jordan. "Oral Recollections as Mechanisms for Investigating the Social and Political Philosophy of Septima Poinsette Clark," in William S. Brockington, ed., *The Proceedings of the South Carolina Historical Association.* Aiken, SC: The University of South Carolina at Aiken, 1987.

The papers of Septima Poinsette Clark are archived at the Robert Scott Small Library, College of Charleston, Charleston, South Carolina.

Ella Josephine Baker

December 13, 1903 — December 13, 1986

Geneva Gay

Ella Josephine Baker was born in Norfolk, Virginia. She was a diligent and consistent social activist, fighting for human freedom, equality, and justice. Although her primary constituent group was African Americans, especially those in the South, she was concerned about the civil rights of all oppressed people. She did not restrict her efforts to a single type of oppression or discrimination, but worked to combat these on multiple fronts, particularly in the social, civic, economic, and political arenas. By job description and philosophical orientation, Ella Baker was a "grass-roots activist" who promoted informed decision-making and locally based participatory democracy. Prominent civil rights organizations, her frequent employers, became the medium through which she practiced and transmitted her social action ideology and methodologies.

Baker consistently devoted her efforts to educating, organizing, and facilitating local groups to understand the politics and economics of their own circumstances, to realize the power of and need for social action, and to use collaborative strategies to confront injustices. She deliberately avoided the media spotlight and high-profile leadership positions. Instead, Baker preferred to work behind the scenes and help others realize their potential for self-leadership. Her life was closely intertwined with the history of the modern day labor, civil rights, peace, and economic justice movements, and she worked with many of the well-known luminaries of the time. Among these were Thurgood Marshall, Walter White, Roy Wilkins, Martin Luther King, Jr., Rosa Parks, and several other leaders whose public service careers were launched in the early days of the Student Nonviolence Coordinating Committee (SNCC) of the 1960s. But, most of her time, energy, and efforts were directed toward ordinary and unknown people, teaching them how to do for themselves instead of following the leadership of others.

Baker's struggle for human freedom, dignity, and equality was a family inheritance, a deeply felt value, and a skillful craft cultivated throughout a lifetime. Her active involvement in these causes, which began when she was a young child, never wavered. She was born into a family that demonstrated and taught her determination, independence, resistance, pride in Blackness, a deep sense of community, and caring for and sharing with others.

Baker first demonstrated this legacy of courage, strength, determination, and rebellion against injustices as a young child in various incidents that are related in her biographies. As a young college student, she challenged a regulation at Shaw University that forbade males and females from walking together across campus. She refused the request of the college president for her to sing for some visiting dignitaries, not wanting to be "shown off" in a public display for whites. She decided against becoming a teacher because she considered this career choice too politically timid: It was the easy way out; what African American female graduates were expected to do.

Baker showed no reluctance to challenge prevailing norms and authority figures; had no patience for rhetoric without substance and concomitant action; resented other people making decisions for her and refused to do likewise for others; and was known for doing the unexpected. Undoubtedly, these personal traits, along with her political ideology and operational style, endeared her to young social reformers coming of age during her tenure as a civil rights activist, but was the source of much consternation on the part of older, more established, and conservative members of the same movement.

After graduating from Shaw University in 1927 with a degree in social science, Baker moved to New York. At that time, Harlem was the center of black cultural expression and creation. Baker was a voracious learner; she soaked up the new knowledge, styles, expressions, relationships, and ideologies raging around her. She did not follow conventions about where young, unescorted women were supposed to go (or not) and how they were supposed to conduct themselves. Wherever there were meetings, discussions, or other gatherings that promised intellectual stimulation, she sought them out, especially if they dealt with issues of social justice. It did not matter if they were located in Harlem or not, and whether the people present were all male, or all white. These interactions introduced her to a wide variety of

89

people and ideas, helped her to crystallize her own philosophical and political beliefs, and craft her approaches to social change.

These ideas were exemplified in the activist work that Baker did for the next fifty years or so. Her life work can best be described as an "organizer" for social change, work that involved education and activism. Her activities were both various and distinguished, but their underlying goals and strategies remained the same: Using well-organized, well-informed, and well-trained groups of ordinary people to achieve social change was her mission.

When forced to make choices about where to place her energies, invariably Baker sided with young, and rank-and-file members in organizations, whether at the local or national level. She thought these constituencies offered new revitalizing and energetic perspectives, potentials, and contributions for addressing stubborn social injustices. She repeatedly admonished advantaged members of communities not to separate themselves from the masses, explaining that protecting one's rights was closely connected with protecting the rights of the most vulnerable, disadvantaged, and powerless members. Baker modeled this behavior in her work with the NAACP, where she fought a diligent battle to democratize the internal operations of that organization by advocating more clearly defined job responsibilities and salary schedules for staff positions, by encouraging branch representatives to be more actively involved in determining NAACP national programs and practices, and by diversifying the rank-and-file membership. She took the NAACP message to the people wherever they were, including pool-rooms, boot black parlors, bars, and grills because she wanted to educate a diverse constituency to the work of this organization.

This notion of close connections between the particular and general, the few and the many, in dealing with social justice dilemmas extended to peace issues as well. For example, in a 1943 radio broadcast, Baker connected the African American struggle against social and political injustices with the fight for democracy for all Americans. Two years later in another broadcast she linked achieving democracy internationally with its accomplishment domestically. In making this argument she declared,

> America cannot hope to lead the peoples of the world to freedom, justice, and equality without achieving for all of its own citizens a full measure of these virtues. Hence, the fate of the minority groups in America is bound with the fate of the peoples of the world; and the prevalence of human freedom and peace throughout the world will be conditioned by the extent to which democracy and freedom are enjoyed by all Americans, regardless of race, creed, or color.[1]

In her work as a facilitator of social change, Baker was as much a pragmatist and a realist as she was a radical and a nonconformist. She understood clearly that when the limited resources of individuals are combined and aggregated they become powerful forces. She applied this understanding in promoting group action and in raising funds to support social justice initiatives. Fundraising was a critical element of her activism and she served this function for all organizations with which she worked. All her fundraising plans involved soliciting small donations from large numbers of people, thereby maximizing the responsibility, participation, and empowerment of the masses in social reform movements.

Baker made significant contributions as an "activist organizer" between 1928 and 1974. She:

- Wrote for the *American West Indian News, Pittsburgh Courier, Norfolk Journal and Guide*, and the Judkins news service. She wrote primarily on the social and economic conditions of African Americans.
- Chaired the Consumer Education Division of the Workers' Education Project of the New York Works Progress Administration (WPA).
- Participated in numerous local community activities in New York City, such as the Youth Committee of One Hundred, the Young People's Community Forum established under the sponsorship of the Harlem Adult Education Committee, and campaigns to get the Harlem branch of the New York City Library to hire African Americans.
- Organized and was the first leader of the Negro History Club, and later staff member of the 135th Street Branch of the New York City Public Library. In the latter capacity she concentrated on parent education.
- Served as Field Secretary and Director of Branches for the National Association for the Advancement of Colored People (NAACP), where she was responsible for conducting fundraising campaigns and membership drives and organizing leadership training conferences with local units primarily in the southern region (including Florida, Virginia, Mississippi, Georgia, Alabama, and North Carolina).

- Helped found In Friendship, a liberal-labor coalition, which supported southern school desegregation and the Montgomery, Alabama bus boycott. She also helped to found Parents in Action, which attacked de facto segregation in the New York City Public Schools.
- Helped organize and was the first director of the Southern Christian Leadership Conference (SCLC). Her responsibilities were to coordinate and serve as the liaison for the nonviolent movements and voter registration campaigns throughout the South.
- Helped found and was advisor to the Student Nonviolent Coordinating Committee (SNCC). In this capacity she fought for the right for the members of this group to be independent of other organizations (e.g., CORE, NAACP, Urban League), make their own decisions, and determine their own courses of action, and mentored them along the way.
- Consultant to the Southern Conference Educational Fund (SCEF) which involved primarily organizing educational conferences and workshops on civil rights and civil liberties.
- Chaired the Washington, DC, and Atlantic City, New Jersey, offices of the Mississippi Freedom Democratic Party (MFDP), which challenged the right of the official Mississippi Delegation to the 1964 Democratic Party Convention to represent African Americans.

Although Ella Baker rejected the teaching profession, she became a teacher in the truest sense of the word. She taught a generation of young adults to be critical thinkers, knowledgeable problem solvers, morally courageous freedom fighters, and astute social activists. She taught these lessons, not by dictate, but by example and facilitation. Throughout her career Baker avoided the limelight, but nonetheless she was a guiding force and shining star for those whom she mentored as a social activist. Well into her seventies she was still "creating a whirlwind. Moving people, stirring them to greater efforts, trying to build a mass movement for change."[2] In her commitment to the cause of human freedom and social justice, Baker fought injustices of all kind wherever she found them.

Although she had no children of her own, Ella Baker "mothered" (in the sense of grooming, guiding, and nurturing) the children and youth of the Civil Rights Movement. She taught them how to be conscientious and competent freedom fighters. At a memorial for her in 1986, Bob Moses, one of her "political trainees," asked

for all of Ella's children to come forward; hundreds responded. Joanne Grant, her biographer and also a "political child," recalled that many of those who stepped forward to declare their affiliation were youngsters, but some were Baker's contemporaries. Many of her "children" went on to make enormous contributions in promoting social justice, thus serving as fitting tributes to Baker, the person and the social activist.

Notes

1. Joanne Grant,. Ella Baker: *Freedom Bound* (New York: John Wiley and Sons, 1998), 67.
2. Grant, 217.

References

Cantarow, Ellen. *Moving the Mountain: Women Working for Social Change*. Old Westbury, NY: Feminist Press, 1980.
Dallard, Shyrlee. *Ella Baker: A Legend Behind the Scenes*. Englewood Cliffs, NJ: Silver Burdett, 1990.
Grant, Joanne. *Ella Baker: Freedom Bound*. New York: John Wiley & Sons, 1998.
"Fundi." *The Story of Ella Baker* (Video). Produced and directed by Joanne Grant. Fundi Productions, 1981.
NAACP Papers. (1940-1955). Reel 1, Part 17 and Reel 31, Part 18.

The papers of Ella Baker are archived at the Schomburg Branch of the New York Public Library.

Marion Thompson Wright

September 13, 1904—October 26, 1962

MARGARET SMITH CROCCO

Marion Thompson Wright began her life in Newark, New Jersey, as the youngest of four children. She attended grammar school in Newark and moved on to Barringer High School as one of only two African American students at the city's most prestigious secondary institution. She graduated at the top of her class and accepted a scholarship to Howard University, where she graduated magna cum laude. She then received a fellowship to study for a master's degree in education at Howard, where she wrote a master's thesis examining the segregated public school systems of sixteen southern states. Charles Thompson, Dean of the School of Education, advised Wright to continue her education further and look more deeply into the matter of school segregation in a doctoral dissertation.

Wright returned home to do a certificate program at the New York School for Social Work, later part of Columbia University. The curriculum there emphasized education and social work in support of the settlement-house movement. During the Depression, Wright worked as a caseworker for the Newark Department of Welfare and the New Jersey Emergency Relief Administration. In 1933 she began a Ph.D. program in history and educational sociology, one of no more than about forty students and only a handful of African Americans matriculating for this degree at Teachers College at that time. In joining history with sociology to study current social problems like segregation, Wright followed in the footsteps of W.E.B. DuBois and E. Franklin Frazier, scholars who used these disciplines to explain the status of African Americans in contemporary society. George Counts, a faculty member at Teachers College, was a prominent proponent of using educational sociology as a moral enterprise bent on improving the human condition. Wright studied under Frazier and Counts and shared a conviction that academic knowledge should be used to make American society more democratic.

In 1938, Wright asked Merle Curti to serve as her dissertation sponsor. Curti had taught at Beloit and Smith Colleges before being recruited to Teachers College in 1938 by his friend, George Counts. A pacifist and socialist, Curti was one of the first white historians

to consider Black History as part of social history. By this time, the work of Carter G. Woodson and Charles Wesley in the Association for the Study of Negro History and Life (ASNHL) had been widely disseminated in black schools through "Negro History Week" and the *Negro History Bulletin*. During Wright's subsequent career, she would contribute significantly to the foundation laid by Woodson and Wesley in promoting Black History in the schools.

Wright's dissertation (1941), "The Education of Negroes in New Jersey," was an exhaustive and highly original piece of scholarship. Wright followed Curti's model in dealing comprehensively with the social, political, and intellectual forces that shaped black education in the state. She demonstrated the negative and powerful impact racial segregation had on children in the southern half of the state while extolling the more favorable circumstances of largely integrated education in the northern half.

Like Counts, Wright believed that the purpose of education was to build a new social order, one that might bring equality to African Americans through schooling. Wright trusted that the democratic process could fulfill its potential of social and racial justice for all citizens. She believed scholarship linked to advocacy could be pivotal in improving democratic education for all the nation's citizens.

In 1944, Wright's dissertation was cited by Gunnar Myrdal in *An American Dilemma*, a book that used social science data to illuminate the ill effects of school segregation. This approach was adopted by the NAACP in arguing *Brown v. Board of Education*. Wright argued that discriminatory practices placed a stamp of inferiority upon black children that inhibited development of a well-integrated personality and sense of personal worth in them. The Supreme Court ultimately found such logic compelling in deciding *Brown v. Board of Education*.

After completing her dissertation, Wright returned to Howard University as a faculty member in the School of Education. She continued to contribute regularly to journals associated with Black History and education, such as the *Negro History Bulletin*, *Journal of Negro*

Education, and *Journal of Negro History*, work disseminated to teachers and students in black schools under the auspices of the ASNLH. She also argued for greater public acknowledgment of the contributions made by black women's organizations to civil rights work. She was a contributing editor to the *Afro American Woman's Journal*, the organ of Mary McLeod Bethune's National Council of Negro Women.

As an educator of social studies teachers who combined history with psychology and sociology, Wright pioneered an interdisciplinary approach to the field. Her involvement with the American Teachers Association and the National Education Association, as well as the Association of Social Science Teachers in Negro Colleges, focused on Black History and to black women's contributions to civil society.

Despite these achievements, Wright's was not a happy life. Throughout her career, she struggled for professional recognition. In addition, her personal circumstances were difficult, including two failed marriages, and estrangement from siblings and even her two children. On October 26, 1962, Wright succumbed to a lifelong battle with depression and took her own life. She left behind a legacy of scholarship and activism nurtured by her faith in the promises of democracy for all the nation's citizens.

References

Crocco, Margaret Smith. "Shaping Inclusive Education: Mary Ritter Beard and Marion Thompson Wright," in Margaret Smith Crocco and O. L. Davis, Jr. eds. *"Bending the Future to Their Will": Civic Women, Social Education, and Democracy*. Lanham, MD: Rowman and Littlefield, 1999, 93-125.

Crocco, Margaret, Petra Munro, and Kathleen Weiler. *Pedagogies of Resistance: Women Educator Activists, 1880-1960*. New York: Teachers College Press, 1999.

Women's Project of New Jersey. *Oral Histories with Friends of Marion Thompson Wright*. Rutgers University Special Collections, New Brunswick, New Jersey, 1988.

Wright, Marion Thompson. *The Education of Negroes in New Jersey*. New York: Teachers College Press, 1941.

Nelda Mae Davis

October 5, 1904—August 8, 1986

Cheryl J. Craig

Nelda Mae Davis helped organize Houston, Texas, councils of social studies educators for white and black teachers as well as the Prince George's County, Maryland Council for the Social Studies. She is best known for her contributions in the areas of geography and gifted and talented education, and the many regional and national roles she played in the development of NCSS.

Born in Wiggins, Mississippi, Nelda was the fourth child of Ward Hampton Davis, a Mississippi merchant, and Pearl Pertha Foote, a housewife. Raised a Methodist, Nelda Davis graduated from Gulfport (MS) High School in 1922 and then moved to Houston in order to attend the former Rice Institute, now Rice University. She graduated from Rice in 1926 with majors in history and English and minors in education and biology.

After receiving a Texas first class high school teaching certificate, Davis began her thirty-year career with the Houston Independent School District (HISD). For many years, she taught social studies and English at Johnston Junior High School. Diane Ravitch, one of her most prominent former students and a well-known educational historian, has recalled Nelda Davis as one of her most influential teachers. Ravitch remembers Davis as a "tall, gangly, wonderful, no-nonsense teacher who commanded the respect of students."[1] She credits her former teacher with instilling in her a deep appreciation for the roots of institutions.

In 1950, Davis began to take graduate courses at Teachers College, Columbia University, the University of Houston, and the University of Texas at Austin. She subsequently received a master's degree from the University of Houston. The HISD superintendent then appointed her as the district's supervisor of secondary social studies.

When Davis began her district wide leadership role, HISD had been embroiled for some time in ideological battles between ultra-right wing conservatives, led by the Houston Chapter of the Minute Women of the U.S.A. (who were immersed in the Cold War ideology of Senator Joseph McCarthy) and liberal progressives and centrists who had been branded in the 1940s as "subversives" and "communists." These struggles manifest themselves at the University of Houston, in the city's

Methodist Church, the school board, and in labor unions.[2] Local right-wing zealots believed that "leftists" and "communists" were responsible for "new teaching philosophies and methods, [and] new classroom courses such as the dreaded 'social studies' and 'language arts.'" They also blamed their opponents for "textbooks that mentioned the Soviet Union, for labor unions, [and] for Blacks thinking that they just might have civil rights."[3] In 1953, extremist forces on the Houston school board ousted the district's deputy superintendent after only one year of service. His unwarranted removal resulted in a major NEA investigation that brought to the surface the dogmatism and extremism present in Houston.[4]

The tense educational situation within which Davis became Supervisor of Secondary Social Studies did not die down. Rather, it continued to generate heat. The Houston Minute Women, along with other ultra-conservative groups, actively searched for suspected communists in HISD schools. The school district's board frequently overruled the textbook adoptions suggested by teachers appointed under Davis's authority, texts that routinely were accepted elsewhere in Texas and the nation. For example, in 1954, it rejected *Economics of Our Time* (McGraw Hill) in favor of *Understanding Our Free Economy* (Van Nostrand), a book that ranked 5th in committee balloting among the district's teachers.

In a 1956 Houston newspaper article titled "Big Battle Set Over School Desegregation," Dallas Dyer, a school board member and Houston Minute Woman, objected to events which transpired at the 1955 NCSS annual meeting in New York City that she had heard about. She proposed that the school board review the programs of national meetings before it authorized spending taxpayers' money to send people like Davis and others to meetings.

During the 1955-56 school year, Superintendent William Moreland was planning for HISD's possible compliance with the *Brown v. Board of Education* ruling by the U.S. Supreme Court. Davis contributed to his report to the school board (1955-1956), describing how she had worked with separate groups of white and "colored" teachers and had hosted discussion sessions about industrial growth in the Houston-Gulf Coast area.[5] She also noted that the Houston Council of Social Studies had increased its membership to 212, and that the Sam Houston Council of Social Studies for black teachers had also been launched. She also reported about her work with NCSS, including her role as chair of a session on the rapid learner and the start of her three-year term on the executive board of the journal *Social Education*.

In 1956, HISD's curriculum review committee met and recommended that social studies be abolished and the constituent subjects be taught separately. Furthermore, it urged that world history and geography be delayed until tenth grade. *Time* magazine reported that these curricular changes would "keep Houston's younger generation safe from learning anything at all about three-fourths of the globe."[6]

This setback to Houston's social studies program and progressive pedagogies deeply chagrined Davis who had worked tirelessly to nurture the subject area and cultivate community in the Houston schools. The turn of events, moreover, proved to be just the beginning of what can only be interpreted as a series of personal assaults on Davis. Two board members demanded that the acting superintendent fire several teachers; among those specifically named was Davis. Houston's superintendent refused to comply with this directive. However, Trustee Dyer convinced the board to deny Davis's expense request to attend the NCSS meeting in Cleveland, Ohio. Davis, a 29-veteran of the Houston schools, was scheduled to make a presentation on rapid learners. Dyer killed Davis's request by charging that speakers with "un-American" backgrounds would appear at the NCSS conference. Furthermore, Dyer made clear that all teacher requests to attend meetings affiliated with the NEA would be denied as part of official board policy. Davis paid her own expenses and attended the NCSS meeting.[7] When she returned to Houston, Davis dutifully completed the school year and later retired from HISD with thirty years of service and a full pension from the state.

Although others might have considered her retirement as the conclusion to a career, Davis did not. She moved to Maryland and became Supervisor of Secondary Social Studies in Prince George's County. Later, she became a member of the county's school board. Davis also founded the Prince George's County Council for the Social Studies, served on the NCSS board of directors, and participated on many state committees. Davis

additionally co-authored a geography textbook, *The Wide World*, as well as *How to Work with the Academically Talented in Social Studies*, which was part of the popular NCSS *"How To Do It" Series*.[8]

Davis died in Washington, DC, in 1986. A fund was established in Maryland to honor her unwavering support of social studies, NCSS, and the path she cut for others to follow in the states of Texas and Maryland.

Notes

1. Diane Ravitch, Personal communication, February 23, 2001.
2. Eric Gerber, "Red Rhetoric Redux," *Houston Post* (June 13, 1985): 2B.
3. Peter Wyckoff, "When 'Baghdad on the Bayou' was a City on Edge: Those Red-letter Days of Cold War in *Houston Post*," *Houston Post* (June 16, 1985): 11F.
4. D. Carleton, *Red Scare: Right-wing Hysteria: Fifties Fanaticism and Its Legacy in Texas. Austin*, TX: Texas Monthly Press, 1985.
5. Office of the Superintendent (William Moreland). "Annual Report to the Board of Education." Houston, TX: Houston Independent School District, 1955-56.
6. Carleton, 290.
7. Carleton.
8. Davis, Nelda M. *How to Work with the Academically Talented in the Social Studies*. "How To Do It" series. Washington, DC: 1966.

Helen McCracken Carpenter

July 31, 1909—October 20, 1997

Lynn M. Burlbaw

Helen McCracken Carpenter provided leadership in the National Council for the Social Studies during a turbulent and challenging time for social studies teachers. She served on the Curriculum Committee (1951 and 1952), on the board of directors (1952 and 1953), as vice-president (1954-55), and as president (1956). This period saw the rapid "baby boom" growth of the school-age population as well as the rise of anticommunist hysteria, exemplified by the McCarthy hearings and the Cold War. Both of these trends affected the members and operations of the NCSS, and Carpenter was instrumental in crafting organizational responses to them.

The growing membership of NCSS created a governance challenge for the organization's leadership. By 1955, NCSS membership had grown to a little over 6,000 members, approximately 11 percent of whom were student members. Governance of NCSS, which had been directed by members who attended the business meeting at the annual NCSS conference, had

> become too unwieldy for any really serious consideration of Association policies. If an issue should arise, its consideration would easily be dominated by the members who live in the convention city. Others who live at a distance have little opportunity to be informed about the affairs of the Association or to have a voice in its deliberations. When the members of the Association have no opportunity to discuss the policies of the Association, the officers can have no real sense of representing or profiting from the thinking of the membership.[1]

The solution to this dilemma of under-representation was to establish a house of delegates, in which representatives from affiliated state, regional, and local councils would determine NCSS policy. Carpenter participated as a member of the board of directors in advancing this plan in 1954. The new governance structure was adopted at the annual meeting of NCSS in 1956, while Carpenter was President. The representational form established under her leadership continues to this day.

Carpenter was also instrumental in providing leadership to protect the rights of social studies teachers. Believing that ethical and competent teachers needed

the flexibility and support to teach what they believed was most important, the members of the NCSS Committee on Academic Freedom promulgated a series of statements on the "Freedom to Learn and Freedom to Teach." These statements, adopted by the board of directors of NCSS, explicated the meaning of schools in a free society.[2] They also provided guidelines which teachers could use to prevent censorship and to defend against professional attacks. Carpenter was either on the board of directors or president of NCSS when these statements were adopted.

The statements were not only assertions of right, they also enumerated teachers' responsibilities to society. The December 1956 statement began:

> We believe that most Americans agree with us in our conception of freedom to learn and freedom to teach. However, communication between the school and the community frequently is not good. Anything which aids the people in understanding what the schools are doing, and why they are doing it, will strengthen the position of the school and render attacks on individual teachers or programs less likely.
>
> It is a definite responsibility of the teaching profession at all levels to be as certain as possible that there are no disloyal persons within its membership. Likewise it is a responsibility of the profession to oppose aggressively investigations that damage individual reputations and lower the morale of our teachers.[3]

Carpenter also had a lifelong interest in identifying the skills needed to analyze and evaluate historical information. To this end, she wrote several "How To Do It" teaching guides and wrote chapters for or edited the 17th, 24th, and 33rd NCSS yearbooks, which focused on skills and skill development.[4]

Under Carpenter's leadership of the curriculum committee in 1952, NCSS published additional volumes in the curriculum series entitled "Social Studies in ..." for a variety of school-age audiences. During her term on the committee, regular features on curriculum began to appear in *Social Education*. These publications were designed to highlight changes needed in social studies as a result of evolving demographics in the schools.

Carpenter also wrote *Gateways to American History: An Annotated Graded List of Books for Slow Learners in Junior High School* (1942, updated and reprinted in 1983); was co-author of a textbook series published by Scribner in 1950, *Building a Free Nation*; and prepared a set of listening guides, "Leads to Listening" for Enrichment Records, based on the Landmark Books published by Random House.

During her years of NCSS leadership and publication, Carpenter was chair of the Department of History and Government at Trenton State Teachers College (today called The College of New Jersey). She received a B.A. at Ohio Wesleyan University, where she was Phi Beta Kappa, and a M.A. and Ed.D. from Teachers College, Columbia University. She taught in the public schools of Ohio and at Ohio Wesleyan, District of Columbia Teachers College (later known as Federal City University), Rhode Island State University, and (during the summers) at Teachers College, Columbia, and Syracuse Universities. She was a member of various educational honor societies and professional organizations throughout her life. She died in 1975, at the relatively young age of sixty.

Notes

1. Merrill F. Hartshorn, "Notes and News," *Social Education* 20, no. 5. (May 1956): 226.
2. National Council for the Social Studies, "Freedom to Learn and Freedom to Teach" *Social Education* 17, no. 5 (May 1953): 217-219; Helen McCracken Carpenter et al., "Directors' Resolutions," *Social Education* 20, no. 2 (February 1956): 53; Committee on Academic Freedom, "Action to Uphold Freedom to Learn and Freedom to Teach" *Social Education* 20, no. 8 (December 1956): 371-372.
3. Committee on Academic Freedom, 371.
4. Helen M. Carpenter and M. Young, *Reading to Learn History: Suggestions for Methods and Materials.* 17th Yearbook. (Washington, DC: NCSS, 1946); Helen M. Carpenter, ed. *Skills in Social Studies.* 24th Yearbook (Washington, DC: NCSS, 1953); Carpenter, Helen M., ed. *Skill Development in Social Studies.* 33d Yearbook (Washington, DC: NCSS, 1963).

References

Carpenter, Helen M. *Gateways to American History: An Annotated Graded List of Books for Slow Learners in Junior High School.* New York: Wilson, 1942, rev. 1983.

Carpenter, Helen M. "Teaching World History to Poor Readers," *Social Education* 15, no. 3 (May 1951): 223-35, 241.

Moore, C., Helen M. Carpenter, L. G. Paquin, F. B. Painter, and G. M. Lewis. *Building a Free Nation.* New York: Charles Scribner, 1950.

Ruth Elizabeth Ellsworth

October 4, 1908—

Linda S. Levstik

As a social studies educator, Ruth E. Ellsworth worked to enable children to understand local, national, and global perspectives "to know that we are in the world." Her experiences as a student and teacher led her to strive for a view of culture and society that considers other nationalities and that recognizes the citizen's obligation to his or her community.

Ruth Ellsworth's interest in education was nurtured in a family of educators. Her mother, Zora, taught Latin. Her father, Frank, directed a laboratory school at Western Michigan University and served on its faculty. Ellsworth received a teaching certificate in 1928 and a bachelor's degree in 1930 from Western Michigan University. She taught in Alma, Michigan, and Bronxville, New York. After completing a master's degree at Teachers College, Columbia University in 1938 and a doctorate at Northwestern University in 1949, she taught at Wayne State University in Detroit, Michigan. She remained there until her retirement in 1977.

Unlike her experience at Northwestern, where the only woman on the faculty was the coordinator of student teaching, a number of women were members of the faculty at Wayne State. "There were quite a few very active women there," Ellsworth recalled. "They served on university committees and exerted a fair degree of influence. Overall, we had good relationships with other faculty." Rather than focus on being a woman in a largely male-dominated profession, Ellsworth explained, "I just did it."

During this period, Ellsworth was very active in NCSS and as a social studies scholar. Throughout most of her tenure with NCSS, Ellsworth found the organization to be fairly conservative. In her view, members tended not to address social issues or to emphasize international or global study. Instead, disciplinary issues predominated, especially as the "structure of the disciplines" movement absorbed attention in the 1960s. While Ellsworth considered the disciplines fundamental to social studies curricula, her own interests focused on inquiry in the context of an integrated social studies program "because [integrated study] provides a more rounded view of culture and society."

As did other women interested in elementary social studies, Ellsworth faced several challenges as a member of NCSS. First of all, she was at some disadvantage because of the lack of attention paid to elementary social studies. "Elementary social studies was an underdog," she explained. There was little emphasis on any aspect of teaching and learning social studies in the early grades. Ellsworth thought that this was related to an over-emphasis on decontextualized reading skills, "especially simple word recognition," in the elementary curriculum. Unable to compete for time with reading, social studies often disappeared from the elementary classroom. As a result, Ellsworth noted, children were left with few resources for making sense of their world. In her scholarship, and especially in her work on community studies and international connections, Ellsworth sought to provide teachers with ways to counteract this trend. She co-edited the 26th NCSS yearbook, *Improving the Social Studies Curriculum,* and contributed chapters on elementary social studies to two other NCSS publications. Other articles focusing on elementary social studies appeared in *The Elementary School Journal, Social Education,* and *The Journal of Geography.* She enjoyed the writing, she said, because she enjoyed the work she was doing.

A second issue facing any new professor was visibility within NCSS . "Basically, you had to have a sponsor," Ellsworth recalled. Usually doctoral advisors sponsored their students in NCSS activities. From Ellsworth's point of view, a new social studies professor's position in NCSS depended on the power and influence exerted by his or her major professor. Ellsworth's advisor was helpful, but she also found an active group of women scholars, including Helen McCrackenCarpenter, Mary Kelty, and Jean Fair. These women, she noted, had an impact in the profession because they wrote books. Ellsworth, too, focused much of her scholarship on editing and contributing to NCSS Yearbooks and Curriculum Series.

Besides her work in NCSS, Ellsworth took leadership positions in several professional associations, including the Association for Supervision and Curriculum Development, the National Education Association, and the Association for Childhood Education. In addition, she served as an officer in a number of Michigan educational organizations, speaking at local P.T.A. meetings, organizing programs, and providing leadership on committees and boards. She also developed a solid list of civic accomplishments, serving as president of the Detroit branch of the Women's International League for Peace and Freedom, chair of the Qualifications Committee, member of the Inter-Group Council for Women as Public Policy Makers, chair of the Detroit UNICEF Committee, and member of the Detroit League of Women Voters.

After her retirement Ellsworth continued her involvement in a number of these activities. For example, for five years she served as head of the UNICEF shop in Detroit. In 1985, Ellsworth established the Frank and Zora Ellsworth Scholarship at Western Michigan University. The College of Education awards the scholarship each year to a junior or senior elementary education or Latin major. Ellsworth continues to meet with recipients and keeps track of their careers.

References

Allen, A., and Ruth E. Ellsworth. "Program and Material Evaluation in the Social Studies," *The Elementary School Journal*, 49 (1964): 161-163.

Eikenberry, Alice, and Ruth E. Ellsworth. "Organizing and Evaluating Information," in Helen McCracken Carpenter, ed. *Skill Development in Social Studies*. 33d Yearbook. Washington, DC: NCSS, 1963, 74-93.

Ellsworth, Ruth E. "Contributions from Studies of Child Development," in L. E. Klee, ed., *Social Studies for Older Children: Programs for Grades Four, Five, and Six*. Washington, DC: NCSS, 1953, 34-44.

-----. "Trends in Organization of the Social Studies," in J. U. Michaelis, ed., *Social Studies in Elementary Schools*. 32nd NCSS Yearbook. Washington, DC: NCSS, 1962, 107-130.

-----. "Critical Thinking: Its Encouragement," *The National Elementary Principal* 42 (1963): 24-29.

-----. Personal communication, August 24, 2000.

-----. and Ole Sand, eds. *Improving the Social Studies Curriculum*. 26th NCSS Yearbook. Washington, DC: NCSS, 1955.

Focus on scholarship. Western Michigan University website, www.wmich.edu/coe/edutoday/focusonScholarships.html.

"Ruth E. Ellsworth Biographical Data Sheet." Association of Faculty Women, Walter P. Reuther Library, Archives of Labor and Urban Affairs and University Archives, Wayne State University, 1959.

Maxine Dunfee

April 6, 1913–

MARY E. HAAS

Maxine Dunfee is known internationally as an advocate for problem solving, values, and ethnic and international education in the elementary curriculum. She was born in Council Bluff, Iowa, to Anna Bess Remy and Edwin James Dunfee, II. In writing informally to her family about "notable" events in her life, she described walking in her best dress with neighborhood children to Avenue B School to begin kindergarten, learning about the world through souvenirs and pictures her father brought home from Niagara Falls, and celebrating the end of World War I by waving a flag at an impromptu parade on November 11, 1918. After this joy came sad memories of the flu epidemic and attending her father's funeral.

As a result of her father's death, the Dunfee siblings were separated; Maxine went to live with her father's parents. After several years the family was reunited. As a high school student Dunfee excelled, graduating from Red Oaks High School in 1930 as valedictorian. Junior college often served as an alternative to four-year colleges for students without funds during the Great Depression. Upon graduation from Southern Community College, Dunfee passed the county teacher exam. She began teaching fifteen students across eight grades at the rural Bleak Hill School. She held two other teaching posts before accumulating sufficient savings to complete her baccalaureate degree at State University of Iowa, Iowa City. Upon graduation, she accepted an invitation to become a fourth grade teacher in the campus Laboratory School. She continued to teach there while earning a master's degree.

In 1942 Dunfee joined the faculty of the University School at Indiana University in Bloomington. Four years later, she became a faculty member of the University's School of Education and taught courses in social studies and science methods and mathematics education. She completed a doctorate in education in 1949. She earned the rank of full professor in 1962 and retired in 1984. In 1982 Indiana University presented Dunfee with its highest teaching honor: the Frederic Bachman Lieber Distinguished Teaching Award. For her years of work with Pi Lambda Theta, the Indiana University chapter (Iota) presented her with its Distinguished Service Award.

Students and colleagues remembered Dunfee as a caring teacher who empowered her students. She demonstrated the style of teaching that she advocated and supported her students' efforts, identifying individual strengths and encouraging them long after graduation. Dunfee specialized in elementary social studies and frequently presented at NCSS annual conferences. She engaged students in active and thoughtful learning based upon "big ideas" (concepts and generalizations) from multiple social sciences disciplines, encouraging them to use these "big ideas" to solve real problems in the world. She developed her ideas about values education and the importance of socializing children to respect the multiethnic character of American society through her publications.

Contributions to the Elementary Commission of the Association for Supervision and Curriculum Development brought her an invitation to attend the Asilomar World Education Conference in March 1970 and a role in the founding of the World Council for Curriculum and Instruction (WCCI) in 1972. Over the years, WCCI had developed into a nongovernmental organization (NGO) of the United Nations, with a membership of more than 1,000 curriculum specialists in fifty nations. Between 1981 and 1993, Dunfee served as WCCI's unpaid executive secretary. In appreciation for her services, she was awarded WCCI life membership.

References

Dunfee, Maxine. *Elementary School Social Studies: A Guide to Current Research.* Washington DC: Association for Supervision and Curriculum Development, 1970.
-----. *Elementary School Science: A Guide to Current Research.* Washington, DC: Association for Supervision and Curriculum Development, 1967.
-----. "Needed Research in Social Studies: Open Classrooms, Inquiry, and Values Education." *Journal of Social Studies Research* 4, no. 2 (Summer 1980): 47-50.

The author conducted interviews with Claudia Crump; Maxine Dunfee; Elizabeth Peterson; Norman Overly; Piyush Swami, WCCI president (1999); and Estela C. Matriano, WCCI executive director (1993-present).

4.
Embracing the
"New Social Studies":
1961-1975

Introduction

MARGARET SMITH CROCCO

Four women served as presidents of NCSS during the years 1961-75: Stella Kern (1963), Adeline Brengle (1966), Jean Fair (1972), and Jean Claugus (1975). During these years, practitioners of the social studies reacted to the Cold War, its eruption in the Vietnam conflict, and the educational implications of these events. On the home front, women earned college and advanced degrees in sufficient numbers to continue serving as teachers and, to some extent, professors of social studies education despite persistent discrimination practiced by the most prestigious graduate and professional schools.

Of the four women ascending to the NCSS presidency during the period, three were teachers (Brengle, Claugus, Kern) and one was a college professor (Fair). The ongoing cultural assumption that women would sacrifice their careers and educational goals to secure marriage and family life seems not to have inhibited the professional paths of these women presidents and the two college professors, Fannie Shaftel and Edith West, profiled in this chapter.

This time period began with the promise of John F. Kennedy's pronouncement of a "New Frontier" in space and ended with the United States' withdrawal from Vietnam. The assassinations of John F. Kennedy, Robert Kennedy, Martin Luther King, Jr., and Malcolm X, along with numerous urban riots left the nation reeling. Whatever cultural confidence characterized the United States as the period began quickly eroded as political and social strife divided Americans.

The scientific and technical challenge presented when the Soviets launched Sputnik into orbit in 1957 was used by educators and politicians to advocate elevating academic standards in U.S. schools. Combined with pressures from the U.S./Soviet arms race and the ongoing threat of nuclear holocaust, unprecedented levels of public and private resources were deployed to improve science education. New geopolitical alignments encouraged the U.S. Office of Education, the National Science Foundation, private foundations, and professional organizations to promote the social sciences through grants for enhancing the teaching of economics, anthropology, geography, and political science in the nation's schools.

Chicago schoolteacher, Stella Kern, in her 1964 NCSS presidential address, called on social studies to meet the challenges presented by new national priorities:

> Yet, the social studies are falling farther and farther behind in the race with mathematics, science, and technology, and there is a time lag, often a long one, as schools strive to keep pace with our rapidly growing culture.... Science is taking us to the moon, and we haven't learned to live peacefully on earth.... We face an insistent question: "Can enough Americans learn enough soon enough to meet the challenges confronting us?"[1]

Publication of the 1958 NCSS yearbook, *New Viewpoints in the Social Sciences*, edited by Roy A. Price, presaged the direction of changes in the field for at least a decade to come.[2] In this volume, scholars in history, geography, political science, economics, sociology, anthropology, and social psychology outlined the major trends in their disciplines. The clear message was that social studies teachers should utilize this information to revamp their approaches to curriculum.

Dorothy McClure Fraser, past president of NCSS and editor of the "Annual Review of Curriculum Materials" then published in *Social Education*, noted the increasing amount of attention devoted to people and cultures around the world, in particular, the non-Western world. In the 1964 issue of this review, she also set aside a special section on materials for teaching about Communism:

> Widespread realization that the international Communist movement poses a grave threat to our freedom and to our representative form of government has created a favorable climate of opinion for dealing with this vital topic in our nation's classrooms.[3]

In addition to this attention to Communism, *Social Education* regularly devoted entire issues to the social sciences. For example, in December 1966, Clyde Kohn of the University of Iowa and head of "The High School Geography Project" guest edited an issue on this subject.[4] In February 1968, the journal focused on anthropology, a discipline growing in popularity on college campuses in the post-World War II years.[5]

Fraser's regular commentary in *Social Education* on social studies research and curriculum translated the contemporary intellectual currents into a teacher-friendly format. She highlighted the significance of concepts and generalizations to the teaching of social studies,[6] the value of instruction based on inquiry and multimedia learning materials,[7] and the importance of sequence in social studies skills and curricula across grade levels.[8]

Interpreting and Teaching American History, the 31st NCSS Yearbook, dealt with trends up to 1961. Even in the discipline of history, the centerpiece of the social studies since its inception, pressures from the social sciences called for reinvention of approach. In 1963, NCSS and the American Council for the Learned Societies published *The Social Sciences and the Social Studies*, a book that emphasized the importance of area studies in a global age.[9] Calls for using the social sciences to refashion the social studies resulted in numerous U.S. Office of Education-funded curriculum projects across the country to bring innovative curriculum from the social sciences into the schools.

Given the Cold War climate, educational matters were seen as having a heightened association with national security. The pages of *Social Education* offer ample evidence of the sense of urgency within educational circles. Many articles published in the sixties, such as "The Crisis Threatening American Education"[10] and "Social Studies Requirements in an Age of Science and Mathematics,"[11] provide evidence of the national mood.

As a consequence of this sense of national educational crisis, historians of education note, "[T]he most significant educational consequence of Sputnik ... was the impetus it gave to federal financing of public education."[12] The first massive infusion of federal aid into education was the 1958 National Defense Education Act (NDEA). Although this legislation originally provided money for science, mathematics, and foreign languages, by the next decade, funding expanded to include the social sciences. Throughout the sixties, NDEA monies underwrote hundreds of summer institutes on these subjects that accommodated more than 5,200 schoolteachers nationwide each year.

The new federal initiatives relied heavily on disciplinary experts, with variable, although typically quite limited, involvement of educational leaders. The influence of the former could be seen in the shape of both the NDEA and the 1965 Elementary and Secondary Education Act, a program that has been described as "by far the most influential piece of educational legislation in American history."[13] These and other funding sources led directly to programs that collectively came to be known as "the new social studies." In projects associated with this label, the influence of social science could be discerned in an emphasis on inquiry in pursuit of knowledge, active participation of students in the learning process, and engagement with the raw materials of the disciplines.

The book that provided a theoretical framework for much of this curriculum revitalization was Jerome Bruner's brief, but highly influential *The Process of Education*, published in 1960.[14] Bruner's work arose from a conference in 1959 held at Woods Hole, Massachusetts on math and science education, sponsored and funded by the National Academy of Sciences, the American Association for the Advancement of Science, the Carnegie Corporation, the Rand Corporation, the U.S. Office of Education, and the National Science Foundation. Despite the emphasis there on teaching and learning, "largely excluded [from the conference] were classroom teachers and 'educationists.'"[15] The absence of educational expertise did not inhibit the Woods Hole participants from making numerous prescriptions for subject matter, curriculum, and methods deemed suitable for the schools.

Psychologist Bruner offered principles of learning in *The Process of Education* that were quickly adopted by social studies scholars interested in reforming the field. Much of what Bruner advocated, such as learning through "discovery," was hardly new to the social studies. However, the scientific patina of these prescriptions made them irresistible to many advocates of reform at the time. Bruner also emphasized that schooling should inculcate in students an understanding of the distinctive structures of the disciplines.[16] As a result, many social studies projects of the sixties adopted these goals as their main emphasis.

The "new social studies" and "new history," as they came to be known, reflected the optimistic belief that scientifically sanctioned approaches would transform social studies teaching and learning from kindergarten through twelfth grade. The new curriculum projects were also intended to redress the alleged intellectual vacuousness of the "life adjustment" emphasis in many curricula, so roundly criticized by Arthur Bestor and others in the forties and fifties.[17]

The Amherst Project, for example, emphasized extensive use of primary sources, with highly detailed curriculum materials created for units in 11th grade U.S. history. Edwin Fenton's Project Social Studies, a federally funded effort, emphasized inductive teaching and the structure of the disciplines.[18] The Anthropology Curriculum Study Project, Sociological Resources for the Secondary School, and Man: A Course of Study (MACOS) were all funded by the National Science Foundation and/or the U.S. Office of Education.[19] Clyde Kohn's High School Geography Project, supported by the Ford Foundation, resulted from a rare coming-together of both educational and disciplinary specialists. In 1963, the Social Science Education Consortium was established at Purdue University as a source of and clearinghouse for social science-oriented school curriculum, with funding from the National Science Foundation and the U.S. Office of Education.[20]

Several other initiatives and influential critiques of the social studies emerged at this time. At the Harvard School of Education, Donald Oliver led a project, funded like those above by the U.S. Office of Education, which focused on public issues.[21] Indiana University professor and later NCSS president Shirley Engle advocated development of an overall "structure" for the social studies based on nine recurring themes.[22] Byron Massialas offered teachers rationale, principles, and examples of teaching through the inquiry method.[23] In an influential essay, Lawrence Metcalf examined the deficiencies of the social studies curriculum and gave advice about how they might be corrected.[24] Paul Hanna provided a comprehensive approach to the elementary curriculum built around the theme of expanding communities.[25]

The women profiled in this chapter shaped, implemented, tested, and translated for teachers the reform efforts associated with "the new social studies." Stanford University professor Fannie Shaftel advocated roleplay and simulation as teaching tools of particular importance for critical thinking about controversial issues such as race relations.[26] Edith West directed a center at the University of Minnesota associated with Fenton's work. As West describes it:

The Center has tried to provide better balance among the disciplines than in the past. This has meant reducing the amount of time devoted to American history in the K-14 sequence. It has also meant giving considerable attention to ideas and materials from the field of anthropology. Indeed, the concept of culture becomes the unifying concept for the entire curriculum. This curriculum places heavy emphasis upon comparative study—from a comparison of families around the world in the elementary grades to a comparison of total cultures (including their economic and social systems) in the senior high school.[27]

Contributions to *Social Education* by Adeline Brengle, Jean Fair, and Stella Kern reflected concerns with the heightened demands being placed on teachers. As a longtime member of the NCSS Board of Directors and as NCSS president, Jean Claugus proposed renewed professional emphasis on topics she believed important to enhancing the capacity of teachers for change: academic freedom and tenure, active involvement with regional and national social studies organizations, and improved understanding of ethnic studies. In their presidential addresses, both Brengle and Kern highlighted the challenges of quality teaching in the tumultuous climate of the sixties. Brengle also used her role as NCSS president to encourage interest in global education.[28]

As professor of education at Wayne State University, Jean Fair directed the NCSS research committee in the mid-sixties towards research on social studies teachers, a priority she maintained as NCSS president in 1972. Her 1965 research committee report on social studies teachers noted that: "The big questions have been around for a long time." Dealing successfully with these questions, she concluded, meant "coming to grips with problems about the kinds of social studies curriculums for which teachers are needed today."[29] Fair succinctly states the prevailing sentiment that new forms of social studies were, indeed, demanded by a new age. Who would decide what those new forms would be remained a matter of some contention.

Notes

1. Stella Kern, "Quality Teaching: The Challenge of the Sixties," *Social Education* 28, no. 3 (March 1964): 138-140.
2. Roy A. Price, ed., *New Viewpoints in the Social Sciences* (Washington, DC: NCSS, 1959).
3. Dorothy McClure Fraser, "Annual Review of Curriculum Materials," *Social Education* 28, no. 4 (April 1964): 214-224.
4. Clyde Kohn, guest editor, *Social Education* 30, no. 8 (December 1966).
5. Malcolm Collier, guest editor, *Social Education* 32, no. 2 (February 1968).

6. Dorothy McClure Fraser, "Annual Review of Curriculum Materials," *Social Education* 33, no. 5 (May 1969): 575-591.

7. Dorothy M. Fraser, "Status and Expectations of Current Research and Development Projects," *Social Education* 29, no. 7 (November 1965): 421-435.

8. Dorothy M. Fraser, ed., "Review of Curriculum Materials," *Social Education* 32, no. 4 (April 1968): 362-385.

9. Bernard Berelson, ed., *The Social Sciences and the Social Studies* (New York: Harcourt, Brace and World, 1962).

10. Eugene McCreary, "The Crisis Threatening American Education," *Social Education* 26, no. 4 (April 1962): 177-180.

11. Emlyn Jones, "Social Studies Requirements in an Age of Science and Mathematics," *Social Education* 27, no. 1 (January 1963): 17-18.

12. Wayne Urban and Jennings Wagoner, *American Education: A History*, 2nd ed. (NY: McGraw Hill, 2000), p. 293.

13. Urban and Wagoner, 328.

14. Jerome Bruner, *The Process of Education* (New York: Random House, 1960).

15. Hazel Hertzberg, *Social Studies Reform*, 1880-1980: A Project Span Report (Boulder, CO: Social Science Education Consortium, 1981), 97.

16. Ibid.

17. Wayne Urban and Jennings Wagoner, *American Education: A History*, 2nd ed. (New York: McGraw Hill, 2000), 291.

18. "Announcement for Project Social Studies," *Social Education* 26, no. 6 (October 1962): 300; see also Edwin Fenton, *Teaching the New Social Studies in Secondary Schools: An Inductive Approach* (New York: McGraw Hill, 1966).

19. Hertzberg, 102-3.

20. "Mission and History," Social Science Education Consortium web page, ssecinc.org/Pr_SSEC.htm, accessed on August 25, 2001.

21. James P. Shaver and Donald W. Oliver, "Teaching Students to Analyze Public Controversy: A Curriculum Project Report," *Social Education* 28, no. 4 (April 1964): 191-194.

22. Shirley H. Engle, "Thoughts in Regard to Revision," *Social Education* 27, no. 4 (April 1963): 182-4, 196.

23. Byron G. Massialas and Jack Zevin, *Creative Encounters in the Classroom: Teaching and Learning through Discovery* (New York: John Wiley, 1967).

24. Lawrence Metcalf, "Some Guidelines for Changing Social Studies Instruction," *Social Education* 27, no. 4 (April 1963): 197-201.

25. Hertzberg, pp. 105-106.

26. Fannie Shaftel, "Roleplaying: An Approach to Meaningful Social Learning," *Social Education* 34, no. 5 (May 1970): 556-560.

27. Edith West, "University of Minnesota: An Articulated Curriculum for Grades K-14," *Social Education* 29, no. 4 (April 1965): 209-211.

28. Jan L. Tucker, "NCSS and International/Global Education" in O. L. Davis, Jr., ed., *NCSS in Retrospect*, Bulletin No. 92 (Washington, DC: NCSS, 1996): 45-53.

29. Jean Fair, "Research in the Education of Social Studies Teachers," *Social Education* 29, no. 1 (January 1965): 15-20.

Stella Kern

September 26, 1900—April 8, 1993

ANDREA S. LIBRESCO

Stella Belinda Kern served as president of the National Council for the Social Studies in 1963. She was a public school teacher whose career encompassed diverse experiences, all connected by her efforts to reach out to different groups of people to improve the quality of social studies education.

Born in Metamora, Illinois, Kern taught in the Chicago public schools throughout her career (1923-66), during which time she received her bachelor's from University of Chicago (1932) and her master's from DePaul University (1937). In the Chicago system, she worked as a teacher (1923-41), in the bureau of curriculum (1941-50), as a secondary teacher at Waller High School (1950-66), and as chair of the social studies department (1951-66). In addition to her public school career, she worked as a cooperating teacher at Mundelein College, DePaul University, and University of Chicago (1950-66). After retiring from the Chicago public schools, she continued to teach in a Title I project at Jacksonville University (1967).

Kern was the recipient of several awards and fellowships throughout her career. She was one of twenty-five teachers nationwide selected for the Scandinavian Life Experience Tour, sponsored by NCSS and Denmark (1952). She received the Chicago Council of Foreign Relations Award (1957) and continued to pursue her interests abroad when she was awarded the Irma F. Imboden Scholarship to study in Geneva, Switzerland (1958). Kern also served her profession as an editor of the *Illinois Councilor* (1947-50) and as chair of the executive board of *Social Education*, the journal of the NCSS (1956-60).

Throughout her career, Kern was extremely active in a variety of professional organizations. She was a member of the order of the Eastern Star, the American Association for the United Nations, and the Academy of Political Science. She was on the executive board of the Illinois Council for the Social Studies and president of her chapter of Delta Kappa Gamma (where she also served as chair of the scholarship and foreign fellowship committees). She was a member of both the Illinois and National Education Associations where she served as delegate to the World Confederation of Organizations of Teaching Professions (1956-64, 1968). Kern was president of the Chicago Teachers History Association (1949-52) and of NCSS (1963).

As president-elect of NCSS, Kern planned the annual convention, identifying the goal as expanding areas of interest to elementary teachers. As NCSS president, Kern was committed to reaching out to other organizations to improve the profession. She began a correspondence with the American Association of School Administrators and the National Association of Secondary School Principals to form a joint committee, "How to Raise Higher Standards for Teaching Students." In addition she began an inquiry into collaboration with the Citizen Education Center at Tufts University and sent a representative to the board of directors of The Nation Assembly, the mission of which was research and education in civil liberties.

As NCSS president, Kern was devoted to identifying and addressing the needs of the "slow learner" in social studies. To that end, she created a questionnaire that she sent to three hundred presidents of state and local councils and other leaders in the field of secondary social studies to ascertain if any classes met the needs of slow readers in their school. Forty percent of those surveyed indicated that they did offer remedial classes. Based on these data, Kern requested that NCSS undertake a program of research and create materials for slow learners; in addition, she argued for an overhaul of teacher training programs so that teachers entering the profession would be able to teach remedial reading within the context of social studies.

Kern's presidential address, "Quality Teaching: The Challenge of the Sixties," dealt with issues that are still with us today, one of which is whether teachers should emphasize fact-based or higher-level thinking. She expressed her concern that the Sputnik phenomenon and the resultant Education Defense Act were causing the social studies to fall "farther and farther behind in the race with mathematics, science and technology"; however, she warned against remedying this deficit with drills. "Teachers must be more concerned with arousing curiosity than with filling the memory, and more concerned with fact-development than with fact giving."

Given her interest in foreign affairs, it is not surprising that a second focus of Kern's address was how to foster a sense of global tolerance and citizenship. She commented, "Today students must have some understanding of the larger world. They must learn to accept their responsibility to participate as effective citizens in it. [We must develop] thinkers who have a concern for others." In keeping with her interest in slow learners, Kern expressed her concern about addressing the needs of average and at-risk students. She reminded her colleagues to work for "quality education for all students, not just the gifted." Finally, she pointed out that one necessary strategy for addressing all of the aforementioned issues was to improve the quality of teacher education programs. She noted, "The first requisite of quality teaching is quality teachers."

As evidenced by her 1963 presidential address and her many professional responsibilities, Kern was an educator committed to working continually to improve the quality of social studies education. Yet even as she gave her time and energy to lead the many educational organizations with which she was involved, she continued to teach a full load throughout most of her career. In fact, at the start of her tenure as NCSS president, she continued to carry five classes and a homeroom. Stella Kern devoted forty-three years to her students and colleagues in the Chicago public schools; at the same time, she sought to affect the lives of social studies students and teachers throughout the country.

References

Kern, Stella. "A Memorable Experience." *Social Education* 17, no. 3 (1953): 120.
-----. Correspondence to Merrill F. Hartshorn, NCSS Executive Secretary." New York: NCSS archives, Teachers College, Columbia University, 1963.
-----. "Quality Teaching: The Challenges of the Sixties." *Social Education* 28, no. 4 (March 1964): 138-40.
-----. "WCOTP Discusses Teacher Shortage." *Social Education* 21, no. 5 (June, 1959): 353-54.
Who's Who in the Midwest, 1965-1966. Vol. 9. Chicago, IL: A. N. Marquis, 1967.

Adeline Brengle

August 27, 1903 –

PAT NICKELL

Adeline Brengle, a high school history teacher and president of the National Council for the Social Studies (NCSS), embodied a high standard of service, acting on behalf of her community, her profession, and her world.

Brengle was born in Orleans, Indiana, on August 27, 1903, to William Sherman and Cora (Dean) Brengle. She received her bachelor's (1926) and master's (1927) degrees from Indiana University and furthered her education at Harvard University during the summer of 1938 and American University during the summers of 1945 and 1953.

She began her teaching career at Salem (Illinois) High School at which she taught history from 1927-1940. Her career continued at Bloomington (Indiana) High School, 1940-65. She served as an exchange teacher at Slough High School for Girls in Slough, Buckinghamshire, England, in 1946-47. She left Bloomington and moved in 1965 to the Chicago suburbs and taught at Elkhart (Indiana) High School until she retired from public school teaching in 1970.

During her career as high school teacher, she was active in both curriculum initiatives and several professional organizations. From 1960 to 1964, she served on the Indiana Social Studies Curriculum Revision Committee. In 1946 and again in 1960, she served as president of the Indiana Council for the Social Studies. She was active in the Indiana Teacher's Association and served on the Executive Committee from 1958-1963, chairing this committee in 1962. She also served on the Resolutions Committee of National Education Association in 1968-69. Of keen importance to social studies educators, she served as president of the National Council for the Social Studies in 1966.

Adeline Brengle's service to social studies perhaps is illuminated best through her NCSS presidential address, delivered at the 1966 annual meeting and subsequently published in *Social Education* (1966). Her year in the social studies spotlight afforded her an opportunity to serve as a teacher advocate. Thus, she gave voice to the concerns of her fellow practitioners who were frustrated by a lack of resources and support for their work in classroom with the nation's children.

Exercising the prerogative of a president to choose his [sic] own subject for his presidential address, and mindful of the fact that seldom is the voice of a public school classroom teacher heard in this position, I have elected to present some problems which persistently plague social studies teachers—problems which I have not previously had the opportunity to discuss publicly.

She discussed ten problems that prevented teachers from being effective and successful. Among these were pressures associated with changes in curriculum to "new social studies" approaches: lack of time and collegial support; and poor communication among students, teachers, and school administrators. Unfortunately, Brengle's pleas and admonitions were not heard clearly beyond the walls of the convention hall. That high school teachers continue to share many of these concerns would indicate that her pleas went largely unheeded.

In this address, she frequently referred positively to "the new social studies." Not only did this phrase reflect the time period during which she served as NCSS president, it also attested to the currency of her knowledge about the field. Thus, although she acknowledged that few teachers found time to teach "the new social studies," she was likely an exception to the rule. Importantly, she testified that new ideas, research, and theory do reach the classroom when teachers have both the opportunity and the interest to be active in professional opportunities beyond their schools and communities.

Upon retirement from school teaching, Brengle began her second teaching career at Tunghai University in Taiwan, where she taught history for five years. Following her sojourn in Taiwan, she traveled around the world, returning to Slough High School in England, 30 years after having taught there.

Modeling the role she longed for her students to assume, Brengle exemplified civic virtue in her local communities and beyond. She served as an elder in her local Presbyterian church and has been a longtime volunteer. In addition, she has served as a docent for the Northern Indiana Historical Society and, most recently,

has served for ten years as the volunteer librarian for
her retirement community.

References

"Adeline Brengle." *Who's Who of American Women.* 4th ed. Chicago,
    IL: Marquis Who's Who Inc., 1966-67.
Brengle, Adeline. "Persistent Problems of the Social Studies Class-
    room Teacher." *Social Education* 31, no.4 (April 1967): 303-
    306.
Stowe, Gene. "On Her Mission, Books, Learning, Are Never Re-
    tired." *South Bend Tribune.* Indiana, September 3, 1996: C7.

Jean Fair

July 21, 1917 –

JANET ALLEMAN

Jean Fair served as president of the National Council for the Social Studies in 1972. She is author of numerous scholarly works in the field. Born and reared in Evanston, Illinois, she received a bachelor's degree (1938) in history and social science from the University of Illinois and a master's degree (1939) in history from the University of Chicago. Subsequently, she taught social studies and history at Evanston Township High School for six years, and at the University of Minnesota high school another year before returning to the University of Chicago to take a Ph.D. (1954) in curriculum under the tutelage of Ralph Tyler. That fall, she returned to Evanston Township High School at which she taught advanced placement courses in history and served as a consultant in the areas of curriculum and evaluation.

From 1958-62, she taught summer courses at the University of Missouri in Kansas City and, in the fall of 1959, continued her career at Wayne State University in Detroit, Michigan. (During the process of her interviews for a higher education position in 1958, she received a form letter from a prestigious institution that rejected her application because she was a woman.) Fair retired from Wayne State in 1984, having served as Chair of Social Studies Education and Coordinator of Doctoral Programs in Curriculum and Instruction.

Fair maintained throughout her career a high level of involvement in both state and national organizations. She served as president of the Michigan Council for the Social Studies in 1966, was elected to National Council for the Social Studies Board of Directors in 1959-62 and again in 1972-75, and was Vice-President and President-elect in 1970-72. She currently serves on the editorial board of the *Michigan Social Studies Journal.*

History, current events, curriculum, decision-making, skill development, democratic values, and evaluation have always ranked high on the list of Fair's interests. Among her first publications was a chapter, "Current Events in World History," in the NCSS 20th Yearbook (1949). In this chapter, she asserted that the study of current events can help young people think critically, grow in the ability to interpret data in various forms,

judge the advocacy of the data, and suspend judgment when they have insufficient evidence. She expressed the importance of having students judge proposed solutions to problems as well as forming and proposing solutions of their own. Fair admitted that current events programs were difficult to develop; however, she believed that they were vitally important and contributed to the effectiveness of world history courses.

Fair's belief in teachers and their powerful role in educating children and youth was modeled through her own remarkable practice at Evanston Township High School as well as reflected in her writings throughout her career. In the 26th NCSS yearbook (1955), she applauded classroom teachers who develop curriculum. She labeled that change in professional responsibility as one of the significant developments in modern education. She stated that "the teacher's greatest function is to guide learning so that the experiences lived by students in realistic situations enable them, in addition to learning facts, understandings, and values, to have opportunities to acquire good citizenship by actually living it."

One of Fair's most significant contributions to the field of social studies was the thirty-seventh yearbook (1967), *Effective Thinking in the Social Studies*, which was co-edited by Fannie R. Shaftel. She wrote the chapter "Implications for Junior and Senior High Schools" in which she identified basic questions that teachers should address if active thinking is to occur in the classroom. In the chapter, she provided curricular models for planning thoughtful discussions and illustrated several interactive patterns of classroom implementation.

In her 1972 NCSS Presidential address, Fair reminded social studies educators that "This is a period of pervasive, even revolutionary change. It is uncertain that society, or the institutions of education, or social studies education in particular are 'with it.'" She advocated cooperative learning, multi-age learning, flexible schedules for high school students, and shared decision-making.

After serving as president, Fair continued to influence social studies education by serving on the NCSS Board of Directors (1972-75) and chairing the steering committee of the NCSS Project for Review of National Assessment. Her interests in assessment continued in Michigan as she and others began work on the early trials of assessments of student achievement in the social studies. Her initial writing of Goals and Objectives for Social Studies in Michigan was adopted for the state with only minor changes after widespread review.

As Professor Emeritas of Education at Wayne State University, Fair co-chaired with Stanley Wronski an NCSS ad hoc committee to examine the controversial attack on global education. She wrote in the committee's report, "Curriculum materials must avoid content that is more unsettling than young people can handle, but [must challenge] what is familiar and common." This point of view is also reflected in her approach to teaching about racial justice through classroom learning.

References

Fair, Jean. Interview conducted with Janet Alleman. Dearborn, Michigan, June 22, 2000.

-----. "Current Events in World History." In Edith West, ed., *Improving the Teaching of World History*, (Washington, DC: NCSS, 1949: 138-144.

-----. "Implications for Junior and Senior High Schools," in Jean Fair and Fannie Shaftel, eds. *Effective Thinking in the Social Studies* (Washington, DC: NCSS, 1967): 167-229.

-----. "The Choice Before Us." *Social Education* 38, no. 4 (April 1973): 292-298.

-----. "Skills in Thinking," in Dana G. Kurfman, ed. *Developing Decision-Making Skills* (Washington DC: NCSS, 1977): 29-68.

Kern, Stella and Jean Fair. "Teachers and Children Improve the Curriculum," in Ruth Ellsworth and Ole Sand, eds. *Improving the Social Studies Curriculum* (Washington DC: NCSS, 1955): 85-111

Wronski, Stanley and Jean Fair. "Global Education: In Bounds or Out?" *Social Education* 52, no. 4 (April/May, 1987): 242-249.

Jean Tilford Claugus

August 18, 1920 —

Barbara Slater Stern

Jean Tilford Claugus served as President of NCSS in 1975 and as originator and first chair of the Fund for the Advancement of Social Studies Education in the 1980s. Looking back over the many facets of her professional career, she believes passion for democratic citizenship has been the animating force behind her many efforts towards improving social studies education.

The daughter of a Presbyterian minister, Claugus lived in Xenia, Ohio, until her junior year in high school when the family relocated to Cincinnati. In 1938, she graduated from the city's Withrow High School and enrolled at the University of Cincinnati from which she earned a bachelor's degree in history in 1942, a B.Ed. in Elementary and Secondary Education in 1943, and an M.Ed.in History and Secondary Education in 1949. She returned to Withrow High School in wartime 1943 as a student teacher. When her supervising teacher was drafted, Claugus became his replacement.

She remained at Withrow for twelve years and taught many subjects, including the course "Problems of Democracy." Her master's thesis was a comparative study on different approaches to teaching this course. In addition to her teaching responsibilities, Claugus worked with extracurricular organizations on issues that remain of concern in schools today: social development of students; involvement of parents in their children's education; controversies over allowing athletes to "play without passing" (a battle which the coaches won and she lost); school reorganization and the establishment of an advisory system utilizing homeroom teachers; and the encouragement of in-service education for teachers.

In 1952, Claugus received a Ford Foundation grant that enabled her to spend a year traveling throughout Western Europe to compare education systems. A highlight of the year was a trip from West Berlin into East Germany. She has reported that this year was a defining moment in her career. She was able "to observe and speak with people who had been in war; watch places recovering and, by actually being there, could see the problems of the times." She recounted that the experiences gathered from her travels helped her to make history real for her students. In addition, she shared her observations about the war with many educational groups throughout the Cincinnati area.

After twelve years as a classroom teacher, Claugus became a supervisor of social studies, grades 7-12, in the Cincinnati schools. Her mentor, Helen Yeager, was active in NCSS and believed that supervisors should be involved in professional organizations. Thus influenced, Claugus first became active in the Ohio Council for the Social Studies (OCSS), then in NCSS. Claugus recognized the importance of this mentoring experience by mentoring others whom she observed as having leadership potential. Later, as president of NCSS, she appointed talented young people, especially minorities and women to NCSS committees.

Continuing her NCSS involvement, Claugus progressed through the ranks from the House of Delegates to Board of Directors, the Executive Board, and the Presidency. She defined her role and mission within NCSS as a "facilitator." She was concerned with process, accountability, and fairness. NCSS membership had declined for the eight quarters preceding her presidency; its budget was running a deficit; the professional staff was in disarray; and the location of NCSS headquarters had provoked controversy. During her presidency, she helped redefine the nature of NCSS as a professional organization and assisted the headquarters' staff to become accountable for its focus on that mission. Her "gift of love" to NCSS was a policy manual for the Council.

The manual codified the roles of the officers, the standing and advisory committees, personnel policies, publications programs, and the purposes of NCSS. When Claugus left the presidency, membership was climbing, the budget was balanced, the office reorganized, job descriptions and accountability measures were established, and plans for the location of the headquarters were almost completed.

In the months preceding her term as NCSS president, Claugus married and moved to Sacramento, California, to start what she calls "her third career." As a volunteer working for the California Council for the Social Studies, Claugus monitored legislative actions and committee and state initiatives that involved social studies education. She also developed a policy manual for the legislative liaison of the California Council for the Social Studies, a position that had not existed before she became the volunteer liaison.

During her tenure on the NCSS Board of Directors, issues of academic freedom and the censorship of textbooks and teaching materials were hotly disputed. Claugus advocated that social studies professionals control content, methods, materials in the classroom. Her career reflected an interest in making social studies more active, participatory, and innovative, reflecting her commitment to citizenship education as a key means of preserving and enhancing democratic life.

References

Boller, Paul and Tilford, Jean. *This is Our Nation*. St. Louis, MO: Webster Publishing, 1961.
Claugus, Jean Tilford. "Extended Careers, Not Retirement." *Social Education* 51, no. 5 (September, 1987): 380.
-----. "What is Ahead for the Social Studies?" Speech at the annual meeting of NCSS, Atlanta, Georgia, November, 1975.
----- "The Fourth 'R' [Reality]." Speech to the membership at the annual meeting of NCSS, Atlanta, Georgia, November, 1975.
Claugus, Jean Tilford. Telephone interviews with the author. 29 March, 2000; 5 May 2000; 15 June 2000; 23 June 2000.
----- Personal correspondence with NCSS (including articles, speeches, policy manuals, and letters) provided to the author by Jean Claugus.

Papers related to Jean Claugus' NCSS presidency are available in the NCSS Archives, Special Collections, Milbank Library, Teachers College, Columbia University.

Fannie Raskin Shaftel

September 30, 1908—March 21, 1999

BETH C. RUBIN

Fannie Raskin Shaftel was an innovator in the social studies who pioneered the use of role-playing to cultivate democratic values and respect for diversity in elementary and secondary school students. Born in Los Angeles, California, Fannie Raskin attended public schools there and earned her bachelor's degree and teaching credential from the University of California at Los Angeles (1928). After teaching elementary school for six years, she pursued a master's degree at Teachers College, Columbia University. Shaftel returned to California and served for eight years as elementary curriculum coordinator for the Pasadena city schools in which she instituted many progressive reforms.

Later, with her husband George and four-year-old son, David, Shaftel moved to northern California to pursue doctoral studies in education at Stanford University. She wrote her dissertation on the use of role-playing in teaching, receiving an Ed.D. degree in 1948. Stanford immediately offered Shaftel a position on the faculty of its School of Education, which she accepted. She taught at Stanford for twenty-seven years, specializing in social studies education in the elementary curriculum. Her particular interest was the use of the social studies as a means by which students might better understand themselves and each other and, in so doing, create a more smoothly functioning democracy and a more peaceful world.

In the late 1940s and early 1950s, Shaftel prepared teachers in role-playing techniques under the auspices of the Intergroup Education in Cooperating Schools Project funded by the National Conference of Christians and Jews. Her seminal work, *Role-Playing the Problem Story*, was co-authored with her husband, a freelance writer. It was published in 1967 and swiftly became a classic in its field. Also in 1967, Shaftel co-edited the yearbook of the National Council for the Social Studies, *Effective Thinking in the Social Studies*. She chaired the Commission on International Understanding for the National Education Association, and was part of a 1972 Stanford task force on the improvement of the education of minority students. In 1973, she participated in a study sponsored by the World Bank and the Fullbright Commission in order to make recommendations for the reform of education in Spain. She also served as Director of the Stanford Workshop on Intergroup Relations and was a consultant to school districts, the Peace Corps, and the National Education Association. In 1976, she received UCLA's Corinne A. Seeds Award for her "significant contribution to young people in the field of education."

Shaftel continued her education and public service work after her retirement. In Honolulu, where she and her husband moved upon retirement, she worked as a consultant to the Hawaii State Department of Education. She also served on the Board of Directors of the Hanahauli School. She returned to California with her husband a few years before her death at the age of 91 at the Sharon Heights Nursing Home in Portola Valley, California.

A major theme in Shaftel's life work was the introduction of role-playing into the social studies curriculum. Role-playing is an instructional method in which students, acting as characters in "problem stories," confront various ethical dilemmas and have free rein to test alternatives and determine the best course of action. Such enactments, she wrote in 1967, help children "to become 'inner-directed'" as well as "to live well in groups and develop intelligent concern for others." She believed that the development of such qualities was crucial to the members of a modern society that had achieved great progress, but had also gained the potential for self-destruction. She saw a connection between how individuals treated one another and the ability of societies to coexist, and believed that improvement of the former was a way of taking positive action on the latter. Shaftel disseminated her theory and strategies for role-playing to classroom practitioners through her courses, workshops, filmstrips, curricular materials, and academic writings. Shaftel took care to offer teachers materials that were useful and accessible to them. *Role-playing for Social Values* contained forty-six different "problem stories" for role-play, each accompanied by explanations and directions for use. The problem stories were divided into four major themes: "individual integrity," "group responsibility," "self-acceptance," and "managing one's feelings." Earlier chapters included a wealth of material of interest to classroom teachers, such as discussions of how to prepare children for role playing, the logistical organization of role-playing in the classroom, using role-playing as a learning method for "disadvantaged children," how to sequence role-playing thematically, and how to extend its use. Such attention to the instructional concerns of teachers revealed Shaftel's remarkable sensitivity to the demands of practice.

Still, Shaftel was no atheoretical curriculum planner. The first half of *Role-Playing for Social Values* is devoted to theories of role playing and of play in general. She grounded the strategy in a broader field, situating it within the context of citizenship education in a democratic society. She delved into "role theory" to provide teachers with a theoretical approach to understanding the ways in which their students enacted roles in the problem situations. The inclusion of such material indicates Shaftel's respect for classroom teachers as competent, intellectually curious professionals who could understand and make use of the leading social science theories of the day.

Shaftel's special talent was in working directly with students and teachers and by all accounts, she was a skilled and charismatic educator. As a professor at Stanford, she brought her non-traditional pedagogical approaches to the university classroom. She encouraged discussion and exchange of ideas and used her role-playing techniques in the college classroom, creating unusual learning experiences for students. In 1969, Shaftel was the first recipient of the Stanford School of Education award for excellence in teaching. She was a teacher first, amid a faculty increasingly dominated by researchers.

Shaftel's work was in the tradition of the social educators of the progressive era in education. She was part of a cohort of like-minded women social studies educators, including Hilda Taba, Rachel Davis Dubois, and Alice Miel, who studied at Teachers College and went on to academic and professional careers in social studies education. Like these women, Shaftel worked on two fronts throughout her career, the academic world and the public school classroom. Shaftel's studies at Teachers College, the seat of progressive education in the 1930s, put her in the company of progressive era luminaries such as John Dewey and George Counts. As curriculum coordinator for the Pasadena city schools at the height of the Progressive Movement in education in the 1930s, she adapted the project-based approach of the Progressives to the California context: for example,

students constructed an adobe house at a local arroyo as part of a study of local Mexican culture.

Later in her career, Shaftel sought to incorporate these progressive values with the more conservative reforms of the late 1950s and early 1960s. Those years emphasized a "disciplinary" approach to "social science" education, in which students were to learn about the various social science disciplines, rather than to address the social education concerns of citizenship and democracy education. Shaftel mediated the two approaches, writing that the strengths of the various social science disciplines should be brought to bear on the quest to "better understand the individual-in-society and group behavior," in order to "develop healthy group climates" both within the classroom and in society at large. In such ways, she reconciled the call for a disciplinary approach to the social studies with the earlier ideals of the social education movement. In the 1960s and 1970s, Shaftel became especially concerned with multicultural education and adapted her methods to those ends.

References

Shaftel, Fannie R. "Cultural Understanding in a World Community." *Educational Leadership* 19, no. 8 (May 1962): 535-41.
-----. and George Shaftel. *Role-Playing for Social Values: Decision-Making in the Social Studies.* Englewood Cliffs, NJ: Prentice-Hall, 1967.
Gross, Richard E., John D. Krumboltz and Alberta E. Siegel, "Memorial Resolution for Fannie Raskin Shaftel." Unpublished paper, Stanford University, Stanford, California, 1999.

Edith West

February 22, 1917 — November 14, 1991

ALLEN GLENN AND WILLIAM E. GARDNER

Edith West made significant contributions both to NCSS and to the field of social studies education. She was a member of the NCSS Board of Directors, edited a yearbook on the teaching of world history, and served on several editorial boards and committees. She also was a professor of social studies education at the University of Minnesota, co-authored a high school textbook, co-authored a college textbook on social studies teaching methodology, directed a major curriculum development project, and was an acknowledged leader of social studies education in Minnesota throughout her career.

Born in Hibbing, Minnesota, West graduated from John Marshall High School in Minneapolis. From the University of Minnesota, she received the Bachelor of Arts degree *cum laude*, with a major in history, in 1938. The next year she returned to the university to earn a Bachelor of Science degree with a teaching certificate in social studies.

After graduation, she taught for three years in schools in northern Minnesota, then at University High School, the University of Minnesota's laboratory school. She earned a master's degree (1945), and two years later went to Iowa State Teachers College, at which she supervised student teachers as well as taught high school social studies. She returned to Minnesota in 1948, earned a Ph.D. in 1951, and became the social studies department head at University High School. She spent the rest of her career at the University of Minnesota.

West was first and foremost a teacher. She believed that history and the social sciences were eminently useful subjects, ones that contained knowledge and skills that would enable students to understand and analyze social and economic life. Teaching high school students was central to her life; and she taught high school history and social problems until the last few years of her tenure at Minnesota. She believed strongly that social knowledge had great potential for students of all abilities and was a master at finding interesting and informative reading materials for students with limited reading ability.

To her, the primary goal of social studies teaching was to stimulate students to think critically. Toward that end, she used a wide range of teaching materials: film,

pictures, printed material, and court records. Free, wide-ranging classroom discussions and small group projects were the means by which she guided students to take responsibility for their viewpoints.

For several decades, West dominated the social studies landscape in Minnesota. For twenty years, she served as executive director of the Minnesota Council for the Social Studies (MCSS) and as editor of the *MCSS Bulletin*. She also authored several articles for each edition of the *Bulletin* and usually wrote about resources, particularly new books of fiction related to social studies topics. Her methods classes at the university were comprehensive; always her emphasis was on the teacher as resource, advisor, and tutor. Her students took teaching jobs all over the state and constantly looked to her for guidance and support.

One of her most significant contributions to the social studies came through her directorship of the Minnesota Project for the Social Studies. This project was one of the original "new social studies" projects funded by the U.S. Office of Education under then President Lyndon B. Johnson. West conceived the project, wrote the proposal, recruited the participants from social science and education and was its main leader for more than a decade of development, implementation, and evaluation. The Project officers developed a K-12 curriculum that was discipline-based, but that used important concepts from all the social sciences. The curriculum proposed several radical departures from conventional programs. It was concept-based and designed to implement current theories of how concepts develop. It introduced material from all of the social sciences in the elementary grades and replaced the "holiday" and "great men and women" topics so common at the time. Of particular importance was the role of the behavioral sciences—sociology, anthropology, economics, and political science—in the social studies curriculum. Anthropology was prominent in the elementary grades; sociology was emphasized in grade seven; a political science course was included in grade eight, and an economics course was featured in grade nine. A highly analytic treatment of American history, a course in area studies, and another in value conflicts and policy decisions constituted the last years of secondary school social studies offerings. The curriculum emphasized teaching students to analyze documents and data from history and the social sciences. Concepts were often introduced in the primary grades with learning reinforced later on. Schools wishing to join this curriculum reform movement sent teachers to summer workshops at which project materials were examined for trial the next year. Seminars were held during the academic year for teachers who used the new materials, and information was collected on pupil achievement. West initiated, conducted, or supervised each of these sets of activities. Her presence was the factor necessary to ensure involvement of classroom teachers and supervisory staff.

Although her efforts centered on the social studies classroom, she also published influential scholarly works and contributed across a wide range of social studies activities. Her methods text for social studies teaching stressed practice as well as theory and was especially useful to in-service and beginning teachers. The 20th NCSS yearbook on teaching world history that she edited treated various ways to organize a world history course. It introduced many teachers to the area studies approach. West used her only sabbatical furlough to study competency-based teacher education programs and programs of continuing education for in-service teachers being developed in several states.

In 1979 West took early retirement from the university, occasioned by her long battle with arthritis. She moved to Colorado in hope of benefiting from a drier climate. Although she continued to be active in social studies education, her health slowly deteriorated and she died of osteoporosis in 1991. Her influence on the field remains powerful and lasting.

References

West, Edith, and Dorothy M. Fraser, *Social Studies in Secondary Schools.* New York: Ronald Press, 1961.

West, Edith, D. Meridith, and Edgar B. Wesley, *Contemporary Problems Here and Abroad.* Boston, MA: D. C. Heath, 1947.

West, Edith, ed., *Improving the Teaching of World History.* 20th Yearbook of the National Council for the Social Studies. Washington, DC: NCSS, 1949.

5.
Debating Future Directions: 1976-1984

Introduction

MARGARET SMITH CROCCO

As social conditions change, so, too, do educational arrangements, as both Ellen Lagemann and O. L. Davis, Jr. among others, have noted.[1] It is probably safe to say that social studies, more than any other school subject, has been influenced by social context. Since social studies deals with human society, and since its mission lies in producing citizens for a democracy, it seems plausible that its shape and substance will be responsive to developments within the entity it takes as its central concern. At the same time, the field will also reflect changing emphases within the scholarship of its related academic disciplines.[2]

In the 1920s and 30s, demographic and social factors precipitated curriculum reform leading to the birth of a new field called "the social studies." Likewise, between 1976 and 1995, demographic and social changes brought demands for inclusion, visibility, and power by groups at the base of the social hierarchy and barely visible within the educational arenas of curriculum and leadership: women, people of color, gays, lesbians, and the disabled. At the same time, a "knowledge revolution" dramatically altered the subjects, questions, theories, and issues seen as legitimate within academic discourse.[3]

New approaches to scholarship at the college level created academic fields devoted to ethnic studies, women's studies, multicultural education, gay and lesbian studies, and disability studies. Taken together, these developments challenged the ways of knowing, teaching, learning, and operating taken for granted by most social studies educators during the first fifty years of the field's history. During the second half of this time period, conservative reactions to these developments brought retrenchment in society, politics, and the academy.

"The new social studies," a reform effort that focused on inquiry and the incorporation of science approaches, responded tentatively to the social changes of the sixties, the decade in which they debuted.[4] By the seventies, a number of new social studies curriculum projects turned to topics reflective of the new cultural milieu. At the same time, *Social Education* gave greater coverage to current events, with articles on the Vietnam War, racial minorities, urban crises, environmentalism, and women.[5] A renewed interest in citizenship education manifested itself in projects on law-related education and the effects of civic education on political socialization processes, emphases that could be traced, in part, to the Watergate scandal.[6]

Over its history, the immediate response of NCSS to events within the cultural context generally has been muted. Researchers looking for a high degree of correspondence between the issues engaging NCSS and contemporary events will not find a great deal of evidence, either in NCSS official publications or in archival materials, for regular and sustained engagement with the "hot topics" of the day. According to two reports on this subject, both social and professional crises have been underplayed in the pages of *Social Education* since its inception.[7] During the convulsive decades of the sixties and seventies, however, some coverage of the topics mentioned above can be found in the journal's pages. Overall, a kind of cultural lag seems to exist in which gradually and then only rather broadly does the field begin to reflect the tenor of the times.

For example, during the seventies, several articles conveyed the message that social studies needed to make suitable adjustments to trends in adolescent psychology, social relations, and schooling. In 1970, Hazel Hertzberg's "The Now Culture: Some Implications for Teacher Training Programs" kicked off a section devoted to reorienting social studies teacher education to the "irrepressible 'Now' culture" which she describes in these terms:

> For what we are faced with is no less than the emergence of a new and seemingly permanent sub-culture, attached to but distinct from the dominant culture: a sub-culture whose preoccupation is with nowness, whose homeland is education, and whose constituency is the young.[8]

Numerous events helped contribute to the significant social changes affecting women during the last three decades of the 20th century. The year 1973 marks the Supreme Court decision in *Roe v. Wade* acknowledging a constitutionally protected right of privacy that includes the right to abortion. "Second wave feminism" also emerged during these years as one response to what was called "the growing gap between ideology and reality,"[9] or between sex role strictures and the way many women led their lives. Although its emergence was often linked to the struggle for civil rights,[10] seventies-style feminism also harkened back to the unfulfilled goals of the first Women's Rights Movement that had culminated in women's suffrage. As the national rhetoric over the rights of African Americans circulated more widely during the sixties and seventies, it became apparent to many that women's economic, political, and social situations had advanced little since passage of the 19th Amendment.

After World War II, U.S. society propagated gender ideology and popular culture blandishments that offered women highly idealized versions of marriage and family. Such messages were aimed at all women to varying degrees, as they clearly cut across lines of race, class, religion and ethnicity. A public opinion poll indicated that the majority of Americans felt that women whose husbands made enough money to support their families should not work.[11] Nevertheless, by 1960, about 40 percent of U.S. women did work, a proportion that had doubled since 1940. During these years, a higher proportion of African American women held jobs outside the home than did white women. By the seventies, a chasm between sex role socialization and the realities of women's lives contributed to a new feminist movement.

Struggles over ratification of the Equal Rights Amendment (ERA), passed by Congress in 1972, evoked historical recollection of the doomed fate of a similar measure sponsored by the National Woman's Party in 1923. Within two days of the passage of the 1972 bill, six states ratified the amendment, but by 1978 momentum had stalled completely, with only thirty-five of the needed thirty-eight states joined in support of the ERA. Despite an extension of the deadline to 1982, time elapsed with no further states on board. ERA died, despite widespread public support for its goals.[12]

The significance of the ERA Amendment overshadowed passage that same year of Title IX of the Education Amendments of 1972. One feature of this measure denied funds for men's sports in schools and colleges unless an equal amount was provided for women's sports. In 1972, women were only 2 percent of college varsity athletes. Student fees from both men and women students supported the travel budgets of male athletic teams, while women's teams received 0.5% of the college's athletic budgets.[13]

While relatively unheralded, Title IX has produced extraordinary results since its debut.[14] The number of women participating in intercollegiate athletics has increased by a factor of four since 1971. By 1996, 2.4 million high school girls competed in sports, representing 39 percent of all high school athletes, and contrasting with only 300,000 or 7.5 percent in 1971, an eightfold increase.[15]

Social studies teachers and scholars sought ways to be responsive to what many perceived as a convulsion of social events during the 1960s and 70s. Educators found themselves knocked off familiar moorings in trying to explain the course of American history to a new generation. As women clamored to change familiar patterns of gender relationships in work and family life, they also challenged the sexism inherent in other institutions of which they were a part.

In 1970, in his "Report of the President," Shirley Engle questioned why the Task Force on Racism and Social Justice did not deal with "the question of women's rights," and commented that the NCSS board "felt this was no time to overlook such a vital question." He then called upon NCSS to establish "an advisory committee on social justice for women with responsibilities paralleling those given to the Advisory Committee on Racism and Social Justice."[16]

As a result, NCSS established the Advisory Committee on Social Justice for Women during the early seventies. The women who participated in this committee had all been affected by the women's movement. The goals of this committee included efforts to get sessions about women into the NCSS program and the annual conferences of the state social studies affiliates; to publish curriculum materials about women; and to deal with equity issues in NCSS, such as encouraging women to run as candidates for major organizational offices.[17]

Reviewing the publications of feminist scholars within social studies like Carole Hahn and Jean Dresden Grambs during this period shows an outpouring of work dealing with sex roles, sex discrimination, and teaching about women.[18] In 1973, David Sadker, Myra Sadker, and Sidney Simon published an article, "Clarifying Sexist Values," in *Social Education* that appeared alongside other timely analyses, for example, an article concerning teachers' knowledge about ethnic groups and another about teaching migrant workers.[19] In 1975, Carole Hahn, on the faculty at Emory University and a member of the NCSS Advisory Committee on Social Justice for Women, edited a special section of *Social Education*, "Eliminating Sexism from the Schools: Implementing Change."[20] Numerous other articles also appeared in this decade on women and U.S. history textbooks, sexist language, women in European history, and women's lives in Asia.[21] In 1976, NCSS published *Teaching about Women in the Social Studies: Concepts, Methods, and Materials*, Bulletin 48, edited by Jean Dresden Grambs,"[22] Overall, between 1975 and 1995, *Social Education* published at least five special topic issues related to women.[23] In the 1980s, the NCSS Advisory Committee on Social Justice for Women evolved into a Special Interest Group concerned with women's issues.

The NCSS House of Delegates passed resolutions, albeit somewhat belatedly, supporting the ERA (1977), encouraging its rapid ratification (1981), and backing Title IX (1981). However, a resolution concerning sexism, racism, and ethnocentrism in the curriculum failed to pass the House of Delegates in 1970.[24]

Between the years 1921 and 1984, fourteen women served as NCSS president. The first three were Bessie Pierce (1926); Ruth West (1939); and Mary Kelty (1945): In short, one woman served as president in each of these three decades. From 1950 to 1984, eleven women served as NCSS president: Myrtle Roberts (1951); Dorothy McClure Fraser (now Hemenway; 1954); Helen McCracken Carpenter (1956); Eunice Johns (1960); Stella Kern (1963); Adeline Brengle (1966); Jean Fair (1972); Jean Claugus (1975); Anna Ochoa (1978); Carole Hahn (1983); Jean Craven (1984). Between 1985 and the present, six women have served as NCSS president: Mary McFarland (1989); Margit McGuire (1991); Charlotte Anderson (1992); Pat Nickell (1996); Susan Adler (2000); and Adrian Davis (2001).

This pattern may not be surprising to those familiar with NCSS, given the organization's mixed constituency, with teachers, administrators, and professors all comprising its ranks. Furthermore, in selecting a president, consideration seems to be given to professional status as well as geography and other factors, with an informal rotation across these categories guiding selection. Until recently, the histories of the National Education Association or the Association for Supervision and Curriculum Development reflected a similar pattern of male leadership despite a large female constituency up. Still, NCSS elected its first female president, Bessie Pierce, in 1926, significantly earlier than other professional groups in the academic disciplines such as the American Historical Association, which had its first female president in 1943 and its second only in 1987.[25]

Today, women's numbers in administrative ranks in education are still relatively low (although growing). The National Center for Educational Statistics reported in 1993-94 that although women represent 73% of all schoolteachers, they hold only 35% of all principals' positions.[26]

In higher education, distribution of leadership positions is skewed by gender to an even greater degree. One of the reasons for this may be the fact that, as late as the 1970s, women earned only 15 percent of all doctoral degrees.[27] However, by the 1980s, at least in education, women took more doctorates than men.[28] Throughout these two decades, women's positions on college faculties held steady at about one-fifth, gradually increasing in the nineties but still concentrated at the lower academic ranks.

In the seventies, the Women's Equity Action League, led by Bernice Sandler, brought class action suits against 250 institutions of higher education charging sex discrimination in hiring, promotions, and salaries.[29] As a later report authored by Sandler put it, college classrooms were characterized by a "chilly climate" for women, whether they be students or faculty.[30] Such factors may help explain why women have held the NCSS presidency only twenty times over the last eighty years.

The women's movement had two major impacts on academic life during this period. First, access and equity issues loomed large for many working women. They pushed to open up opportunities so women could pursue any occupation for which they were qualified. They fought against the barriers associated with the "glass ceiling" in institutional hierarchies, such as those in educational administration. In the seventies and eighties, this ceiling could have been the position of department chair or assistant principal in a school, or department head or dean at the college level. Today, a glass ceiling exists in the area of the college presidency. The American Council on Education reports that in the year 2000, only 19% of all college presidents were women. While a low figure, this proportion represents a doubling of the percentage since 1986.[31]

A second emphasis within the academic women's movement constituted a more radical undertaking. As feminist critiques of knowledge construction, institutional modes of operation, and governance structures gathered steam, some feminists wished to reconstruct the academic enterprise thoroughly. These women felt schools and colleges needed to accommodate what was called "women's ways of knowing"[32] as well as give attention to "caring."[33] Central to this effort was transformation of curriculum by exposing its normative, patriarchal underpinnings, thereby making room for women's experiences as well as those of other "marginalized" groups.

Mary Kay Tetreault clarified the issues at stake in terms of social studies curriculum with her important article, "Rethinking Women, Gender, and the Social Studies."[34] In this piece, she laid out five types of history that reflected differing treatments of women in the curriculum: male-defined history, contribution history, bifocal history, histories of women, and histories of gender. In moving from male-defined history to histories of gender, the curriculum provides broader attention to the significance of women, ultimately reflecting an understanding of gender's impact on all human societies. The fifth phase or "histories of gender," Tetreault argued, would present a "multifocal, relational, gender-balanced perspective ... that weaves together women's and men's experiences into multilayered composites of human experience."[35]

Both equity and curriculum emphases figured prominently in the careers of the women profiled in this chapter. As a faculty member at the University of Maryland, Jean Dresden Grambs contributed to the establishment of one of the first Women's Studies Program in the nation. She was a trailblazer in introducing subject matter dealing with women, the life cycle, and the aged into social studies teacher education curriculum. Hazel Hertzberg and Deborah Partridge Wolfe worked with aspects of what we would today call "multicultural education." Hertzberg focused on Native Americans and Wolfe on African Americans. June Chapin (with Janet Alleman) co-authored a textbook, *Voices of a Nation*, that was one of the first in the social studies to take seriously the histories of women, along with racial and ethnic minorities.[36]

As we have seen, NCSS expressed a commitment to curriculum inclusion of racial and ethnic minorities early in this period. In 1971, Anna Ochoa served on a team that wrote a position statement on social studies curriculum, called "The Task Force on Social Studies Curriculum Guidelines," which read in part:

Furthermore, the knowledge utilized by the school has reflected the biases of the white middle class and has distorted the role of minority groups. Such distortions have prevented white people as well as members of minority groups from fully knowing themselves and their culture. Such practices are clearly inconsistent with the requirements of individuals in an increasingly complex, pluralistic society.[37]

This statement reflects sensitivity to matters of cultural pluralism as regards curriculum; gender had not yet registered as an issue for official consideration, but the later work of the Advisory Committee on Social Justice for Women built on efforts such as the one Ochoa pioneered.

Since the founding of NCSS in 1921, official publications scarcely reflected the fact that women were half the world's population; had, in one sense, half of all life experience; and since the thirties, had been the majority force in the social studies field, writ large. For example, Hazel Hertzberg's 1981 history, *Social Studies Reform, 1880-1980*, still a standard text in the field, is virtually silent on the subject of gender,[38] as is Bulletin 92, *NCSS in Retrospect.*[39] In the latter document, published in 1996, the women's rights movement is not included as one of the "social crises" with which NCSS has had to deal.[40] The seventies and early eighties, therefore, represent a marked departure from this general pattern of neglect.

Janice Trecker's 1971 article, "Women in United States History High School Textbooks," launched the era's consideration of women as subject matter in the pages of *Social Education.*[41] In 1977, Anna Ochoa edited a section of the journal focusing on "Books About and By Women."[42] The reviews included one by Jean Grambs on a work about U.S. women's history and another about a book written by Grambs and Walter Waetjen on sex role differences. In the early eighties, two editions of *Social Education* featured cover stories on the women's movement (1983) and Eleanor Roosevelt (1984).[43] In 1984, Mary Kay Tetreault published a second review of the treatment of women in U.S. history textbooks, following up on changes since Trecker's 1971 analysis. Two other articles about women's history also appeared in that edition, one dealing with women's biographies and another on resources for teaching women's history.[44]

Most of the women profiled in this chapter contributed, albeit in different ways, to bringing women into more prominent consideration by the social studies. For some, support of women's issues had more to do with equity and an end to discrimination than with scholarship on sexism or developing materials to balance the curriculum in terms of gender. For others like Grambs, women's issues became a primary focus of scholarly work. In a memorial statement published in *Social Education* in 1990, Judith Torney-Purta wrote:

Jean [Grambs] did not merely stand as a model or advocate for women; she voiced and wrote about her conviction that scholarship about women should be taught in social studies classrooms in an intellectually honest and historically defensible way. She did not confine herself to counting how many women were pictured in the texts, but rather with the preparation of teachers to deal with the real issues that concern women, minorities, and immigrants in the history curriculum.[45]

Alongside their interests in promoting curricular change, many of the subjects of this chapter were also committed to equity for minorities. June Gilliard, one of the first African American women to work in a leadership position with the National Council on Economics Education, published a critique of the cultural bias found in the National Assessment of Educational Progress (NAEP) tests in 1974.[46] Dorothy Skeel registered her concern over the merger of Peabody College for Teachers with Vanderbilt University by organizing a protest of faculty and students in 1979. Skeel was a strong advocate for students who were ethnic minorities or who came to Tennessee from overseas; she felt the merger might weaken the historic openness of Peabody to such groups. Deborah Partridge Wolfe served as the first female African American Education Chief of the Committee on Education and Labor for the U.S. House of Representatives. Her life work was devoted to using education as a tool of democracy for African Americans and other disenfranchised groups.

Both Anna Ochoa and Jo Ann Sweeney pursued many interests during their careers, but are most notable for their investment of time and energy in global education and teacher education. Sweeney researched student understanding of economic principles from both multicultural and cross-cultural perspectives. Ochoa's parents fled the Soviet Communist regime in 1922; perhaps it is not surprising, therefore, that she developed a lifelong interest in academic freedom as well as global education.

The subjects of this chapter all served in a variety of leadership positions in social studies and other professional organizations. While not all of them identified openly with women's issues during their careers, each demonstrated a concern for diversity and equity across social groups, both in the work they did and, by all accounts, by the way they lived their lives as well.

References

1. Ellen Condliffe Lagemann, *An Elusive Science: The Troubling History of Educational Research* (Chicago, IL: University of Chicago Press, 2000); O. L. Davis, Jr., ed., *NCSS in Retrospect*, Bulletin 92 (Washington, DC: NCSS, 1996).
2. Davis, 113.
3. Thomas Kuhn, *The Structure of Scientific Revolutions* (Chicago: University of Chicago Press, 1962). From today's vantage point, Kuhn's thesis concerning the shifting of "paradigms" precipitated more rapid and far-reaching changes in the humanities than in the sciences.
4. Hazel Whitman Hertzberg, *Social Studies Reform 1880-1980: A Project Span Report* (Boulder, CO: Social Science Education Consortium, 1981), 116-117.
5. Hertzberg, 123-136.
6. Hertzberg, 139-142.
7. Jack L. Nelson and William R. Fernekes, "NCSS and Social Crises," in O. L. Davis, Jr., ed., *NCSS in Retrospect* (Washington, DC: NCSS, 1996), 89-99; June R. Chapin and Richard E. Gross, "A Barometer of the Social Studies: Three Decades of Social Education," *Social Education* 34, no. 7 (November/December, 1970): 788-95.
8. Hazel Hertzberg, "The New Culture: Some Implications for Teacher Training Programs," *Social Education* 34, no. 3 (March 1970): 272.
9. Jane Sherron DeHart, "The New Feminism and the Dynamics of Social Change," in Linda Kerber and Jane Sherron DeHart, *Women's America: Refocusing the Past*, fifth ed. (New York: Oxford University Press, 2000), 589-617.
10. Ruth Rosen, *The World Split Open: How the Modern Women's Movement Changed America* (New York: Viking, 2000).
11. DeHart, 595.
12. DeHart, 543.
13. DeHart, 543.
14. For a fuller description of Title IX and its effects, see Winifred D. Wandersee, *On the Move: American Women in the 1970s* (Boston, MA: Twayne, 1988), 118-120.
15. U.S. Department of Education, "Title IX: 25 Years of Progress-June 1997," accessed at www.ed.gov/pubs/TitleIX/part2.html on August 9, 2001.
16. Shirley H. Engle, "Report of the President," November 5, 1970. NCSS Archives, Series III-B, Box 1, folder 8, Special Collections, Millbank Library, Teachers College, Columbia University.
17. This information is based on a phone interview with Carole Hahn by Margaret Smith Crocco on August 30, 2001.
18. A full biography for Carole Hahn has not been included because much of her influence on social education was manifested after the cut-off date of 1984. However, as noted, she did serve as chair of the NCSS Advisory Committee on Women and Social Justice in the seventies and as NCSS president in the early eighties. Her publications from this period (including many dealing with sexism, equity, and curriculum issues as regards gender) appeared in *Social Education*, *Social Science Record*, *Journal of Research and Development in Education*, and *Theory and Research in Social Education*.
19. David Sadker, Myra Sadker, and Sidney Simon, "Clarifying Sexist Values," *Social Education* 37, no. 8 (December 1973): 756-61; also in that issue, see James A. Banks, "Teaching for Ethnic Literacy: A Comparative Approach," 738-51; and Wayne Mahood, "The Plight of the Migrant," 751-56.

20. Carole Hahn, "Eliminating Sexism from the Schools: Implementing Change," *Social Education* 39, no. 3 (March 1975): 133-150.

21. Janice Law Trecker, "Women in U.S. History Textbooks," *Social Education* 35, no. 3 (March 1971): 249-61; Elizabeth Burr, Susan Dunn, and Norma Farquhar, "Women and the Language of Inequality," *Social Education* 36, no. 8 (December 1972): 841-46; Mary W. Matthews, "A Teacher's Guide to Sexist Words," *Social Education* 41, no. 5 (May 1977): 389-98; Mildred Alpern, "Images of Women in European History," *Social Education* 42, no. 3 (March 1978): 220-228; Bonnie R. Crown, "Women's Lives in the Asian Tradition," *Social Education* 43, no. 4 (April 1979): 248-61.

22. Jean Dresden Grambs, ed., *Teaching about Women in the Social Studies: Concepts, Methods, and Materials*, Bulletin 48 (Arlington, VA: NCSS, 1976).

23. Margaret Laughlin, "Recent Challenges and Achievements, 1982-1995," *Social Education* 59, no. 7 (November/December 1995): 438-442.

24. William G. Wraga, "Struggling toward Professionalization, 1968-1982," *Social Education* 59, no. 7 (November/December 1995), 429-437.

25. Joan W. Scott, *Gender and the Politics of History* (New York: Columbia University Press, 1987), 186.

26. National Center for Education Statistics, U.S. Department of Education, "1995 Digest of Education Statistics: Schools and Staffing Survey, 1993-94." Accessed online at nces.ed.gov/pubsold/D95/dtab066.html on August 10, 2001.

27. DeHart, 543.

28. Lagemann, 223.

29. Wandersee, 104

30. Bernice R. Sandler and Roberta M. Hall, *The Campus Climate Revisited: Chilly for Women, Faculty, Administrators, and Graduate Students* (Washington, DC: Association for American College and Universities, 1986).

31. American Council of Education, "ACE Study Shows Gains in Number of Women College Presidents, Smaller Gains for Minority CEOs," *ACE News*, September 11, 2000. Accessed online at www.acenet.edu/new/press_release/2000/09September/college-president.html on August 9, 2001.

32. Mary Belenky, Blythe Clinchy, Nancy Goldberger and Jill Tarule, *Women's Ways of Knowing: The Development of Self, Voice, and Mind* (New York: Basic Books, 1986).

33. Nel Noddings, *Caring: A Feminine Approach to Ethics and Moral Education* (Berkeley, CA: University of California Press, 1984).

34. Mary Kay Tetreault, "Rethinking Women, Gender, and the Social Studies," *Social Education* 51, no. 3 (March 1987): 170-178.

35. Tetreault, 173.

36. Janet Alleman and June Chapin, *Voices of a Nation* (Palo Alto, CA: Field Educational Publications, 1972).

37. NCSS Task Force on Curriculum Guidelines, "Social Studies Curriculum Guidelines," *Social Education* 35, no. 2 (December 1971): 853-874.

38. Hazel Hertzberg, *Social Studies Reform, 1880-1980* (Boulder, CO: Social Science Education Consortium, 1981).

39. O. L. Davis, Jr., ed. *NCSS in Retrospect* (Washington, DC: NCSS, 1996).

40. Jack L. Nelson and William R. Fernekes, "NCSS and Social Crises," in O. L. Davis, Jr., ed. *NCSS in Retrospect* (Washington, DC: NCSS, 1996), 89-103.

41. Janice Law Trecker, "Women in United States History High School Textbooks," *Social Education* 35, no. 3 (March 1971), 248-335.

42. Anna S. Ochoa, "Book Reviews: Books About and By Women," *Social Education* 41, no. 3 (March 1977): 251-52.

43. Howard J. Langer, "The Women's Movement: What N.O.W.?" *Social Education* 47, no. 2 (February 1983), 112-123; Joan Hoff-Wilson, "Eleanor Roosevelt: A Centennial of Remembrance and Reappraisal," *Social Education* 48, no. 7 (November/December 1984): 521-543.

44. Sheryl B. Robinson, ed., "Women in American History," *Social Education* 48, no. 7 (November/December 1984): 551-54; Sandra Styer, "A Selected List of Women's Biographies for the Social Studies," *Social Education* 48, no. 7 (November/December 1984): 554-567.

45. Judith Torney-Purta, "Jean Grambs: A Memorial," *Social Education* 54, no. 4 (April/May 1990): 232.

46. Barbara Ivory Williams and June Gilliard, "One More Time: NAEP and Blacks," *Social Education* 38, no. 5 (May 1974): 422-25.

Hazel Whitman Hertzberg

September 16, 1918 — October 19, 1988

ANDREW DEAN MULLEN

Hazel Manross Whitman Hertzberg was an educator of teachers, historian, and curriculum theorist. She wrote a comprehensive history of the social studies field (the first to appear in nearly half a century) in addition to a wide variety of other scholarly writing. She was also well known for her work on Native American history.

Hertzberg was born in Brooklyn, New York and spent most of her professional life in the New York City metropolitan area. Her college education was interrupted by her involvement in numerous social and political causes, including advocacy for Mississippi sharecroppers, the American Socialist Party, and independence for India. Her marriage to fellow activist Sidney Hertzberg in 1941 and the subsequent birth of two children further delayed her pursuit of formal education. She was awarded a B. A. from the University of Chicago (1958), shortly after beginning to teach junior high social studies in suburban New York. Concurrent with teaching, she earned an M. A. from Teachers College, Columbia University (1961). She served on the faculty of Teachers College from the completion of her doctorate (Columbia, 1968) until her death from cancer in 1988.

While a junior high school teacher, Hertzberg participated in one of the first federally funded "New Social Studies" projects. She helped develop a new seventh-grade curriculum for New York State under the auspices of the Anthropology Curriculum Study Project (ACSP, 1962-1968). Her academic study of Iroquois culture in New York State marked the beginning of a lifelong scholarly interest in Native American history and resulted in publications such as *The Great Tree and the Longhouse: The Culture of the Iroquois* (1966) and *The Search for an American Indian Identity: Modern Pan-Indian Movements* (1968). From her ACSP effort sprang also a number of the central educational concerns and questions that dominated her professional thinking: questions concerning the ideal relationship of history and the non-historical social sciences in the social studies curriculum, the study of previously marginalized groups in schools, the process and politics of curriculum reform, and the changing nature of social studies as a field.

In 1970, Hertzberg was invited to join the Social Science Education Consortium (SSEC), which was at that time a *de facto* national academy of social studies theorists. Her participation in SSEC forums convinced her that the social studies field was becoming increasingly amorphous and directionless. Her effort to provide historical perspective on the field to fellow SSEC members led eventually to a shift in her professional focus from Native American history to social studies curriculum history. In 1981, she published a preliminary history of the field, *Social Studies Reform, 1880-1980*, which remains the fullest treatment of the topic. A more interpretive history was left incomplete at the time of her death.

Throughout the 1970s and 1980s, Hertzberg supported efforts to provide greater coherence and definition to the social studies curriculum. Among other activities, she was an active member of the National Commission on Social Studies in the Schools (conceptualized 1984-85) and the Bradley Commission on History in the Schools (created 1987). On both commissions, she was a voice for strengthening the teaching of history and for building lasting connections between historians and teachers.

Altogether, Hertzberg's less-than-linear career reflects clearly the larger social studies field as it was during her professional prime. Her dabbling in economics, anthropology, urban sociology, women's history—to name but a few of her fleeting enthusiasms—closely mirrors what others have referred to as the "smorgasbord" or "grab-bag" social studies of the period. Her constant calls for coherence, vision, and shared sense of purpose express her own professional turmoil as much as the state of a field to which she often referred as, at best, intrinsically ambiguous.

While better at diagnosing than resolving the fuzziness of the field, and while not attempting to articulate a formal philosophy of social studies, Hertzberg expressed throughout her career a fairly consistent set of responses to the curriculum issues of her day. The core of social studies, she believed, traditionally had been—and should remain—the study of history. Properly taught, history provided the tools, habits of mind, and information that citizens needed to work effectively for the public good. Although certain of her contemporaries perceived the study of history to be in opposition to the development of citizen-activists, Hertzberg saw no necessary tension in her position. Enlightened and effective citizenship had been and should remain the purpose of social studies, but that was to be accomplished with historical study as the means. Attempts to teach citizenship directly, divorced from disciplined historical study, too often degenerated into a dry study of governmental structures or into vacuous propaganda. Likewise, she disparaged attempts to teach history as an end in itself, apart from its traditional public purposes.

If historical instruction oriented to exploring questions related to the public good were to be the core of the social studies, what role were the non-historical social sciences to play in the social studies curriculum? As an "ex-economist and would-be anthropologist," Hertzberg appreciated the insights and analytical tools of the social sciences, but argued that they were most meaningful to students when synthesized within the rubric of history. Her curriculum plan for seventh-grade New York State history, in which anthropological, sociological, and geographical concepts and tools were infused in a larger chronological study of history, provided one concrete response to the question of how to organize the social sciences for teaching purposes.

Apart from her advocacy of history in the schools, Hertzberg's devotion to curriculum history represented an implicit argument for the usefulness of history for educators. Tracing the history of the field of social studies, she believed, helped to clarify her own thinking and provided her with inspiring professional role models. Her initiation of the "Foundations" department in *Social Education* in 1987 was one step toward helping other social studies educators discover the riches of the field's "usable past." For the marked renewal of interest in the history of the social studies since her death—including, indirectly, the existence of the present volume—Hertzberg must be given a certain amount of the credit.

References

Hertzberg, Hazel W., *Social Studies Reform, 1880-1980*. Boulder, CO: Social Science Education Consortium, 1981.

-----. *Teaching a Pre-Columbian Culture: The Iroquois*. Albany, NY: New York State Department of Education, 1968.

Mullen, Andrew Dean, "Clio's Uncertain Guardians: History Education at Teachers College, Columbia University, 1906-1988." Ph.D. dissertation. Columbia University, 1996.

The papers of Hazel Whitman Hertzberg are archived at Teachers College, Columbia University, New York.

Jean Dresden Grambs

April 6, 1919—September 30, 1989

Joseph M. Cirrincione and Richard Jantz

Jean Dresden Grambs was a leading educator who promoted women's issues in social studies. Her research and teaching on women's issues won her research grants in the early 1960s and resulted in an extensive list of articles and books. She reached out to administrators, professors, and public school teachers in her work, serving as consultant, director of workshops, and author. She was a role model and activist at the university level, assuming major offices and helping to establish one of the nation's first women studies programs.

Grambs was born in 1919 in Pigeon Point, California. In 1940 she received an A. B., awarded with Phi Beta Kappa recognition, from Reed College in Portland, Oregon. Her initial teaching experience was at the secondary level in San Leandro and San Andreas, California. She attended graduate school at Stanford University where she received an M. A. (1941) and Ed. D. (1948). She remained at Stanford as a faculty member until she moved to the Washington, DC, area in 1953. Initially she was a lecturer at George Washington University, and subsequently, the supervisor of adult education in Prince George's County (Maryland) from 1955 to 1958. During this period, she also worked as a lecturer at the University of Maryland. In 1961, she became associate professor of secondary education in the College of Education, University of Maryland. She was promoted to professor six years later. In 1979, she moved to the college's Department of Human Development and Learning, remaining there until her death in 1989.

Grambs' more than seventy articles, books, papers, and other creative efforts testify to her role as a dedicated educator and researcher. She was well known for her major textbook, *Modern Methods in Secondary Education*, co-authored with John Carr (1979). She had an uncanny ability to anticipate issues and emerging areas of concern in education. In addition to her wide range of scholarly activity in secondary education, she also provided leadership in areas in which issues of equity, justice, and opportunity were of paramount concern. Her early work in the 1940s and 1950s focused on intergroup relations, addressing issues of prejudice, desegregation, and equal opportunity in education. She also began to research questions concerning sex differences and sex-roles in education.

In the early 1960s, Grambs received a series of grants to examine the educational implications of sex differences in public schools. This pioneering research led to the publication of two major articles (1963 and 1965) heralding a concern for women's issues in social studies education and schools in general. Her research and publication in this area continued into the late 1970s, at which time she extended her writing to consider women in administration, their choice of academic fields, and their experiences as working mothers.

Grambs sought gender equality throughout the educational environment. She conducted a major literature review with Walter Waetjen in 1963 on gender differences. This work focused upon differences between males and females not only in academic achievement in the public schools, but also as evidenced comprehensively in classrooms. The review is considered by many to be groundbreaking work. The ideas and conceptualizations presented therein became the foundation for *Sex: Does It Make a Difference?* (1965), co-authored with Walter Waetjen. Grambs' particular interest in the status of women in the social studies was reflected in her role as editor for an NCSS publication *Focus on Women in the Social Studies: Concepts, Methods and Materials* (1976).

Grambs' engagement with women's issues extended beyond research and publication, carrying over into groundbreaking activities at the University of Maryland. She was the first woman vice-chair of the Campus Senate, chair of the Faculty Council, and president of the campus American Association of University Professors. She led the first Women's Studies Committee in 1973. Moreover, she was one of the founders of the undergraduate and graduate programs in Women's Studies at the university and served as a member of the Women's Studies Advisory Board from 1976 until her death.

Grambs' concern for those underrepresented in the school curriculum eventually led her to address the question of an aging population. In this area of inquiry, like her other pursuits, she developed a solid research agenda, won grants, and generated publications on older women and older teachers. She also produced curriculum materials on aging and was a driving force in the development of the Center on Aging at the University of Maryland.

Grambs was a visionary as well as a committed activist. She promoted intergroup relationships, sought rights for minorities and immigrants, challenged sex role stereotypes, and pushed for equality. She was an advocate and educator who challenged the profession for more than forty years.

References

Jean Grambs and Walter Waetjen. "Sex Differences: A Case of Educational Evasion?" *Teachers College Record* 65, no.3 (December 1963): 261-71.

-----. *Sex: Does It Make a Difference? Sex Roles in the Modern World.* North Scituate, MA: Duxbury/Wadsworth Press, 1965.

Jean Grambs, ed. *Focus on Women in the Social Studies: Concepts, Methods and Materials.* Washington, DC: NCSS, 1976.

Jean Grambs and John Carr. *Modern Methods in Secondary Education,* 4th ed. New York: Holt, Rinehart and Winston, 1979.

Deborah Partridge Wolfe

December 22, 1916—

STEPHANIE D. VAN HOVER

Olive Deborah Juanita Cannon Partridge Wolfe has been a teacher, school administrator, university professor, and federal legislative aide. As an African American woman, her contributions often went unrecognized. Still, she persisted in her work for equality and equity in educational practices and for racial justice in American life.

Born in Cranford, New Jersey, Wolfe received a bachelor's degree in social studies education from Jersey City State Teachers University (1937) and a master's degree in teacher and rural education from Teachers College, Columbia University (1938). While she pursued these degrees, she taught adult education at night in Cranford, New Jersey (1936-38) and spent two summers teaching the children of migrant workers on the eastern shore of Maryland (1936 37).

After her graduation from Teachers College in 1938, Wolfe joined the faculty at Tuskegee Institute, Alabama (1938-50). There, she established and served as principal of two laboratory schools (1938-43). She also worked as supervising teacher (1938-50), faculty member (1938-50), and head of the Department of Elementary Education (1938-50). She directed a new graduate program during the last five years of her tenure at Tuskegee (1945-50). She received her Doctor of Education degree (1945) from Teachers College, Columbia University, during a two-year leave of absence from Tuskegee while her husband, Henry Roy Partridge, fought in World War II. Upon her return to Alabama, Wolfe became the first faculty member at Tuskegee to possess an earned doctorate. Her son, Henry Roy Partridge, Jr., was born on April 23, 1947. Her marriage to Henry Roy Partridge ended in 1951. She married Estemore Alvis Wolfe in August, 1959 (divorced, 1966).

In 1950, Wolfe joined the faculty of Queens College, City University of New York. Throughout the 1950s and 1960s, Wolfe also served as visiting lecturer at a number of other institutions, including Grambling College, New York University, Fordham University, University of Michigan, Teachers College, Columbia University, and the University of Illinois.

In 1962, Wolfe took a leave of absence from Queens College to become the first female African American named chief of the Committee on Education and Labor for the U.S. House of Representatives, then chaired by Congressman Adam Clayton Powell. Wolfe acted as the liaison between the House of Representatives and the Department of Health, Education and Welfare on all educational matters. She researched and drafted legislation, arranged and attended hearings, wrote reports, provided members of the committee with pertinent information, and briefed her counterpart in the Senate. During her tenure, Congress passed thirty-five laws relating to education, including the Economic Opportunity Act of 1964, the Higher Education Facilities Act of 1963, and the Elementary and Secondary Education Act of 1965. She returned to Queens College in 1965, at which she taught until her retirement in 1986.

Between 1937 and 1986, Wolfe published more than sixty-five journal articles and, in 1945, authored the *Handbook for the Student Teachers of Tuskegee Institute*. Additionally, she contributed to and edited the proceedings associated with educational legislation considered by the U.S. House of Representatives Committee on Education and Labor between 1962-65. Throughout her career as an educator, Wolfe's scholarly writings consistently focused on curriculum issues related to democracy and education and specifically addressed rural education, culturally deprived children, migrant workers, human relations, and social justice.

Wolfe argued that the basic and abiding moral purpose of democracy is respect for the individual human being and recognition of the equality of each person regardless of race, creed, gender, or social class. She expressed concern that the culture of schools reflected the controlling ideas, values, and sentiments of middle-class white society and overlooked the pressing needs of migrant children, rural students, inner-city African American students, and other "culturally deprived" groups. She asserted that education should serve as the great equalizer in American society and recommended culturally relevant curricular approaches designed to address the needs of all students for an understanding of democracy and equality of education.

Wolfe understood curriculum as the summation of all the activities of the child and maintained that the child's needs, interests, and capacities should serve as the central core of the curriculum. In order to create meaningful and relevant educational experiences, teachers needed to relate subject matter to the social and cultural background of students and attempt to understand how each child learned. Several of Wolfe's articles addressed the need to teach human relations in order to create a more democratic society and to combat prejudice.

Wolfe stresses the need to move beyond writing and talking about democracy toward "doing democracy." To this end, Wolfe continues to be involved in numerous societies and educational organizations that reflect her interest in achieving social justice and quality education for all, including: Non-Governmental Representatives to the United Nations for Church Women United, National Alliance of Black Educators, National Council of Negro Women, American Council on Human Rights, National Association for the Advancement of Colored People, American Association of University Women, Zeta Phi Beta Sorority, League of Women Voters, and the New Jersey State Board of Higher Education.

In the 1960s, Wolfe studied theology at Union Theological Seminary and was ordained to the Christian ministry in 1970. She currently serves as associate minister of First Baptist Church in Cranford, New Jersey. From 1989-91 she taught feminist theology as a visiting scholar and lecturer at Princeton Theological Seminary. In recognition of her many lifelong accomplishments, Wolfe has been awarded twenty-six honorary doctorates.

Wolfe's contributions to social education include her teaching, scholarship, social activism, community involvement, and government service. Through all of these activities resounds her advocacy of a curriculum for children that emphasizes democracy, diversity, and tolerance.

References

Partridge, Deborah C. "Working Together for Better Human Relations," *Journal of Educational Sociology* 26, no. 7 (March 1953): 303-310.
Van Hoven, Stephanie D. "Deborah Partridge Wolfe's Contributions to Social Education." Ph.D. dissertation, University of Florida, 2001.
Wolfe, Deborah Partridge. "Curriculum Adaptations for the Culturally Deprived," *Journal of Negro Education* 31, no. 2 (Spring 1962): 139-151.
-----. "Valuing the Dignity of Black Children: A Black Teacher Speaks," *Childhood Education* 46, no. 7 (April 1970): 348-350.
-----. "Teaching: A Lifetime Commitment," *Kappa Delta Pi Record*, 35, no. 2 (Winter 1999): 86-88.

For more information on the career of Deborah Partridge Wolfe, see The Black Women Oral History Project and "Women of Courage" photography exhibit at Schlesinger Library at Radcliffe Institute, Harvard University.

June Chapin

May 19, 1931—

KAREN RILEY

June Roediger Chapin is a teacher educator, researcher, and long-time champion of the social studies. She co-authored an early social historical and multi-cultural textbook, *Voices of a Nation* (1972), written for use in secondary classrooms, which treated the perspectives of women, immigrants, African Americans, Chinese, Hispanics, Native Americans, and others. She served as editor of *The Social Studies Review*, published by the California Council for the Social Studies, during the 1970s. She also served for a number of years as an officer of the local San Mateo Social Studies Council. At the national level, Chapin served as a board member and the program chair of CUFA (College and University Faculty Assembly) at its San Francisco meeting in the 1970s, and as a member of the NCSS Textbook Committee and liaison to the NCSS House of Delegates during the same decade. Her content analysis of three decades of *Social Education*, published in that journal in November 1970, noted significant changes in the field over the years. A member of NCSS since 1954, Chapin has attended nearly every annual conference since 1965.

Chapin's career as a social studies educator and NCSS member spans more than 40 years, during which she taught social studies in Chicago public schools, and later in northern California public schools and colleges. After her retirement in 1996, June volunteered as an ombudsman for patients in California nursing homes. Her fundamental belief is that the goal of social studies education is to promote active participatory citizenship, a position that continues to guide her actions and interests.

Chapin was born and reared in Chicago, Illinois, the daughter of an auto parts store owner and a full-time homemaker. One of the top ten graduates in her high school class of 400, she enrolled at the University of Chicago in 1949 and took a B.A. in liberal arts (1952) and an M.A. degree (1954) in social sciences. During her graduate studies, she came under the influence of Earl Johnson who introduced her to NCSS. He maintained that membership in the organization was "a must for anyone entering into the field of social studies." Like Mary Kelty, also a graduate of the University of Chicago, Chapin was influenced by Ralph Tyler's approach to the curriculum. Hence, her writings reflect a strong attention to social studies skills.

Chapin began her professional life as a second and third grade social studies teacher in Chicago in 1954. She taught elementary social studies for one year and then took a position in 1955 as a high school social studies teacher at Phillips High School, a predominantly African American public school. In 1956 she moved with her husband, Ned Chapin, to northern California, and subsequently taught "Core," a combination of language arts and social studies, for four years at Hoover High School, Redwood City. In 1960, she left public school teaching to pursue a doctoral degree at Stanford University. There she studied with Richard E. Gross, who later became president of NCSS. She was also influenced by the work of Paul Hanna, whose "expanding horizons" approach to the social studies continues to influence elementary school programs, and by Fannie Shaftel, an exponent of role playing in the social studies. Chapin received her doctoral degree in 1963.

In 1964, she started her career in higher education at San Francisco State University. From 1965-67, she taught at the University of Santa Clara. She then accepted a position at the College of Notre Dame in Belmont, California, working there for the next 29 years, until retiring in 1996. As a university instructor, Chapin authored more than two dozen articles on topics ranging from social studies skills to controversies about the new history standards. She also authored and co-authored twelve social studies textbooks for K-12 students as well as college methods textbooks. Her eighth grade social studies textbook, *Quest for Liberty*, sold over 300,000 copies, and her *Elementary Social Studies* for the college level is now in its fifth edition.

Chapin's work also influenced the "New Social Studies" movement. Between 1965 and 1970, she served as leader of an implementation team for sociological resource materials and as director of three National Science Foundation institutes for secondary teachers in the San Francisco Bay area. Despite her hard work, Chapin believes that the impact of the sociology program for secondary classrooms was only indirect. She believes that most of the New Social Studies projects suffered in two critical areas: 1) conceptual and reading levels were too advanced for students; and 2) teacher education was inadequate for successful program implementation. She next turned her attention to the world of computer technology. Always on the cutting edge of educational issues, Chapin secured two federal grants to study the state of technology in higher education. In 1969, she wrote *The Financial Support and Usage of Computer Centers in Higher Education, Final Report*, followed closely in 1971 by *Interactive Patterns of Computer Support and Usage, Final Report*.

Chapin continues to assess the role of computers in social studies classrooms, which she believes should serve as a tool for student learning. She notes, "the public has decided that we will have them [computers] regardless [of whether] they are really effective in student learning." Therefore, "teachers need to be familiar with technology usage, while schools must develop comprehensive technology plans, including strategies for updating both hardware and software."

References

Alleman, Janet E. and June R. Chapin. *Voices of a Nation*. Palo Alto, CA: Field Educational Publications, 1972.

Chapin, June R. Personal communication, 2000.

-----. Raymond J. McHugh, and Richard E. Gross. *Quest for Liberty*. Palo Alto, CA: Field Educational Publications, 1971.

-----. and Rosemary G. Messick. *Elementary Social Studies*. New York: Longman, 1999.

Shaver, James P. *Handbook of Research on Social Studies Teaching and Learning*. New York: McMillan, 1991.

Anna Sultanoff Ochoa-Becker

October 5, 1933—

Frances E. Monteverde

The sixth woman to serve as President of the National Council for the Social Studies, Anna Ochoa exerted vigorous leadership for four decades at all levels in social education. Five areas bear her enduring stamp: the democratization of the goals of social studies education; teacher education; the defense of academic freedom; global education; and the assessment of social studies, K-12.

Born and reared in Windsor, Ontario, Canada, Anna was the only child of Vera and David Sultanoff, who had fled Soviet Communist rule in 1922. She attended local public schools and, after her high school graduation in 1951, she commuted to study at nearby Wayne State University (WSU) in Detroit, Michigan. Completing a major in social studies and a minor in English, she received a Bachelor of Science degree from WSU in June 1955. She married shortly thereafter and became a U.S. citizen in 1958.

Teaching credentials in hand, Ochoa launched a twelve-year career in Michigan that portended a dynamic professional and intellectual future. From 1955 to 1957, she taught social studies in elementary and junior high grades at the Bendle Schools in Flint. During the next ten years, she held social studies positions, grades eight through twelve, in the Grand Blanc Community Schools. As an officer in the local teachers' association and chair of high school social studies (1961-1967), she honed her leadership and organizational skills. Her department's faculty and program won praise throughout the state. In 1966, she organized a countywide Model United Nations for 600 students from fifteen schools. A year later, in an overseas program sponsored by Michigan State University (MSU), she taught social studies methods at the American School in El Salvador.

Her professional growth coincided with intellectual advancement as well. By 1963, she received her M. A. for studies in history and political science at the University of Michigan at Ann Arbor. From 1964 to 1967, she earned additional credits at Wayne State and attended summer workshops at MSU and Teachers College, Columbia University. She met Shirley Engle, a social studies leader who taught at Indiana University.

During the next three decades he inspired her as a mentor, colleague, friend, and co-author.

The dissolution of Ochoa's marriage in January 1966 led her to redefine her career goals. At age 34, with 12 years of successful teaching to her credit, she left Michigan to teach fourth grade in Freemont, California, and to reconsider her options for the following school year.

In summer 1968, Ochoa enrolled at the University of Washington (UW) at which she earned a Ph. D. under the guidance of NCSS leader John Jarolimek. By the time of her graduation in June 1970, she had shifted her professional focus to elementary social studies and broadened her scope of service to the national level. As a doctoral student, she coordinated the teacher education component of the Tri-University Project, an experimental program for elementary teachers.

After designing the social studies guidelines for the State of Washington in 1969, she and Gary Manson joined Gerald Marker and Jan Tucker to finalize the NCSS Curriculum Guidelines that were disseminated in *Social Education* (December 1971). Using the state document as a basis, she strove to maintain an issues-centered orientation, to stress intellectual skills, and to incorporate values in the decision making process. Although the nation moved in a more conservative climate later in the decade, NCSS approved the document with minor revisions, as published in *Social Education*, April 1979.

Ochoa taught graduate and undergraduate social studies education as assistant professor at the University of Wisconsin in Milwaukee for one year (1970-1971). During that year, she began a four-year stint on the NCSS Publications Board (1971-1974). She also contributed to the establishment of *Theory and Research in Social Education* (*TRSE*) in 1972. An independent journal of the College and University Faculty Assembly (CUFA), which is an NCSS-affiliate, *TRSE* publishes refereed reports of research and theoretical articles.

Ochoa moved to Florida State University (FSU) at which she held appointments in the Departments of Social Studies Education and Childhood Education (1971-1976). Under the leadership of department head Byron Massialas, she served as associate head of Social

Studies from 1971 to 1974. Among many projects targeted to improve Florida education were seventeen modules of teacher competencies for middle school social studies assessment. She was elected to the NCSS board of directors (1974-1976) and to CUFA's executive committee. In 1975-76, she became an FSU Associate Professor, but the following academic year, she moved to Indiana University at Bloomington (IUB), at which she taught until her retirement in 1996.

For twenty years, Ochoa formed part of a stellar social studies faculty at IUB that included such luminaries as Shirley Engle, James M. Becker, Gerald Marker, and Howard Mehlinger. Beginning as associate professor in curriculum and instruction, she taught undergraduate and graduate courses in social studies methods as well as global and multicultural education.

By the fall of 1976, she had already started on the path of elected posts that culminated in her 1978 NCSS presidency. In that role, she channeled resources to promote global education, international cooperation among social studies educators, and collaborative projects between U.S. and Japanese educators. In her presidential address, she directly confronted the growing problem of censorship. During her tenure, Ochoa created a coalition of professional organizations and built up the NCSS Defense Fund to buttress academic freedom. Teachers, she reasoned, had an ethical obligation to present diverse views of controversial issues. Thus, to avoid authoritarian indoctrination, academic freedom was crucial. Her persistent advocacy of academic freedom during the 1980s led the National Education Association to invite her to edit its 1990 volume, *Academic Freedom to Teach and to Learn: Every Teacher's Issue.*

From 1980 to 1988, Ochoa won federal research grants for projects that combined her interests in international studies and teacher education. She directed summer institutes to inform Indiana teachers about global issues. To infuse international perspectives into preservice teacher education, she collected and organized creative instructional materials from more than 50 professors at four IU campuses. The contributors and other Indiana teachers took Fulbright study tours to Zimbabwe and Malawi in the summer of 1985. Simultaneous to her appointment as director of undergraduate studies at the School of Education (1985-1988), she secured federal funds with which to develop materials and methods that incorporated research-based skills in teacher education.

Several watershed events marked Ochoa's career in 1988. She advanced to the rank of professor and became Director of Teacher Education, the largest program in the IU School of Education. She participated in the U.S.-Japan Consortium on Teacher Education Research at Osaka. Most significant for the history of social education, however, was the publication, jointly authored by Shirley Engle, of *Education for Democratic Citizenship: Decision Making in the Social Studies.* Begun in 1983, it represented the authors' response to criticisms of education and calls for a return to traditional schooling. They synthesized and clarified more than six decades of debate about the nature and purpose of social studies education.

In 1991, Anna resigned her administrative post and returned as a full-time professor. She mentored junior faculty and focused on affirmative action and peace education. At the end of 1993, she confronted a rare health problem that required surgical intervention and resulted in long-term complications. Undaunted, she critically weighed the options of medical science and applied the same resolve that distinguished her decisions in the past. Ochoa retired in 1996 and, in May, married James M. Becker, an IUB colleague. Retirees of the University, they live on the outskirts of Bloomington, Indiana. She was named IU professor emeritas of education in 1997.

Her last graduate seminar (Spring 1996), "Democracy in Education," symbolized the thread woven into her professional and intellectual fabric. She has described it as "one of the best teaching experiences in my career." A review of her accomplishments reveals lasting effects on social education for democracy. She played a prominent role in drafting the 1971 NCSS Curriculum Guidelines, which laid the foundation for the next 20 years of deliberation. Undoubtedly, her countless hours of labor on publications over the years helped shape the discourse of the field. Her farsighted leadership established *TRSE* as an outlet for research in social studies education. For more than two decades, she asserted and defended teachers' right to teach and the pupils' right to learn rather than conform to contemporary political power. Multicultural education and global studies benefited directly from the projects she personally supported. Throughout her career, she converted theoretical principles into concrete practices. Since 1988, scholars have repeatedly cited her capstone book, *Education for Democratic Citizenship*, as the clear, definitive treatise on issues-centered social education.

References

Engle, Shirley H., and Anna S. Ochoa. *Education for Democratic Citizenship: Decision Making in the Social Studies.* New York, NY: Teachers College Press, 1988.

Ochoa, Anna S., ed. *Academic Freedom to Teach and to Learn: Every Teacher's Issue.* Washington, DC: National Education Association, 1990.

-----. "Now More Than Ever... Decision Making and Related Skills," in Jack Allen, ed., *Education in the 80s: Social Studies.* Washington, DC: National Education Association, 1981.

-----. "The Social Studies Teacher: An Exploration of Ethical Behavior." *Theory and Research in Social Education* 5, no. 2 (August 1977): 70-80.

The papers of Anna S. Ochoa are located in the NCSS archives, Special Collections, Milbank Memorial Library, Teachers College, Columbia University. The bulk of her papers and oral history tapes will be deposited at University Archives, Bryan Hall 201, Indiana University, Bloomington, Indiana. Her employment placement file is at the University of Washington at Seattle.

June V. Gilliard

August 15, 1934 –

Lisa Cary

June Gilliard served as director of curriculum for the Joint Council on Economics Education (later known as the National Council on Economics Education) from 1974 to 1991. She was the author, designer, and creator of numerous curriculum development projects and the editor of curriculum guides that aimed to bring economics education to American students. Born in Enfield, North Carolina, she spent her childhood and attended schools in Durham, North Carolina.

After receiving a bachelor's degree (1954) from Howard University, she took a Master of Science degree in history from the University of Wisconsin, Madison, a year later. She taught social studies and mathematics for nine years in the state's secondary schools. Afterward, she became Associate Supervisor of Social Studies in the State Department of Public Instruction. In 1961 Gilliard was a John Hay Fellow in global studies at Northwestern University. Subsequently, she received a Ph.D. from the University of Washington in 1981.

Gilliard's primary contribution to the field of social studies was her leadership in the field of economics education. She was one of the first African American women to work in a leadership position with the Joint Council on Economics Education. In her role as its director of curriculum, Gilliard advocated providing student citizens with the knowledge and skills to think critically and to solve problems responsibly and effectively. She worked closely on the national curriculum guidelines for grades K-12 in 1988, especially in the area of economics.

She was the spokesperson for the council at the national level and worked to connect the economic education curriculum with national social studies curriculum guidelines. Her colleagues have described her as one who dealt effectively with the bevy of economists who surrounded these efforts. She brought educational imperatives to bear on the discussion of economic theories.

A considerable part of her earlier work focused on research into school desegregation as the grounds for building community through reshaping attitudes held by administrators and teachers. In her "Improving Human Relations in the Desegregated School" (1969), a report of the North Carolina State Department of Instruction, she discussed the need to reshape the schools of the state, drawing from the work of the U.S. Commission on Civil Rights and other sources. Her report called for the attitudes and beliefs of administrators and teachers to be addressed in the following ways: development of committed leadership; community participation; improvement of the quality of education; reduction of interracial friction; desegregation of classrooms; and reformulation of geographic districts to ensure schools serve a balanced population of students on racial and social class criteria.

In a 1974 project, Gilliard additionally addressed the manifestation of racial bias and hegemonic truths in a comparison of the educational achievement of Blacks and non-Blacks. She challenged the cultural deprivation theory that had framed this project and many similar projects of that period. She called for an end to comparisons that reinforced stereotypes.

Gilliard moved from her work in North Carolina to the national scene in the 1970s. This career change reflected Gilliard's continued commitment to equal access of all children to a good education. She worked steadily to compile and develop frameworks and curriculum guides in economics education and to draw together elements from the disciplines of economics, political science, and geography into social studies programs. Gilliard edited *The Community Publishing Company* (1989, rev. 1995), an instructional unit that provided elementary students (grades 3 and 4) with opportunities to use economic content and related skills as they learn about their community. She also edited *The International News Journal (Exploring the Marketplace Series)*. In these efforts, Gilliard continued to connect community and schools as a central tenet of economics education. Working with professors of teacher education and economics, and with public school teachers, Gilliard and her colleagues related lessons and supporting materials to children's everyday experience. Gilliard also co-edited *A Framework for Teaching Basic Economic Concepts* (1995). This framework may be understood as a reflection of Gilliard's lifelong project to improve education through the development of effective and sound curricula for all children.

In her 1993 chapter entitled "Economics in Elementary and Secondary Schools," Gilliard outlined the historical development of economics education in schools and highlighted the issue of addressing diverse students' needs in the new millennium, while avoiding homogenizing tendencies within curriculum design.

Gilliard established a consulting firm, JG Consulting Services, when she left the Joint Council on Economics Education. She was visiting lecturer at the University of Georgia, Athens for one term in 1993. Gilliard resides in Durham, North Carolina.

References

Gilliard, June V. "Economics in Elementary and Secondary Schools," in *Teaching Social Studies: Handbook of Trends, Issues, and Implications for the Future*, Virginia S. Wilson, James A. Little, and Gerald Lee Wilson, eds. Westport, CT: Greenwood Press, 1993, 157-171.

-----. *Improving Human Relations in the Desegregated School*. Raleigh, NC: State Department of Public Instruction, 1969.

Saunders, Phillip, and Gilliard, June V., eds. *A Framework for Teaching Basic Economic Concepts with Scope and Sequence Guidelines K-12*. New York: National Council on Economic Education, 1995.

Williams, Barbara I., and Gilliard, June V. "One More Time: NAEP and Blacks," *Social Education* 38, no. 5 (May, 1974): 422-424.

Dorothy J. Skeel

June 23, 1932—May 1, 1997

RON W. WILHELM

Dorothy June Skeel served as Director of the Peabody Center for Economic and Social Studies Education at Peabody College of Vanderbilt University from 1980 to 1995. In that role she directed projects in global, economic, and law-related education that affected social studies curriculum in Tennessee and the nation. She also chaired the National Council for the Social Studies Task Force on Early Childhood/Elementary Social Studies that produced the NCSS position statement "Social Studies for Early Childhood and Elementary School Children Preparing for the 21st Century" (1988). A native of Erie, Pennsylvania, Skeel taught fifth and sixth grades and special education in public schools after receiving her B.A. (1955) in science and social studies from Edinboro State College. Later she earned an M.A. (1961) in educational administration and a Ph.D. (1966) in elementary education and history from The Pennsylvania State University.

Skeel began her career in higher education as an assistant professor at Kutztown State College in Pennsylvania (1961-1964). There, she taught sixth grade in the Laboratory School in addition to teaching undergraduate courses in social studies methods and children's literature. She joined the faculty at Indiana University in 1966. In 1968-1969, she held a post-doctoral fellowship in social sciences and social studies at the University of Washington. During her years at IU, she also served as visiting professor at the University of Southern Nevada (1968) and the University of Washington (1969). As an associate professor at IU, Skeel chaired (1974-1976) the social studies education program. In 1976, she joined the faculty of George Peabody College for Teachers in Nashville, Tennessee.

Soon after arriving at Peabody, Skeel organized a protest of students and faculty against the merger of Peabody College with Vanderbilt University. At the time (1979), Peabody had a more ethnically and internationally diverse student body than did Vanderbilt. Skeel, already recognized as a strong advocate for ethnic minority and international students, was concerned that Peabody's ethos and teacher preparation programs might be weakened by the merger. Although the decision to merge was not deterred by the protest, Skeel agreed to head the Faculty Merger Committee that was responsible for representing the faculty during discussions with Vanderbilt's Board of Trustees. The merger events highlight important characteristics found in Skeel's writing and professional actions throughout her career. She recognized possibility in each of her students, even when they could not see their own potential. She was a tireless advocate for people who had been marginalized by mainstream society. She taught by her actions and example the importance of finding and using one's civic voice. She also understood the role of honorable compromise in the contested arenas of democratic, public debate.

Skeel remained single throughout her life. The focus of Skeel's professional and research interests centered on developing civic efficacy in children. With her writing and teaching, Skeel and her students focused particularly on the educational needs of children who struggled to overcome inner city poverty and prejudice. Beginning in the 1970s, Skeel explored children's values development. A decade later, she began to concentrate her work on issues of global education and human rights education. She dedicated the last ten years of her life to efforts to teach young people about the U. S. Constitution and Bill of Rights, always within the context of global and human rights education.

During her Vanderbilt years, Skeel directed several statewide Law-Related Education projects (1980-1985) and Economic Education Workshops (1982-1987). She also directed a laboratory experience "Using Research Knowledge to Improve Teacher Education" (1985 1988) in the pre-service teacher education programs. From 1987 until shortly before her death, Skeel held the position of Elementary Department editor for *Social Education*. She served as project director for the Fisk/Peabody Cooperative Teacher Education Project from 1988-1991. Arguably one of her most significant contributions to social studies consisted in her work as state coordinator from 1987 until her death in 1997 of the "We the People" and Bill of Rights competition celebrating the Bicentennial of the Constitution. The project was so important to Skeel that she accompanied a group of high school students from Tennessee to

Washington, D. C. just days before she died of complications from colon cancer upon her return to Nashville. Her untimely death prevented her from completing her term as the first president of the International Association for Children's Social and Economic Education, an organization she helped to found.

Skeel authored nine books, including *Elementary Social Studies: Challenges for Tomorrow's World* (1995), which updated her previous three editions of *The Challenge of Teaching Social Studies in the Elementary School* (1970, 1974, 1979). Her book *Children of the Street: Teaching in the Inner City* (1972) signaled what would develop into a lifelong concern for the education of poor and disenfranchised children. She wrote seven elementary textbooks for first through third grades, including *The People of the United States and Canada* (1972) and *The People of Latin America* (1972). For an American Book Company series, Skeel followed the expanded horizons model of social studies curriculum development to write *Self* (1979), *Others* (1979), *Communities* (1979), *People* (1982), *Neighborhoods* (1982). She also authored more than 20 chapters and reports and some 16 articles in journals such as *Science & Children*, *Social Education*, *Social Science Record*, *The Social Studies Teacher*, and *Foreign Language Annals*. In one of her final publications, "An Issues-centered Elementary Curriculum" (1996), Skeel presented her rationale for construction of a social studies centered on real-life problems, whether past or present. For Skeel an issues-centered, integrated curriculum would provide young children opportunities to gain important problem-solving skills and historical knowledge to be used as they acted to resolve social problems throughout their lives.

Dorothy Skeel's contributions to social studies education were recognized in 1988 by her alma mater, The Pennsylvania State University, with an "Excellence in Education Award." She was elected chair of the College and University Faculty Assembly of the National Council for the Social Studies in 1995. Peabody College of Vanderbilt University established the "Dorothy J. Skeel Award for Outstanding Professional Promise," given annually to the graduating senior in the Department of Teaching and Learning who has shown exceptional promise as a future elementary school teacher. After her death, the International Association for Children's Social and Economic Education established the "Dorothy J. Skeel Memorial Lecture." According to many of her former colleagues and students, Skeel's legacy rests not so much in her publications, as in her advocacy for curricula that develop civic efficacy in students and emphasize human rights and equity for all people.

References

Skeel, Dorothy J. *Children of the Street: Teaching in the Inner City.* Pacific Palisades, CA: Goodyear Publishing, 1972.

-----. *Elementary Social Studies: Challenges for Tomorrow's World.* Fort Worth, TX: Harcourt Brace College, 1995.

-----. "An Issues-Centered Elementary Curriculum," in Ronald Evans and David Saxe, eds. *Handbook on Teaching Social Issues.* Washington, DC: NCSS,1996, 230-236.

Jo Ann Cutler Sweeney

May 27, 1939—December 18, 1996

CINTHIA SALINAS

Jo Ann Cutler Sweeney's contributions to social studies focused on economics education, international social education, and teacher education. Early in her career she chaired the College and University Faculty Assembly (CUFA) of NCSS. Her publications include contributions to thirteen co-authored books, seven chapters in collections, and more than twenty journal articles. Sweeney received her B.A. (1966), M.A. (1968), and Ph.D. (1970, in social science research/social studies education, K-12) from the University of Michigan at Ann Arbor, then launched her teaching career at the University of Texas at Austin (1970-1996). She also served as assistant dean of the College of Education (1988-1990), and chaired the Department of Curriculum and Instruction (acting chair 1989-1990, chair 1990-1996) until an accident at her summer home in Bear Lake, Michigan, abruptly ended her life.

Sweeney taught elementary and secondary social studies methods courses and supervised student teachers throughout her university career. Her six-week, field-based summer practicum (1979-1994) garnered a Freedom Foundation Award. Throughout her career, Sweeney received numerous awards that recognized her teaching excellence. For example, she received the Distinguished Teaching Award at the Laboratory School at the University of Michigan (1967), the Distinguished Teacher Award from The University of Texas at Austin (1970), and the International Paper Company Foundation National Award for the Teaching of Economics (1986).

Over her twenty-six year career Sweeney held a variety of leadership, governance, and editorial positions in professional associations. For example, she served CUFA as chair of the Research in Social Studies Education Committee, as a board member, and as chair of the board for two terms (1971-72 and 1977-78). She served NCSS as a member of the Writing Team for Teacher Education Standards and of the Committee for International and Global Education. Finally, Sweeney served on the editorial board of five social studies journals, including *Theory and Research in Social Education* and *Curriculum and Teaching*.

Sweeney concentrated her research on the importance and approaches of economics education in public schools. Writing about the history of the United States as "essentially an economic one" and about the role of economics in the social studies public school curriculum, Sweeney equated economics education with citizenship education. She encouraged the teaching of economics within the context of current, controversial or pressing social issues. The separation of economics from public policy, politics, history, or other social studies discussions, according to Sweeney, is artificial and ineffectual. Arguing that students would not be engaged by the teaching of economic concepts as sterile and remote ideas, she advocated an awareness of personal and real world experiences that could be extended to understand the economic dimensions of social problems.

Much of Sweeney's research also focused on how students in the United States and from other countries develop an understanding of economic principles. Building upon a framework of relevant instruction and multicultural and global education, Sweeney emphasized the significance of all students' meaningful engagement in economics education and participation in the economic system. She concluded that although teenagers have a profound effect on the economy, superficial "marketing" data ignore their diverse and perceptive beliefs about contemporary society. Her work in Oman, Turkey, Jordan, Korea, and the United States examined how children, through their experiences in schools, learn about themselves and the world in which they live. Two particular studies conducted by Sweeney compared the political socialization and economic insights and perceptions of students in Thailand and Japan, and England and the United States. In sum, Sweeney provided a richer description of students' economic reasoning and choices and highlighted the similarities and differences of students in different countries while simultaneously exposing the relationship between economics education and national and international economies.

Sweeney's influence and research in teacher education and economics education was far-reaching. In 1981, she became director of the Advancement of Economic Education Program, a nationwide network that included more than 250 Centers for Economic Education in the United States. In the early to mid 1980s, she was pivotal in the deliberations that added economics to the high school curriculum in Texas and in the development of the state's economics education standards, *Essential Elements*. She was a member of the author teams of three widely used economics high school textbooks, including *Economics: Principles and Practice, Economics: Free Enterprise in Action, and Economics*.

Beyond her contributions to economics education, international social education, and teacher education, Sweeney's dynamic personality and ability to work with and support other social educators distinguished her as an outstanding member of the community. One of her colleagues at the University of Texas at Austin explained, "It is her gift (there is no other word) for working with people. The research Dr. Sweeney has done in her field is stunning, but its power is perhaps enhanced by her ability to share her work in meaningful dialogue with others."

References

Cutler-Sweeney, Jo Ann, and Alan Garrett. "The Artificial Separation of Economics, Government, and History: Results of a Content Analysis of Fourteen High School Textbooks." Paper presented at the 27th International Atlantic Economic Conference, Barcelona, Spain, 1989.
Cutler-Sweeney, Jo Ann, Jill Cardenas, and Stuart Foster. "The American Economic System: How Teenagers View Their Economy." Paper presented at the American Research Association Annual Meeting, San Francisco, California, 1995.
Cutler-Sweeney, Jo Ann, and Frances Monteverde. "Creating a Civic Culture: Questioning Classroom Assumptions," in Rodney Allen and Byron Massialas, eds., *Critical Issues in Social Studies, K-12*. Belmont, CA: Wadsworth Publishing, 1995.

Conclusion

Margaret Smith Crocco

Three final points demand consideration as we conclude this history of women working in social education. First, we offer this book as a corrective to recent histories in social studies that have underplayed the role of women as well as an invitation to much-needed further scholarship about women's role. Second, we recognize the lack of attention accorded women's issues generally within education, thus acknowledging that social studies is by no means unique in this regard. Finally, we argue that women's inclusion in histories of the field does matter, believing such inclusion important to ongoing and future efforts at gender equity within the social studies.

We came to this project because of shared interest in our field's professional history. At the time of the 75th anniversary of NCSS, we noticed that women merited little mention in publications marking the occasion. Even though many women had long been active in citizenship education, it seemed that their contributions had been hidden, forgotten, or lost.

On one level, this "lacuna" was puzzling. Since the birth of the republic, women involved themselves with citizenship education in this democracy. As the teaching profession became feminized in the 19th century, women taught history and the new social science disciplines at all levels. In the 20th century, across the nation, they labored on commissions and committees, wrote bulletins, textbooks, and task force reports, and even led NCSS as presidents. Still, they remained almost invisible in the recorded histories completed before and after the 75th anniversary.

This oversight struck us as a misrepresentation of our field's history and led to parallel, shared musings about the manner in which history gets written. These exchanges inevitably led us to the work of feminist theorists writing about history, such as Joan Scott, Joan Kelly, Bonnie Smith, and Mary Kay Tetreault, to name just a few.

While ours is not an institutional history of NCSS, the 75th anniversary event did generate a considerable amount of corporate stocktaking and a rekindling of interest in the history of social studies that demanded, we felt, a critique of prior publications in terms of their unbalanced gender portrayal. Interest in the subject of women and the social studies finds confirmation in the many contributors to this volume.

One author, as part of her research for a chapter in this book, posed the question to a female past president of NCSS of whether that association had been an "old boys' club." The former president strongly disagreed with this characterization and offered an alternative analysis, one echoed by another past president.[1] Both women felt it important to make clear that university people dominated NCSS in the forties, fifties, and sixties. Of course, most university people were men. Both presidents recognized that numerically more men than women had served in leadership capacities, but emphasized that first, women were a sizable presence in the organization and, second, they themselves did not at all feel dominated by the men of NCSS.

Thus, it would seem that the answer to the question of why women had been hidden, lost, or forgotten lay more with the approach of contemporary historians than with past realities. Still, as Gerda Lerner notes, "It must be stressed that women have been left out of history not because of the evil intent of male historians, but because we have considered history only in male-centered terms. We have missed women and their activities, because we have asked questions of history that are inappropriate to women."[2] In writing a more inclusive history of social studies, the big question is not "Have women done anything important in social studies?" but, simply, "What have women done in social education and why has it not been better remembered?"

A quick review of Tetreault's approach to rethinking women in history will illuminate some of the historiographic matters involved.[3] Unfortunately, the issues she raises seem not to have permeated practice within the social studies profession; most of the histories written about the field do not adequately consider the issues Tetreault raises.

The first three phases of incorporating women into history lead from male-defined history (women are virtually absent) to contributions history (women acting like men appear in historical accounts) to bifocal history (both males and females are represented in history, but women are seen chiefly as oppressed). In the fourth phase called "Histories of Women," Tetreault poses these questions: "How have women of different races and classes interacted throughout history?" and "What kind of productive work, paid and unpaid, did women do and under what conditions?"

Raising these questions suggests that further work must be done in writing a truly inclusive history of social education in this country. Acknowledging academic hierarchies as well as institutional racism and sexism, and making a commitment to exploring women's roles seriously, new histories of the social studies could take researchers beyond professional organizations, higher education, and even K-12 schooling to the myriad ways in which women have enacted citizenship education at the grassroots level, for example, in parent-teacher associations, settlement houses, and women's clubs.[4]

Tetreault's final phase, "Histories of Gender," focuses attention on equally challenging issues. Tetreault describes such histories in this way:

> A multifocal, relational, gender-balanced perspective is sought that weaves together women's and men's experiences into multilayered composites of human experience. At this stage scholars are conscious of particularity, while at the same time identifying common denominators of experience...They search for the nodal points where comparative treatment of men's and women's experiences is possible ... The conceptualization of knowledge is not characterized by single-discipline thinking but becomes multidisciplinary.[5]

Among the questions that operationalize this phase of historical reconstruction are the following: "What is the intricate relation between the construction of gender and the structure of power?" and "Are the private, as well as the public, aspects of history, presented as a continuum in women's and men's experiences?" and "How can we compare women and men in all aspects of their lives to reveal gender as a crucial historical determinant?" and "How did the variables of race, ethnicity, social class, marital status, and sexual preference affect women's and men's experiences in history?"[6]

Applying these questions to the history and contemporary reality of social studies means asking how it has been a gendered enterprise, in terms of authority, power, organizational structure, curriculum, values, recognition, and remembrance. For example, how did the difficulties women faced in gaining higher education and admission to elite graduate programs as late as the fifties and sixties impact their ability to hold prestigious academic positions that would have afforded them the opportunity to do research, writing, and publication— the clear *sine qua non* of gaining a foothold in historical recollection? Conversely, how were the men who became prominent in our field and other academic disciplines in the last fifty years aided by having wives who typed, edited, organized, and generally supported them in professional pursuits as well as making their personal lives more comfortable?

Furthermore, moving from a history of women in the social studies to a history of gender in the social studies requires acknowledgment by those writing these histories that, when it comes to gender, there is no default option, no gender-neutral standpoint. That is, gender imbricates all of social life, and includes men as well as women. Recognizing our situatedness in writing history will assist in illuminating its multiple perspectives, asking different questions, searching for evidence in different places, and constantly raising the question, "What were the women doing?"

Even today, underplaying or ignoring women's issues is common in academic life. In a 1999 article in *Educational Leadership*, David Sadker, who with his late wife, Myra Sadker, did much of the groundbreaking research on gender equity, commented that many educators ask, "Wasn't that battle fought and won years ago?" As a result, Sadker suggests, "Those who believe in gender equity face an uphill struggle."[7]

In spring 2000, the American Association of Colleges of Teacher Education published a small pamphlet "The Missing Discourse of Gender: Education Reform and Teacher Reform."[8] Reviewing publications on educational reform published within the last twenty years, the authors note:

> It was implausible to us that education reform commentaries, even those with female collaboration, hardly mentioned the gender demographics of the profession, much less attempted to analyze the consequences or impact that those demographics may have on public education or the system that prepares the education workforce.[9]

Neither social studies nor the educational milieu in which it finds itself, therefore, have been characterized by sustained attention to gender. Still, given the nature of inquiry and subject matter in our field, this shortsightedness is particularly troubling, especially in light of the significance of the 20th century to women's history. According to Gerda Lerner,

Viewed in the perspective of the millennia of educational disadvantaging of women, the 20th century represents a watershed, a period of enormous progress. Yet discrimination remains firmly entrenched in the majority of nations and the effects of past discrimination continue to disadvantage women even under relatively advantageous conditions.[10]

As the above statement suggests, the import of any book about women's history, including this modest effort, resonates across time and place. Ongoing research and publication in women's history represent attempts to break the cycle of both forgetfulness and sexism, with its incredibly resilient capacity for reinventing itself to fit the contours of each new age. Knowing the history of women in the social studies serves as a reminder of women's agency and resistance to the norms that would keep women from becoming voices of authority within our society.

Recollecting women's history also suggests that "progress" can be a slippery state, indeed. As we have seen, women advanced educationally, politically, and socially up until 1920, only to find backsliding in subsequent decades from these thresholds of achievement. Only by constantly challenging the patriarchal assumptions that lie at the base of ideas, institutions, and relationships can we make a more equitable society. Although the lessons learned here about such matters apply to the particularities of women's situation in American society, they may also suggest something about women's situation worldwide, since patriarchy exists across time and place. One crucial and self-perpetuating means of breaking the cycle of women's subjugation is through education that remembers women's past and recognizes its significance to women's present and future.

Although we have focused here on social education within a pluralist democracy, women like Anna Ochoa would hasten to point out the degree to which this democracy is interdependent with the rest of the world. While Lerner calls the 20th century a "watershed for women," she also notes that gains for women have been highly skewed towards developed nations. For example, in sub-Saharan Africa, more than 90 percent of women aged twenty-five and over remain illiterate today. Education represents the best hope of women worldwide for progress in improving living conditions, including life expectancy for themselves and their children.[11]

In developed and developing nations, discrimination and its consequences remain an enormous problem. Feminist theorizing offers a powerful tool for reshaping social and cultural attitudes held by both men and women that contribute to women's oppression. Over the last two hundred years, many social educators have committed themselves to social justice.[12] Working to end patriarchy and sexism worldwide should stand alongside the historic call to end racism made over thirty years ago by NCSS and reiterated in a 1992 statement.[13] Prioritizing issues of gender equity needs to be a visible, ongoing element within the social justice commitments of this profession.

We hope this publication will spur further interest in women's many histories as lived and practiced in the arena of social education. We suspect that some women who should have been included in this book may have been overlooked, and we are particularly concerned about the small number of women of color who are featured in its pages. The limitations of this work represent, in part, those of the present community of scholars engaged in this historical reclamation project. Such limitations are also a cause for our collective concern.

We invite colleagues to write their own histories of women and gender across all aspects of our field. Such efforts can steer our profession toward addressing the issues of gender equity faced by so many women today in our own nation and around the globe.

Notes

1. Telephone interviews with Jean Fair and Dorothy Fraser Hemenway by Keith C. Barton, April 2001.
2. Gerda Lerner, *Why History Matters* (New York: Oxford University Press, 1997), p. 119.
3. Mary Kay Tetreault, "Rethinking Women, Gender, and the Social Studies," *Social Education* 51, no. 3 (March 1987): 170-180.
4. See, for example, the recent work of Christine Woyshner, "Teaching the Women's Club Movement in United States History," *The Social Studies* 93, no. 1 (January/February 2002): 11-17.
5. Tetreault, 173.
6. Ibid.
7. David Sadker, "Gender Equity: Still Knocking at the Classroom Door," *Educational Leadership* 56, no. 7 (April 1999): 22-26.
8. Peggy Blackwell, Jane Applegate, Penelope Earley, and Jill Mattuck Tarule, *The Missing Discourse of Gender: Education Reform and Teacher Reform* (Washington, DC: AACTE, 2000).
9. Blackwell, 5.
10. Lerner, 95.
11. Ibid.
12. Margaret Laughlin discussed the 1992 official position in favor of social justice taken by the NCSS House of Delegates in her article, "Recent Challenges and Achievements, 1982-1995," *Social Education* 59, no. 7 (November/December 1995): 438-442.
13. NCSS Task Force Report, *Social Education*, October 1969, NCSS Archives III-B, Box 1, Special Collections, Milbank Library, Teachers College, Columbia University.

Contributors

Janet Alleman	Michigan State University
Sara Bair	Wilson College
Keith C. Barton	University of Cincinnati
Jane Bernard-Powers	San Francisco State University
Mary Black	University of Texas at Austin
Chara Haeussler Bohan	University of Texas at Austin
Lynn M. Burlbaw	Texas A & M University
Lisa Cary	University of Texas at Austin
Joseph M. Cirrincione	University of Maryland
Cheryl J. Craig	University of Houston
Margaret Smith Crocco	Teachers College, Columbia University
Matthew D. Davis	Rowan University
O. L. Davis, Jr.	University of Texas at Austin
Ashley G. DeWaal-Lucas	Indiana University
Sherry L. Field	University of Texas at Austin
William E. Gardner	University of Minnesota
Geneva Gay	University of Washington
Allen Glenn	University of Washington
Mary E. Haas	West Virginia University
Mary Beth Henning	Northern Illinois University
Tyrone C. Howard	University of California at Los Angeles
Richard Jantz	University of Maryland
Linda S. Levstik	University of Kentucky
Andrea Libresco	Hofstra University
Andra Makler	Lewis and Clark College
Michael P. Marino	Teachers College, Columbia University
Frances E. Monteverde	University of Texas at Austin
Andrew Dean Mullen	Westmont College
Petra Munro	Louisiana State University
Murry R. Nelson	Pennsylvania State University
Pat Nickell	Independent Scholar
James Wesley Null	Baylor University
Daniel Perlstein	University of California at Berkeley
Karen Riley	Auburn University
Paul Robinson	University of Arizona
Beth C Rubin	Rutgers University
Cinthia Salinas	University of Texas at Austin
Sherry Schwartz	State University of New York at Geneseo
Dawn M. Shinew	Washington State University
Barbara Slater Stern	James Madison University
Stephanie D. Van Hover	University of Virginia
Kathleen Weiler	Tufts University
Ron W. Wilhelm	University of North Texas
Elizabeth Anne Yeager	University of Florida

Index

This index identifies names of individuals, places, organizations and institutions mentioned in the text of the book. United States government institutions are listed under the letters U.S. (e.g., U.S. Department of Health, Education and Welfare).

D

E

F

G

H

I

J

K

L

M

S

T

U

V

W